Advances in
Parapsychological
Research

1 Psychokinesis

Advances in Parapsychological Research

Volume 1   Psychokinesis
                  Edited by Stanley Krippner

A Continuation Order Plan is available for this series. A continuation order will bring delivery of each new volume immediately upon publication. Volumes are billed only upon actual shipment. For further information please contact the publisher.

Advances in Parapsychological Research

1 Psychokinesis

EDITED BY

Stanley Krippner
Humanistic Psychology Institute
San Francisco, California

MANAGING EDITOR

Rhea A. White

ASSOCIATE EDITORS

Montague Ullman and Robert O. Becker

PLENUM PRESS · NEW YORK AND LONDON

Library of Congress Cataloging in Publication Data

Main entry under title:

Advances in parapsychological research.

  Includes bibliographies and index.
  CONTENTS: v. 1. Psychokinesis.
  1. Psychokinesis—Addresses, essays, lectures. 2. Psychical research—Addresses, essays,
lectures. I. Krippner, Stanley. [DNLM: 1. Parapsychology. BF1031 A244]
BF1371.A35   133.8'8   77-9518
ISBN 0-306-32501-2 (v. 1)

© 1977 Plenum Press, New York
A Division of Plenum Publishing Corporation
227 West 17th Street, New York, N.Y. 10011

Printed in the United States of America

To Gardner and Lois Barclay Murphy,
my inspired teachers, trusted guides,
and devoted friends

Contributors

Jan Ehrenwald, The Roosevelt Hospital, New York, New York

Stanley Krippner, Humanistic Psychology Institute, San Francisco, California

Joseph H. Rush, Boulder, Colorado

Gertrude R. Schmeidler, Psychology Department, City College of the City University of New York, New York

Robert H. Thouless, Cambridge University, Cambridge, England

James M. O. Wheatley, Department of Philosophy, University of Toronto, Toronto, Ontario, Canada

Rhea A. White, Reference Department, East Meadow Public Library, East Meadow, New York

Preface

The history of humankind cannot be charted as a steady linear upward slope but rather as a series of quantum jumps of short duration separated by plateaus of varying duration during which no progress occurred. During these periods of no progress, the revolutionaries who produced the preceding quantum jump pass from the scene, their principles and concepts become concretized as dogma, and a new establishment is born whose sacred duty is the protection of the dogma against the new revolutionaries. The last quantum jump was the scientific revolution of the nineteenth century which laid the groundwork for our present technological civilization, and perhaps more important, also shaped our philosophical view of what is a human being. Since the basis of this scientific revolution was reason, logic, measurement, and total reliance upon the organized senses, the resultant view of the person is that of an automaton, functioning in a clockwork world. The power of this view is evident in the advances made in medical science up until the 1950s. The twin triumphs of sanitation and preventive medicine and the development of the antibiotic concept completely revolutionized the practice of medicine, and by 1950 those of us in the profession were anticipating a new golden age of medicine. But, in fact, the reality has been disaster. The mechanistic view of humanity has led to more and more technological applications of ever increasing complexity and cost and ever decreasing efficiency. The diseases for which these treatments are designed are largely the result of our technological society, which continues to remove people further and further away from their natural biological environment. The scientific revolution and scientific medicine have both failed humanity, and a new appraisal of our situation and a new scientific revolution are in order. The opposition of the scientific establishment to such a new revolution is obvious and determined, and its power is not to be underestimated. What is needed is a new view of the person as a biological organism, a return to the recognition that even the simplest of living things is more than the sum of its parts—more than a machine, and a unique miracle in a world governed by the law of entropy.

The discipline of parapsychology is uniquely suited to lead the new revolution. It deals directly with the core of the living process: the areas which manifestly are more than the sum of the parts. It can deal in a relevant fashion with the overwhelming problem of the failure of scientific medicine by re-evaluating and bringing to the fore those principles of medicine which were swept away by the mechanistic view of scientific medicine. It can lead to a new vision of the human being and his place in the universe. Indeed, it may be the last and best hope we have. The responsibility is heavy, for choosing the wrong path will lead to disaster, and instead of a new revolution, a new dark age, ruled by superstition and fear, will arise. Clearly, the new revolution must be based upon the true scientific principles: careful observation, quantification, verification, development of unifying theories, and respect for true authority coupled with rejection of mere authoritarian doctrine. Mysticism, the evocation of unknowable and unmeasurable forces, must be avoided at all costs. Our knowledge of the physical universe, while admittedly not complete, is extensive and has not been fully applied to the biological world. One example that comes to mind is the whole range of solid-state electronic processes and their possible relationship to life processes. A combined multidisciplinary approach to the nature of life, and humanity in particular, would be most fruitful if centered upon the area of parapsychology.

Parapsychological research has come of age as evidenced by this volume. Here, other disciplines are being integrated with it, dogma is being questioned, and the true principles of science and scientific investigation are being adhered to. Events seem to be moving parapsychology closer to the center stage; the responsibility is great.

Robert O. Becker

Syracuse, New York

Contents

Introduction

Stanley Krippner

1. The Field of Parapsychology

In 1893 Hans Berger, a student of astronomy at the University of Berlin, had an experience which inspired him to study the interaction between mental phenomena and physiological processes. Riding a horse on the narrow ledge of a steep ravine, Berger fell into the path of a mounted battery and came to lie almost beneath the wheel of one of the horse-drawn guns. The battery came to a stop just in time, and he escaped injury. In the evening of the same day, Berger received a telegram from his father asking about his well-being—the only time in his life that he had received such a query. This inquiry resulted from Berger's sister having told her parents that she knew for a fact her brother had been involved in an accident. Berger (1930) later wrote, "This is a case of spontaneous telepathy in which at a time of mortal danger, and as I contemplated certain death, I transmitted my thoughts, while my sister, who was particularly close to me, acted as the receiver" (p. 6).

Berger left astronomy to study medicine, directing his activities toward identifying measurable physiological properties of the brain that represented mental activity. He made his first successful recording of the human electroencephalogram (EEG) in 1924. However, Berger never had the opportunity to use the EEG to investigate telepathy because the Nazis dismantled his laboratory when they rose to power in the 1930s.

Hans Berger's letter represents just one example of parapsychological anecdotes which have accumulated throughout the ages. These occurrences date back to primitive times when people were perplexed by

Stanley Krippner · Humanistic Psychology Institute, San Francisco, California.

dreams which appeared to transmit thoughts of another person, trance states in which they seemed to become aware of distant events, rituals in which future events supposedly were predicted, and meditative procedures which were said to produce direct action on a distant physical object. These occurrences may have been instances of what parapsychologists now call telepathy, clairvoyance, precognition, and psychokinesis.

Collectively, these phenomena are referred to as psi: interactions between organisms and their environment (including other organisms) which are not mediated by recognized sensorimotor functions. The names given to the major psi phenomena include "telepathy" (an organism's acquisition of knowledge concerning another organism's thoughts or mental state without using the known sensory channels); "clairvoyance" (an organism's acquisition of knowledge concerning external objects and events by other than the known sensory channels); "precognition" (the noninferential knowledge of future events); and "psychokinesis" (the influence of an organism, without the use of the known motor functions, on objects or events in the environment). The first three of these phenomena are referred to as "extrasensory perception" (ESP), because they do not appear to depend on the known functions of the senses. The latter phenomenon, psychokinesis (often shortened to PK), does not appear to depend on the known functions of the muscles or motor system.

The study of these phenomena will comprise the subject matter for *Advances in Parapsychological Research*. The first two reviews will summarize research methodology and research results in ESP and PK since the 1880s when scientific methods were first utilized in their study. Each subsequent volume will update the methodological advances and the new results which have emerged since the previous publication. In addition, several chapters will appear in each volume presenting the implications of parapsychological research for other disciplines. Bibliographical material will also be included in every review.

This volume presents complete summaries of research methods and research data in PK. The following review will do the same for ESP. In addition, this volume contains an annotated bibliography of books in parapsychology appearing since 1974. Also included are chapters on the implications of psi for religious studies, philosophy, and psychotherapy.

Since a full-scale review of ESP will not appear until the second volume of the review, some of the major features of ESP research, including history, criticisms, findings, and theories, will be summarized in this introduction for the benefit of readers who are unfamiliar with the now vast literature of the subject.

2. History of Early ESP Research

With regard to experimentation, the Society for Psychical Research (SPR), founded in London in 1882, was the first major organization to assess psi scientifically. The SPR attracted the attention of many distinguished scholars, the most active of whom included Henry and Eleanor Sidgwick, Sir William Barrett, Frederic W. H. Myers, and Edmund Gurney. Similar organizations emerged in other countries, including the American Society for Psychical Research, founded in New York through the efforts of William James and his colleagues. These early investigators focused most of their initial efforts on the task of authenticating individual cases of purported psi. Unfortunately, spontaneous cases can rarely be adequately assessed because of such contaminating factors as coincidence, unconscious inference, sensory leakage, exaggeration after the fact, falsification of memory, and outright fabrication.

Laboratory experiments were designed in an attempt to prevent this contamination from happening. In the early 1600s, Sir Francis Bacon (1627/1952), in his book *The New Atlantis,* made several suggestions for conducting psychical research. He advised that "the motions of shuffling cards or casting of dice" could be used to test the "binding of thoughts." The experimenter could then record whether the subject "hit for the most part." The application of probability theory to the assessment of deviations from theoretically expected chance outcomes was introduced by the French Nobel laureate, Charles Richet (1884, 1923) in ESP experiments involving card-guessing.

The most extensive use of card-guessing procedures was initiated by William McDougall, J. B. Rhine, and L. E. Rhine at Duke University in the late 1920s and early 1930s (Rhine, 1934). By using a 25-card ESP deck with five different symbols, it could be mathematically predicted that five correct guesses would be made by a subject. Therefore, consistently "better than chance" scores would provide evidence for ESP.

In this early work, telepathy was generally tested by having a subject in one room guess the order of cards as they were observed in another room by an "agent" or "transmitter." Clairvoyance involved having a subject guess the order of cards that lay face down with the faces unobserved. After McDougall's death, the Rhines carried on this work and initiated experiments with precognition which involved having subjects make anticipatory guesses as to the future order of the cards before the cards were shuffled or otherwise randomized (Rhine, 1938). In some cases it was difficult to tell whether a subject's "hits" were due to telepathy, clairvoyance, or to some combination of the two; in these cases, the term "general extrasensory perception" was used to describe the phenomenon.

The most highly publicized experiment of that time was designed as a clairvoyance test in which the subject, Hubert Pearce, attempted to guess the order of cards handled in another building by an experimenter, J. G. Pratt. A total of 1850 test "trials" were completed with a deviation from chance associated with a probability of approximately twenty-two thousand million to one (Rhine, 1934, p. 97; and Rhine and Pratt, 1954).

3. Early Criticisms of ESP Research*

J. B. Rhine published his first major work, *Extrasensory Perception,* in 1934, and between then and 1940 a flurry of critical articles appeared, challenging the evaluative methods and experimental conditions used in the card-guessing studies. The criticisms, and the responses to them, are summarized in the most important compendium of the earlier parapsychological research known as *ESP-60* (Pratt, Rhine, Smith, Stuart, and Greenwood, 1940).

The first major issue concerned the validity of the assumption that the probability of success in the card-guessing experiments was actually one in five. This issue was quickly resolved through empirical cross-checks in which subjects' guesses were deliberately compared with target orders for which they were not intended. Although the subjects' guesses for the correct target orders were a highly significant 7.35 per deck of 25, the control cross-check scores were not significant, with an average score of 5.04 per deck.

There were other critiques of the Rhines' mathematics, most of which were dispelled when the president of the Institute of Mathematical Statistics, B. H. Camp, approved the evaluative techniques. In 1937, J. B. Rhine initiated the *Journal of Parapsychology,* a scientific periodical which reported on psi experiments, and employed a statistician to check the mathematics of each article before it was published.

---

*The review of criticisms in this and the following section is largely based on an article by Honorton (1975a). Criticisms of PK research are discussed in detail by Rush and by Schmeidler in their contributions to this volume. The best known critical analysis of PK testing was written by Edward Girden (1962), who claimed that the experiments carried out in this field contained so many defects that the reality of PK could not be considered as established. Gardner Murphy (1962) rejoined that Girden had exaggerated the defects in the tests and had ignored instances in which the defects had been avoided.

Another criticism centered around the possibility of sensory leakage, such as involuntary whispering or unconscious observations of visual cues (e.g., Jastrow, 1939). This hypothesis later received temporary support from the discovery that commercially manufactured ESP cards could, under certain circumstances, be read from the back. The Rhines insisted that defective cards had not been employed in any of the experiments reported in the literature and that, in any case, they could not account for results from studies in which the cards were separated from the subject by such devices as opaque envelopes, screens, or distant rooms.

By 1940, the Rhines and their colleagues (Pratt *et al.,* 1940) had reported 33 experiments involving nearly one million experimental trials under conditions which precluded sensory leakage. The results were statistically significant in 27 of the 33 experiments, a fact which convinced many people that sensory leakage could not account for the results as, for 10 of the experiments, the subject and the "agent" were in different buildings.

Another line of criticism was advanced which held that scoring errors were responsible for above chance results on psi tests. To explore this possibility, Gardner Murphy (1938), an eminent American psychologist who was also a pioneer in parapsychology, analyzed 175,000 trials from actual ESP experiments, finding only 0.10% errors. It was generally concluded that scoring errors alone could not account for the Rhines' astronomically high levels of statistical significance. Nevertheless, the problem still remains, and anyone who conducts parapsychological experiments needs to consider the possibility of scoring error, its prevention, and the necessity of preserving the data for inspection by outside observers.

Another criticism involved improper selection of test data (e.g., Gardner, 1952). It was alleged that the Rhines tested several subjects and only published the results from the ones that gave significant results. It was also charged that an experiment would be cut off when the subjects' scores began to hit chance level, that certain statistically significant segments were used from a large block of mostly nonsignificant data, and that only that type of statistical analysis would be selected that would be likely to show significant results for the data collected. There was some merit in these criticisms, and parapsychologists generally began to include all data collected in their analyses, to determine the number of trials in advance, and to clearly state the type of statistics to be used before the experiment began.

Another criticism centered around the alleged lack of statistically significant findings in parapsychological experiments performed by other investigators. If the Rhines had been the only ones able to produce above-chance results with card-guessing and dice-throwing experiments, there would have been little need to take their results seriously. Between 1934 and 1939, however, 31 ESP studies were reported from other laboratories. Of this number, 21 produced statistically significant results supporting the ESP hypothesis.

4. Recent Criticisms

By 1940, the active methodological controversy was over, with the exception of occasional critiques of specific experiments. The issues raised since 1940 center upon possible anomalies in probability theory and the hypothesis of fraud. Spencer Brown (1953) has suggested that card-guessing experiments provide evidence not of ESP but of fundamental defects in probability theory. For example, Brown stated that tables of random numbers, used frequently by parapsychologists, have been revised before publication to remove certain nonrandom features. This practice, according to Brown, makes such sequences nonrandom and invalidates the use of standard statistical significance tests. Christopher Scott (1958) published an examination of Brown's allegations; he stated that the maximum error due to edited sequences of random numbers would not affect interpretations of results unless they were marginally significant and, in that case, would usually lessen the possibility of confirming the ESP hypothesis.

Although many of the points raised by Brown are still current among critics of parapsychology, the most recent phase of the controversy over psi centers on the possibility of deliberate fraud. This argument was presented by G. R. Price in a 1955 issue of *Science* in which he concluded: "My opinion concerning the findings of the parapsychologists is that many of them are dependent on clerical and statistical errors, and that all extra-chance results not so explicable are dependent on deliberate fraud or mildly abnormal mental conditions" (p. 367). The article was widely distributed and is frequently used to debunk psychical research despite the fact that Price (1972) later retracted his accusations.

C. E. M. Hansel (1966), in a book titled *ESP—A Scientific Evaluation,* proposed that the subjects as well as the investigators could have cheated during parapsychological experiments. Although he gave no evidence of deception, he concluded, "It cannot be stated categorically that trickery was responsible for the results of these experiments, but so long as the possibility is present, the experiments cannot be regarded

as ... supplying conclusive evidence for ESP" (p. 241). Parapsychologists (e.g., McConnell, 1972) who reviewed Hansel's book generally
agreed that fraud should be guarded against but pointed out that
Hansel's accounts of the experiments were less than accurate; in one
case, Hansel had drawn a picture of the Rhines' experimental laboratory
in which hall distances and room placements were grossly distorted.

In 1965, the Rhines left Duke University and organized the Foundation for Research on the Nature of Man (FRNM). In 1974, J. B. Rhine
revealed that a medical researcher at FRNM, Walter Jay Levy, had been
caught tampering with data from an animal experiment. Levy's activities
reinforced the notions of fraud held by many critics of the field.
However, to parapsychologists, the Levy scandal pointed out the need
for stringent controls in laboratory research as well as the need for
cross-validation.

For many scientists, the issue of cross-validation is more important
than any other issue in parapsychology. Since Charles Richet (1884) first
applied statistics to psychical research data nearly 100 years ago, no
experimental procedure has emerged which would invariably produce the
same results no matter who followed it. Furthermore, no mechanism
underlying psi operation has been discovered, although several have been
hypothesized. Finally, no practical use of ESP or PK has been validated
by laboratory research. If any one of these three possibilities should
develop—a repeatable experiment, a mechanism of operation, a practical
use (such as "psychic healing")—parapsychology could leave its place at
the fringes and be swept into the mainstream of scientific inquiry.

5. Correlates of Psi

In the meantime, a number of experimenters (e.g., Rhine, 1969b)
have attempted to identify scoring patterns which might be associated
with ESP and PK. The Rhines claimed to have observed a "decline
effect" with even their superior subjects after repeated testing. A number
of experimenters have found "displacements" from one ESP target to
another, in which a subject fairly consistently guesses the target just
before or immediately after the actual target. Some researchers have
observed "psi-missing" in which subjects make so many "misses" that
their scores are significantly below chance expectation (Rhine, 1969a).

To determine whether ESP and PK scores are associated with other
aspects of behavior, a number of parapsychologists have designed experiments involving various psychological variables. Gertrude Schmeidler and
Gardner Murphy (1946), for example, examined their subjects' attitudes

toward ESP. The subjects who rejected the possibility of ESP received significantly lower scores than did more open-minded subjects. In fact, some of Schmeidler's later experiments demonstrated that skeptical subjects scored in the psi-missing category (see Schmeidler and McConnell, 1958, for a review).

Margaret Anderson and Rhea White (1957) tested over two hundred school children, using symbols from ESP cards. The classroom teachers acted as experimenters, distributing the test materials to the children without knowing the order of the ESP symbols. Anderson and White discovered a significant difference between ESP scores of children who liked their teachers and whom the teachers would include in an "ideal class" versus scores of children who disliked their teachers and whom the teachers would exclude from an ideal class. The former group had a mean score of 5.31 "hits" while the latter had a mean of 4.54.

A number of other studies appeared to converge on the generalization that above-chance ESP scores are likely to result from a mood of comfortable, relaxed, friendly interest, while below-chance (psi-missing) ESP scores are likely to result from a mood of negativism, distrust, resentment, or reserve. A large number of individual differences appear in these studies and, of course, none of these findings has been found to be easily replicable (Schmeidler, 1974).

Less work has been done with PK subjects. R. L. Van de Castle (1958) separated subjects into "spontaneous" and "inhibited" groups on the basis of Rorschach inkblot scores, finding that the former subjects scored higher than the latter group on PK tests, which involved attempted influence of falling dice.

6. Psi Response Factors

In the folk literature, psi is often referred to as a "sixth sense," but laboratory research has failed to identify any sense modality associated with ESP or PK. Thus, attention has been paid in response factors, the circumstances which occur while a person is using psi ability.

One such response factor has been identified as spontaneity; a number of studies suggest that freedom from various kinds of inhibition may be favorable to psi. For example, W. B. Scherer (1948) found that psi performance increased when subjects guessed the identity of an ESP card only when they spontaneously felt the urge to make a response. Scherer's findings help to explain the "decline effect" so often noted as subjects proceed through a lengthy test session.

Previously established memories and associations may also be important response factors in psi performance (e.g., Roll, 1966). When cards containing words and nonsense syllables are used as ESP targets, more hits are generally scored on the words, possibly because nonsense syllables are not in the subjects' memory banks. The same finding emerges from studies done with words in a foreign language and words in the subjects' native tongue; the cards containing the foreign words are less likely to provide hits than the others, even though both types of cards are represented equally and even though the subjects have duplicate cards that they can use as guides. This finding is referred to as the "differential effect" and has been intensively studied by K. R. Rao and his associates (e.g., Rao, 1964).

Earlier work with such subject variables as mood and personality factors led many parapsychologists to explore another response factor, that of free-response ESP versus forced-choice responses. It was thought that if subjects were not restricted to one of five geometric forms in a deck of ESP cards for their responses, the subjects' spontaneity might be activated more fully. This activation may be especially important in creating the comfortable, relaxed mood found by many experimenters to be conducive to ESP. Most free-response ESP tests utilize a collection of magazine pictures, photographs, or art prints. As the subjects do not know what specific pictures are in the collection, they are not consciously focusing on a restricted task. Recently, Honorton (1975b) has described a method of objectively scoring free-response stimuli.

7. Psi-Conducive States

In reviewing the literature on psychical research, many investigators (e.g., Parker, 1975) were struck by the frequency with which altered states of consciousness have been associated with psi. It could be that certain altered states are favorable for many response factors associated with ESP. These factors include reduced attentiveness for external distracting stimulation, reduction of internal distractions through relaxation, and the redirecting of one's focus of attention inward.

Thousands of spontaneous cases of ESP collected by L. E. Rhine (1967) over the years include more which occurred in altered conscious states, such as dreams, than in ordinary waking consciousness. Therefore, a number of parapsychologists have attempted to enhance ESP scoring by studying sleeping subjects, as well as those who have been hypnotized, drugged, placed in sensory bombardment or sensory deprivation chambers, or those undergoing biofeedback training or meditation (Honorton, 1974).

Although few studies have been done with psi and drugs, considerable work has been reported involving hypnosis. Most of these studies have found hypnotic induction to be associated with increased ESP scoring, and some studies have found additional links between ESP and hypnotic susceptibility and/or the depth of hypnotic experience (Honorton and Krippner, 1969).

Another line of investigation has involved psi effects in dreams; the majority of these studies have yielded statistically significant results (Ullman and Krippner, with Vaughan, 1973). Typically, an agent in a distant room would concentrate on a target picture, usually an art print, while a subject went to sleep after having been asked to incorporate the target into his or her dreams. Judging procedures were devised to determine the extent of correspondence between the dreams and the target picture. On one night, in a sleep laboratory, the randomly selected art print was Orozco's "Animals," which portrays two ravenous beasts with bones in the foreground and a black rock in the background. The subject's dream reports included the following statements:

> I was at this banquet . . . and I was eating something like rib steak. And this friend of mine . . . was very conscious of other people getting more to eat than she got. . . . Vermont, Black Rock, Vermont. . . . I was sitting on one of the rocks . . . and I felt like that mermaid from Black Rock. (p. 98).

Freud's (1922) suggestion that telepathic messages can be distorted in dreams could be exemplified by this case. The beasts could have been transformed into the dreamer and her greedy friend. And Black Hills, Vermont, as well as White Rock beverages (with their wood nymph trademark) appear to have both been transformed to match the black rock in the target.

Charles Honorton and his associates (Honorton, Davidson, and Bindler, 1971), in an attempt to identify psi-conducive states of consciousness, designed a self-report scale to study the depth of consciousness alteration among subjects in ESP tests. Subjects were taught to respond with a number from zero to four whenever asked for a report:

> Zero indicates that you are normally alert. . . . One indicates that you feel especially relaxed. . . . Two indicates that your attention is being focused more on internal feelings and sensations. . . . If this shift is not only recognizable but strong, you should report three, and if it is strong and very impressive to you, report four. (pp. 311–312)

ESP performance, in Honorton's studies involving alpha wave, biofeedback, hypnosis, and sensory deprivation, appeared to be a function of the subject's conscious state. Scores of two, three, and four were associated with ESP hits more often than scores of zero or one. Furthermore, "shifts" in consciousness were more often linked with ESP hits than were "steady states" of consciousness, confirming a hypothesis stated by Gardner Murphy (1966) in an important article on the topic.

8. Theoretical Issues

The simplest theory to explain parapsychological findings has been put forward by such critics as C. E. M. Hansel (1966), who claimed that statistically significant data in psi research are produced fraudulently. Taking a less simplistic approach, Christopher Scott (1961) outlined several specific hypotheses, e.g., "Psi occurs only occasionally, but when it occurs it gives . . . complete information" (p. 196). "Psi occurs all the time and consists of a multiplication of the percipient's chance of success by a constant factor" (p. 196), as well as proposed experimental tests.

Lawrence LeShan (1974) has also proposed several testable hypotheses which could confirm his theory of "clairvoyant reality"—the unusual way in which psychics experience the world.

William Roll (1966, 1975) has suggested that "psi fields" exist around people and objects which interact with each other, and with known fields, to produce ESP and PK.

The Soviet biologist V. M. Inyushin (1970) posits the existence of "bioplasma," a hypothetical state of matter, to explain psi. Other Soviet theoreticians include Alexander Dubrov (1976), who feels that living organisms produce psi by controlling their own gravitational fields, and Nikolai Kozyrev (1958), who thinks that time has density and that the future represents that aspect of the present which is less dense.

Arthur Koestler (1972) used insights from theoretical physics to help explain psi. He noted that a positron is conceived of as an electron traveling backward in time, and that this may underlie precognition.

The Columbia University physicist Gerald Feinberg (1975) has noted that the theoretical concept of an "advance wave" which heralds the propagation of light may eventually explain some types of precognition.

Another physicist, E. H. Walker (1974), has used quantum physics in an attempt to explain psi phenomena. The indeterminism in quantum physics has given rise to the search for hidden variables. Walker believes that the most important of these variables is consciousness and has combined this notion with data from neurophysiology to arrive at three data rates of mental events: 10^8 units of information per second for conscious experience, 10^{12} units for unconscious experience, and 10^4 units for the experience of "will."

The parapsychologists facing the most difficult theoretical problems are those who investigate ESP and PK phenomena associated with the possible survival of human personality after bodily death. C. D. Broad (1962, pp. 381–430; 1976) has suggested that stray memories or fragmentary psychic processes may continue to exert effects for a short period of time after death. Other investigators suspect a continuity of human personality either in the absence of the body or through "reincarnation" in another body (e.g., Stevenson, 1974).

In conclusion, it can be seen that psychical research poses many challenges. The data challenge parapsychologists to construct theories as to the mechanisms for psi as well as to find possible applications for the constructive use of ESP and PK. And the data challenge nonparapsychologists to accept them or to find logical reasons for not doing so.

9. References

Anderson, M. L., & White, R. A. A further investigation of teacher–pupil attitudes and clairvoyance test results. *Journal of Parapsychology*, 1957, *21*, 81–97.

Bacon, F. *The New Atlantis.* Chicago: Encyclopedia Britannica, 1952. (Originally published, 1627.)

Berger, H. On the electroencephalogram of man. *Journal für Psychologie und Neurologie*, 1930, *40*, 160–179.

Broad, C. D. *Lectures on psychical research.* New York: Humanities Press, 1962.

Broad, C. D. Personal identity and survival. In J. M. O. Wheatley, and H. L. Edge (Eds.), *Philosophical dimensions of parapsychology.* Springfield, Ill.: Charles C Thomas, 1976.

Brown, G. S. Statistical significance in psychical research. *Nature,* 1953, *172,* 154–156.

Dubrov, A. N. The interaction of biological objects with time and space. *Psychoenergetic Systems*, 1976, *1*, 209–214.

Feinberg, G. Precognition–A memory of things future. In L. Oteri (Ed.), *Quantum physics and parapsychology.* New York: Parapsychology Foundation, 1975.

Freud, S. Dreams and telepathy. *Imago*, 1922, *8*, 1–22.

Gardner, M. *In the name of science.* New York: McGraw-Hill, 1952.

Girden, E. A review of psychokinesis (PK). *Psychological Bulletin,* 1962, *59,* 353–388.

Hansel, C. E. M. *ESP: A scientific evaluation.* New York: Scribner's, 1966.

Honorton, C. Psi-conducive states of awareness. In E. D. Mitchell and others, *Psychic exploration: A challenge for science.* New York: Putnam's, 1974.

Honorton, C. "Error some place!" *Journal of Communication,* 1975, *25*, 103–116.(a)

Honorton, C. Objective determination of information rate in psi tasks with pictorial stimuli. *Journal of the American Society for Psychical Research*, 1975, *69*, 353–359. (b)

Honorton, C., Davidson, R., and Bindler, P. Feedback-augmented EEG alpha, shifts in subjective state, and ESP card-guessing performance. *Journal of the American Society for Psychical Research*, 1971, *65*, 308–323.

Honorton, C., & Krippner, S. Hypnosis and ESP performance. *Journal of the American Society for Psychical Research*. 1969, *63*, 214–252.

Inyushin, V. M. Bioplasma and interaction of organisms. In Z. Rejdák et al. (Eds.), *Symposium on psychotronics*. Downton, Wiltshire, England: Paraphysical Laboratory, 1970.

Jastrow, J. ESP, house of cards. *American Scholar*, 1939, *8*, 13–22.

Koestler, A. *The roots of coincidence*. New York: Random House, 1972.

Kozyrev, N. A. *Prichinnaya ili nesemmitrichnaya mekhanika v lineynon priblizhenii*. Leningrad: Main Astronomical Observatory, 1958.

LeShan, L. *The medium, the mystic, and the physicist*. New York: Viking, 1974.

McConnell, R. A. *ESP curriculum guide*. New York: Simon & Schuster, 1972.

Murphy, G. On limits of recording errors. In The ESP symposium at the A.P.A. *Journal of Parapsychology*, 1938, *2*, 262–266.

Murphy, G. Report on paper by Edward Girden on psychokinesis. *Psychological Bulletin*, 1962, *59*, 520–528.

Murphy, G. Research in creativeness: What can it tell us about extrasensory perception? *Journal of the American Society for Psychical Research*, 1966, *60*, 8–22.

Pratt, J. G., Rhine, J. B., Smith, B. M., Stuart, C. E., and Greenwood, J. A. *Extrasensory perception after sixty years*. New York: Henry Holt, 1940.

Parker, A. *States of mind: ESP and altered states of consciousness*. New York: Taplinger, 1975.

Price, G. R. Science and the supernatural. *Science*, 1955, *122*, 359–367.

Price, G. R. Apology to Rhine and Soal. *Science*, 1972, *175*, 359.

Rao, K. R. The differential response in three new situations. *Journal of Parapsychology*, 1964, *28*, 81–92.

Rhine, J. B. *Extrasensory perception*. Boston: Bruce Humphries, 1934.

Rhine, J. B. Experiments bearing on the precognition hypothesis. *Journal of Parapsychology*, 1938, *2*, 38–54.

Rhine, J. B. Psi-missing re-examined. *Journal of Parapsychology*, 1969, *33*, 1–38. (a)

Rhine, J. B. Position effects in psi test results. *Journal of Parapsychology*, 1969, *33*, 136–157. (b)

Rhine, J. B. Comments: "A new case of experimenter unreliability." *Journal of Parapsychology*, 1974, *38*, 215–225.

Rhine, J. B., and Pratt, J. G. A review of the Pearce–Pratt distance series of ESP tests. *Journal of Parapsychology*, 1954, *18*, 165–177.

Rhine, L. E. *ESP in life and lab: Tracing hidden channels*. New York: Macmillan, 1967.

Richet, C. La suggestion mentale et le calcul des probabilités. *Revue Philosophique*, 1884, *18*, 609–671.

Richet, C. *Thirty years of psychical research*. New York: Macmillan, 1923.

Roll, W. G. ESP and memory. *International Journal of Neuropsychiatry*, 1966, *2*, 505–521.

Roll, W. G. *Theory and experiment in psychical research*. New York: Arno Press, 1975.

Scherer, W. B. Spontaneity as a factor in ESP. *Journal of Parapsychology*, 1948, *12*, 126–147.

Schmeidler, G. R. The psychic personality. In E. D. Mitchell and others, *Psychic exploration: A challenge for science*. New York: Putnam's, 1974.

Schmeidler, G. R., and McConnell, R. A. *ESP and personality patterns*. New Haven: Yale University Press, 1958.

Schmeidler, G. R., and Murphy, G. The influence of belief and disbelief in ESP upon ESP scoring levels. *Journal of Experimental Psychology*, 1946, *36*, 271–276.

Scott, C. G. Spencer Brown and probability: A critique. *Journal of the Society for Psychical Research*, 1958, *39*, 217–234.

Scott, C. Models for psi. *Proceedings of the Society for Psychical Research*, 1961, *53*, 195–225.

Stevenson, I. *Twenty cases suggestive of reincarnation* (2nd ed.). Charlottesville, Va.: University Press of Virginia, 1974.

Ullman, M., Krippner, S., with Vaughan, A. *Dream telepathy*. New York: Macmillan, 1973.

Van de Castle, R. L. An exploratory study of some personality correlates associated with PK performance. *Journal of the American Society for Psychical Research*, 1958, *52*, 134–150.

Walker, E. H. Consciousness and quantum theory. In E. D. Mitchell and others, *Psychic exploration: A challenge for science*. New York: Putnam's, 1974.

Problems and Methods in Psychokinesis Research

1

Joseph H. Rush

1. Introduction

Psychokinesis (PK), sometimes called telekinesis or mind-over-matter, is as old as folklore. The power to affect a physical situation without known physical means has been attributed to shamans, mystics, witches, ghosts, and saints, and it figures prominently in religious and other literature. Yet, it was not until a century ago that investigators of such claims began to evolve methods that could be considered scientific. This development came about, in part, because Spiritualism had assembled an unlikely assortment of ostensibly paranormal phenomena under its aegis and made them fashionable and because contemporary developments in electrical science had impressed scientists and laymen alike with the essentially mysterious nature of the world.

This first century of parapsychology (formerly called psychical research) can be viewed as consisting of three fairly distinct periods. The first, ending about 1930, was a time of exploratory efforts to establish the reality of PK and other paranormal (psi) phenomena. It was dominated by the spiritistic orientation out of which the research had arisen, and its methods were severely compromised by restrictive conditions that the "physical mediums" usually imposed upon the investigators.

The second period began with the statistically controlled ESP and PK experiments with cards and dice that were undertaken at Duke

Joseph H. Rush · Boulder, Colorado.

University in 1930. This type of research dominated the field until interest in PK almost disappeared in the 1950s.

The third period, roughly since 1960, has been characterized by a revival of PK research, by a new wave of interest in spectacular manifestations by PK "stars," and by more sophisticated experimental designs and technology.

Because the purpose of this chapter is not to evaluate the results of PK investigations but to trace the evolution of research methodology, no attempt will be made to mention or summarize all the significant research. Rather, attention will be directed to certain representative investigations for the insight they afford as to the reasons for various methodological developments, their merits, and their defects. Original references and important reprints usually will be given. However, many of the early publications are not readily available. Useful summaries and criticisms of most of the early research may be found in Carrington (1907, 1909, 1939/1975, 1954), Gauld (1968), Geley (1927/1975), Podmore (1902/1963), 1910/1975), and Richet (1923).

2. The Pioneer Period: 1870 to 1930

2.1. Poltergeists

The term *poltergeist* (German: "noisy ghost") refers to spontaneous occurrences of rappings and other noises, movements and breakage of objects, and other physical manifestations that have been reported from many cultures and periods. A. R. G. Owen (1964) has compiled summary reports and discussions of a great many such cases. During the pioneering period of psychical research, two methodologically significant works appeared on this subject.

Sir William Barrett (1911) published a collection of comparatively credible poltergeist cases. He analyzed these as best he could, in view of the uncertain reliability of the material, and arrived at these principal conclusions: some poltergeist episodes involved paranormal phenomena; usually they were associated with a child or young adult; they were sporadic and temporary; and they were closely related to the physical phenomena of spiritualistic séances.

Barrett's contribution to the methods of such investigations thus consisted in collecting and analyzing the records and testimony of others, much as Gurney, Myers, and Podmore (1886/1970) had done with respect to spontaneous psychic experiences more generally. He found little opportunity to investigate poltergeists himself. The methods applied to such investigations by those who reported them amounted to doing whatever seemed expedient to the investigator, rarely experienced in such matters, when unexpectedly confronted with a baffling and suspect situation.

A notable exception to this tendency is summarized by Owen (1964, p. 111) in the case of Karin, a young woman. Soon after her marriage, she had developed hysterical symptoms. As these symptoms had subsided over several years, a secondary personality and poltergeist phenomena had emerged. Hjalmar Wijk (1905) reported observations that he and Dr. Paul Bjerre (1947), a pioneer psychoanalyst, made in the course of Bjerre's attempts to resolve Karin's psychological difficulties. Using hypnosis and analytical techniques, he tried to communicate with the secondary personality and bring about its integration with her normal self. He was able by posthypnotic suggestion to have raps produced at specified times; but he was unable to evoke the secondary personality directly or to integrate it. This isolated therapeutic effort marked an approach to poltergeist and haunting manifestations that would receive more attention a generation later.

2.2. The Physical Phenomena of Spiritualism

The proliferation of physical mediumship confronted scientists with both opportunity and challenge. The opportunity was obvious, to investigate psychic phenomena that occurred more-or-less on order. The challenge was more subtle: to accommodate to the conditions that were held to be necessary for the production of the phenomena and yet obtain valid evidence of their genuineness. That requirement obviously was prerequisite to any meaningful study of the phenomena per se. Physicist William Crookes (1874) saw the problem clearly:

> The spiritualist tells of rooms and houses being shaken even to injury by superhuman power. The man of science merely asks for a pendulum to be set vibrating when it is in a glass case and supported on solid masonry. . . .
> The spiritualist tells of flowers with the fresh dew on them, of fruit, and living objects being carried through closed windows, and even solid brick walls. The scientific investigator naturally asks that an additional weight . . . be deposited on one pan of his balance when the case is locked. (p. 6)

Yet Crookes never found a medium who could or would meet his criteria. Indeed, Frank Podmore (1902/1963, vol. 2, p. 183) could still put the matter succinctly: "The annals of Spiritualism offer no physical phenomena which do not, in the last analysis, depend on the experimenter's unaided senses for their observation, and on his memory for their record." Why were such simple conditions as Crookes proposed not met? Most mediums refused to try such experiments; others agreed, but evaded the conditions; others tried and failed. The German physicist J. C. F. Zöllner (1880), experimenting with the highly dubious medium William Slade, marveled that the spirits, even when failing to meet his prescribed tests, usually gave him still "better" evidence of their own choosing. As an example, when he asked that two separate wooden rings be interlinked, "they" instead put the rings around a table leg—a neat trick, but not physically impossible (Podmore, 1902/1963, vol. 2, p. 193).

Besides the phenomena of the (usually) dark séance, two variations were sufficiently distinctive to justify separate treatment: séances, usually in good light, in which "spirit writing" appeared on slates apparently independently of normal agency or contact; and "spirit photography," by which intrusive images, supposedly of departed friends or relatives, appeared on otherwise normal photographs.

2.2.1. Slate-Writing

Investigations of slate-writing turned out to be almost exclusively exercises in the detection of fraud, contributing little to research methodology proper. Nevertheless, the phenomena they dealt with were superficially so convincing, the explanations so astonishing, and the lessons for all areas of psychic investigation so chastening, that their presentation here appears justified. Podmore (1902/1963) devotes a chapter to the subject and cites numerous other references. Gauld (1968) gives it some attention also. For our purpose, one climactic development will serve to demonstrate the methods that were used and the psychological principles on which they depended for their outrageous success.

Among the clients who came to be mystified by the slate-writing feats of William Eglinton was a young man, S. J. Davey, who at first was deeply impressed. He was in good company. Not merely convinced spiritualists, but even such master magicians as Harry Kellar and "Professor Hoffman," were convinced that Eglinton's phenomena were not produced by trickery. Davey, however, became suspicious and by intensive conjuring practice learned to duplicate the slate-writing feats he had seen. In 1886, in collaboration with investigator Richard Hodgson, Davey "came out" under an assumed name as a slate-writing medium.

His "sittings" were conducted in the prosaic atmosphere of his lodgings. He made no appeal to religious expectancy, considering that unethical. Yet he duplicated most of Eglinton's demonstrations and completely mystified his clients, even some who had been told in advance that they would see only conjuring tricks. Sitters' accounts of what they thought happened, compared with Davey's accounts of what he actually did, are most illuminating (Hodgson, 1892; Hodgson and Davey, 1887).

Gauld (1968) has presented one of these incidents modified from Hodgson (1892, pp. 282—289), conveniently rearranged for such comparison; a portion of it follows. The unbracketed passages are the sitter's account; that in square brackets is what Davey did:

Three tricks are described and, since Davey ran them concurrently, the better to distract his sitter (a certain Mr. S.), I [Gauld] have indicated which portion of the text is related to which trick by inserting the signs (i), (ii) and (iii).

(i) After I had finished examining the slate, Mr. Davey asked me to write on the slate any question I liked while he was absent from the room. Picking up a piece of grey crayon, I wrote the following question: "What is the specific gravity of platinum?" and then having locked the slate and retained the key, I placed the former on the table and the latter in my pocket.

[(i) When Davey returned to the room he asked Mr. S. to examine the table. Whilst Mr. S. was thus occupied, Davey removed the locked slate, probably under cover of a duster which was used for cleaning the slates, and substituted a precisely similar slate (both slates were his own property). He then gave Mr. S. some ordinary slates to wash and dry. During this interval Davey left the room, opened the slates, answered the question, and returned and exchanged the slates once again.

(ii) Davey now took three slates. On one of them, which had not been in the hands of the sitter, and on the under surface of which was a prepared message, he placed a fragment of red crayon. He then covered up this slate with another, and left them on the table in full view. (The third slate he held under the table flap for a while, obtaining writing on its upper surface by the simple expedient of writing on the lower surface with a crumb of pencil attached to a thimble, taking the slate out to show the blank upper surface, and turning it upside down as he replaced it. . . . (i) Davey and Mr. S. then both put their hands on the locked slate on top of the table.]

(i) After the lapse of a few minutes I heard a distinct sound as of writing, and on being requested to unlock the slate I there discovered to my great surprise the answer of my question: 'We don't know the specific gravity, Joey.' The pencil with which it was written was a little piece which we had enclosed, and which would just rattle between the sides of the folded slate.

Having had my hands on the slate above the table, I can certify that the slate was not touched or tampered with during the time the

writing was going on. . . . If the particles taken from the pencil by
friction did not go on the surface of the slate, where could they go?
(pp. 205–207)*

It is essential to note that Davey's success depended not merely on
distracting the sitter's attention, but on doing so in such a way that the
sitter did not notice that he was being distracted. Like most conjuring
feats, these exploited the fact that perception is not at all the direct,
continuous process that it seems subjectively to be. The implications of
these and other such analyses for all phases of psychical research were
profound, but they do not appear to have been widely recognized.

2.2.2. Spirit Photography

Portrait photography and spiritualism became popular at about the
same time, and certain photographers soon began to get "extras" (images
of persons not physically present) on some of their portraits. Sitters
frequently identified extras as likenesses of dead friends or relatives, and
photographers who could produce such images enjoyed recurrent popularity throughout the period we are examining. They enjoyed also the
attentive interest of skeptical investigators, whose reports constitute one
of the more entertaining chapters in the checkered history of psychical
research. Astute detective work revealed many ingenious ways by which
fraudulent images were superimposed upon normal portraits. Mrs. Henry
Sidgwick (1891) published an early critical essay on the subject. Fred
Barlow and W. Rampling-Rose (1933) wrote of their investigations of
photographic fraud, and Harry Price (1936) included a chapter on the
subject, with many references.

Since none of these investigations developed impressive evidence for
paranormal photography and many found clear proof of fraud, spirit
photography—like slate-writing—might appear to hold only cautionary
significance for PK methodology. However, a few reports appear to
deserve more serious consideration. Charles H. Cook (1916), a Denver
minister, obtained pictures with a medium who merely sat passively
while Cook handled his own plates but used the medium's camera and
accessories. Cook took the plates to another place for development.
Unfortunately, these experiments were published 15 years after they had
been done, and it is not clear to what extent Cook's account was
supported by detailed records.

*Reprinted by permission of Routledge & Kegan Paul (London, 1968) and Schocken
Books Inc. from *The Founders of Psychical Research* by Alan Gauld. Copyright
© 1968 by Alan Gauld.

F. W. Warrick (1939), a British industrialist, reported a decade of studies in paranormal photography and related phenomena. His book is extensive and detailed, with many photographs. It includes accounts of many such experiments by other investigators also. Warrick's experiments antedated publication by 10 to 15 years; however, he stated that he had made notes during each experiment and expanded these into a detailed report within two days.

Warrick's account poses the problem of evidence in such matters with classic clarity. Obviously a capable, intelligent, persistent man, he was uncommitted to the spiritistic or any other preconceived hypothesis. He well understood the possibility of fraud, and freely acknowledged that some of his photographs bear peculiarities that strongly suggest fraudulent production. He insisted, however, that the implied fraud could not have been accomplished under the conditions of the experiment. This is the weakest link in his case. His confidence is disturbingly reminiscent of that of observers of Davey's slate-writing feats. Nevertheless, Warrick reported some experiments in which the hands of his medium, Mrs. Emma Deane, had been confined in "stocks"; yet marks and patterns appeared on photographic material, or sometimes plain paper, that was supported on an easel above her hands.

Meanwhile, a professor of literature at the Imperial University of Tokyo, T. Fukurai (1931/1975), began in 1910 a series of experiments in what he termed "thoughtography." Most of his subjects worked in trance and exhibited secondary personalities, but they did not invoke spirits or produce portraits. Almost always the object of the test was to produce on a wrapped and sealed photographic plate a figure or symbol that Fukurai prescribed. He worked extensively with only one subject, a Mrs. Nagao, but personally conducted a few tests with two others, and tested three more through agents or by correspondence.

Fukurai appears to have appreciated the precautions that were necessary to validate the results of such experiments: e.g., varied sources of plates and precautions against tampering with the experimental plates or substituting others. His report, however, reveals that he repeatedly had to compromise his methodological standards because of circumstances (testing by correspondence or through third parties) and because of concessions insisted upon by the subject. His relation with Mrs. Nagao affords an entertaining example of the battle of wits to which investigators of physical phenomena usually were reduced. He, of course, wanted to keep the experimental plates with him throughout his visit to her home. She insisted he leave them unguarded on a table in an anteroom until she was ready for the experiment and upbraided him on one occasion when she discovered that he had kept them in his pocket!

Because of such difficulties, only two successful tests appear by his account to have been fully controlled against fraud. Nor is one's estimate of his experimental sagacity improved by reading his enthusiastic report of later sittings in England with the spirit photographer William Hope, who was exposed repeatedly by other investigators (Barlow and Rampling-Rose, 1933; Price, 1936). Nevertheless, Fukurai deserves a place in the history of PK methodology. Despite his concessions to necessity, he clearly conceived of a well-controlled, nonspiritistic laboratory PK experiment a quarter-century before such a concept was generally adopted.

2.2.3. Dark-Séance Phenomena

Most alleged PK phenomena of this early period occurred in "dark séances." Typically, several investigators or spiritualist clients and the medium, who was the focus of the phenomena, sat around a table in a dark or dimly lighted room. The medium went into a self-induced trance, and various manifestations developed. These typically began with rapping sounds and tilting movements of the table. In many cases, more spectacular effects were reported: levitation of the table or other objects without contact; fleeting lights; cold sensations; touches as if by hands; manipulation of musical instruments or other objects; and even "materializations," apparently substantial simulations of heads, hands, even entire human figures. The more spectacular phenomena nearly always occurred in darkness or at best very dim red light. Mediums insisted that light was dangerous to them and inhibited the phenomena.

Scientific investigation of such manifestations presented severe difficulties, not in designing fraudproof experiments, but because such experiments were rejected by the mediums, or were compromised in the execution, or failed. Investigators almost always were limited to "controlling" the medium by continuous sensory surveillance: i.e., by touching or holding the medium's hands and feet, with such confirmation as vision in dim light could afford. The literature of such investigations is extensive, interesting, and sometimes downright hilarious (e.g., Carrington, 1907, 1909, 1954; Feilding, 1963; McComas, 1935; Richet, 1923; Tietze, 1973a). In some instances it is baffling and evocative of wonder.

2.2.3a. The Battle of Wits. The methodological capabilities and difficulties that attended such limited means of control can be epitomized by the studies of the Italian medium, Eusapia Palladino, who was investigated repeatedly from 1892 to about 1910 by Continental, British, and American scientists. Two of these studies will serve to illustrate the range of investigative approaches and results. In 1895 a committee of the (British) Society for Psychical Research (SPR) conducted sittings with Palladino at Cambridge. The group included F. W. H. Myers and Oliver Lodge, who both ha'd been favorably impressed in earlier sittings with her, and such confirmed skeptics as Henry and Eleanor Sidgwick and Richard Hodgson. From the outset, evasions of control were detected. These were accomplished by a skillful technique, not original with Palladino, of shifting hands or feet until the controllers on both her right and left were induced to transfer their tactual control to a single hand or foot without either noticing what had happened. Thus a hand or foot of the medium was freed to manipulate objects in the near-darkness.

Such substitution of hands or feet appears at first sight incredible. How could two investigators both hold the same hand not know it? First, Palladino allowed the controller on one side to grasp her hand; but she usually insisted on placing her other hand *on* the hand of the other controller. And she usually placed at least one of her feet (in shoes) on the shod foot of the controller. Further, she was continually active during a séance, kicking, swinging her legs, shifting hands from table to controllers' knees to her lap, stroking the hand or arm of the controller with her hand. The difficulty in making sure of tactual control after several hours of such monotonous routine, particularly when distracted by exciting phenomena, is easy to imagine. Further distraction of the Victorian gentlemen's attention may be surmised from the medium's uninhibited disposition of her person during the séance, now falling into the arms of one controller, now flinging a leg across the lap of the other.

When Hodgson took charge of the Cambridge investigation late in the series of sittings, he posed to Palladino as a naive enthusiast and deliberately relaxed the controls enough to allow her to cheat without difficulty. Apparently she seized the opportunity. Myers, probably the most favorably disposed member of the SPR committee, wrote:

> I cannot doubt that we observed much conscious and deliberate fraud, of a kind which must have needed long practice to bring it to its present level of skill. . . . With growing experience . . . and careful observation of the precise conditions permitted or refused to us, the existence of some fraud became clear; and fraud was attempted when the tests were as good as we were allowed to make them, quite as indisputably as on the few occasions when our holding was intentionally left inadequate in order to trace more exactly the *modus operandi*. . . .
> I do not think that there is adequate reason to suppose that any of the phenomena at Cambridge were genuine. [Quoted in Podmore (1910/1975), pp. 97, 98]

In 1908, persistent reports of phenomena with Palladino under good conditions led the SPR to sponsor a second investigation. The Hon. Everard Feilding, Hereward Carrington, and W. W. Baggally undertook the task. Baggally and Carrington were good amateur conjurers. All had extensive experience in investigating physical mediums; none had found any phenomena he believed to be paranormal. This team, with their stenographer and sometimes with guests, held eleven sittings with Palladino in a hotel room in Naples. During each séance, the investigators continually reported changes in their control conditions, phenomena observed, and other relevant information. The resulting shorthand report, together with the investigators' appended comments, is undoubtedly the most meticulous record ever made of such an investigation (Feilding, 1963; Feilding, Baggally, and Carrington, 1909).

The team on a few occasions detected the medium freeing a hand by the substitution trick described earlier. They were much impressed by the skill with which this maneuver could be done, so smoothly that it could not be detected by touch alone. They therefore decided that nothing they observed could be considered evidential unless they had positive control of the medium's hands and feet, or enough light to verify control. The illumination required by the medium varied from darkness to enough to read small print.

The unanimous conclusion of the investigators was that they had observed raps, movements and levitations of tables and other objects, billowing of curtains, lights, inexplicable shapes including on one occasion a hand, sensations of being touched, and other phenomena, all under conditions of control that in their judgment completely precluded fraud. They (Feilding et al., 1909) were as emphatic in this opinion as Myers had been in his contrary estimate of the Cambridge sittings:

> The evidence for the foregoing phenomena varies considerably both in quantity and quality. . . . It was only through constant repetition of the same phenomenon, in a good light and at moments when its occurrence was expected, and after finding that none of the precautions which we took had any influence in impeding it, that we gradually reached the conviction that some force was in play which was [paranormal]. . . . Our conclusions are based on the resultant impressions derived from the whole series. (pp. 340–341)

Yet, as the investigators had recognized, their report could not be as convincing as their experiences had been. Podmore (1909) especially remained skeptical. He developed a detailed analysis supporting his belief that Palladino had managed substitution of hands or feet despite the investigators' vigilance. Further séances, in some of which systematic fraud was reported, preceded Palladino's retirement.

The controversy over Palladino's phenomena, still unresolved, is not immediately relevant to this discussion. The essential point is the inadequacy of the investigative method of the time, even when applied by such highly qualified men as the SPR team at Naples. The method still demanded of the investigators continuous vigilance and accurate sensory interpretations under difficult conditions. It simply was not good enough to support definitive conclusions.

2.2.3b. Improved Methods; Instrumentation. During the 1920s several investigators introduced improved instrumentation to control séances and to register observations of phenomena. Such use of technology was hardly novel. Photographs had been taken in sittings with Palladino and some other mediums. However, instantaneous photos seldom contribute significantly toward understanding how effects were accomplished, particularly if they have been taken at times designated by the medium. In 1874 Cromwell Varley had devised an electrical apparatus for Crookes, to insure that the medium did not free her hands (Medhurst and Goldney, 1964, pp. 95–102; Podmore, 1902/1963, vol. 2). However, it produced ambiguous results (Brookes-Smith, 1965) and does not appear to have been used later. Weight changes of Eusapia and other mediums during the occurrence of physical phenomena had been recorded (Carrington, 1939/1975, p. 102); but controls had been dubious.

Harry Price (1925/1973) reported a series of séances with Stella C., a young woman medium. Price selected the sitters and determined the procedure; the sittings were held in his laboratory. By his account, the red light was always sufficient to see the sitters clearly; and the medium offered no problems of control, being very quiet and also visible. A special "table within a table" was devised as a focus for the phenomena. It consisted essentially of a small wooden table nested inside a cage, except that the top of the small table was exposed. Thus, levitation of the inner table or movement of objects inside the cage by normal means was made very difficult. Under these conditions, very strong physical effects were reported.

A self-registering thermometer, which indicated maximum and minimum temperatures to which it had been exposed, hung on a wall of the séance room. It repeatedly registered minima several degrees lower than the normal room temperature. Inside the inner table Price placed an ingenious device, an electrical pressure switch mounted inside a cup and connected to an external light. The top of the cup was sealed by a soap-bubble film, and a protective glass cover was placed over the cup. Nevertheless, on one occasion the light was turned on and the bubble film found intact afterward.

Price also used a "shadow apparatus"—essentially a lens to project a straight beam of red light several feet onto a viewing screen—in the hope that any materialized or semimaterialized forms crossing the beam would appear in silhouette on the screen. On at least one occasion such a form was reported.

The prolonged investigations of the Austrian medium Rudi Schneider inspired several significant innovations. Price (1930) adopted a control scheme that Baron Albert von Schrenck-Notzing and Karl Krall had proposed. Each person present, including the medium, wore special electrically conducting shoes and mittens that were connected to several red signal lights. So long as the sitters maintained a closed circle by touching hands and feet, the lights glowed. No one could free a hand or foot without breaking one of the light circuits, unless both his neighbors "covered" for him by maintaining contact. This apparently excellent control did not inhibit the production of spectacular physical phenomena.

Eugene Osty (Osty and Osty, 1931, 1932), of the Institut Métapsychique at Paris, then conducted a long series of experiments with Schneider. One of his tests consisted of an apparatus by which a beam of infrared (IR) radiation acted on an electrical detector that controlled several cameras. Interruption of the beam by an object would fire the cameras and presumably photograph the object. Invisible IR radiation was used to avoid the medium's objection to visible light. On several occasions the cameras were triggered; but the photographs (made by visible flash) revealed no trace of anything in the IR beam. However, it is equally plausible that the psychokinetic agency, if such it was, acted directly on a switch or other element in the camera circuit.

Lord Charles Hope et al. (1933) and Lord Rayleigh (1933) conducted experiments with Schneider that were similar to Osty's, in which ostensible obstruction of an IR beam was registered electrically, though the beam was shielded against normal access.

Price also used photography during some of his experiments with Schneider. One of the resulting photographs became the basis of an accusation of fraud by Price, leading to a bitter controversy (Besterman, 1932; Gregory, 1971, 1974; Price, 1936; Tietze, 1973b).

Christian Winther (1928) of Denmark reported experiments with a remarkable medium, Anna Rasmussen. Various effects were obtained, including lowering of thermometer readings. Rather than merely observing whatever happened, Winther concentrated on experiments with pendulums. Changes in the motion of a pendulum are easily observed, and from them calculations of energy and other physical parameters involved in the PK activity could be evaluated. Unfortunately, a pendulum is one of the most sensitive devices to small, repeated mechanical disturbances, such as the unobtrusive shifting of a portion of one's weight from one foot to the other in time with the natural period of the pendulum. Winther recognized this difficulty, but was satisfied that his precautions eliminated such intervention. He obtained, for example, alterations of the motion of one of a pair of pendulums hung on the same support while the other was unaffected. And he emphasized that all of his experiments were carried out in normal room light, even daylight.

Methodologically more significant, perhaps, than these experiments is Winther's account of the psychological conditions during his séances and of the development of the medium's abilities under his direction and discipline. Mrs. Rasmussen behaved as one of the sitters. She liked much talking, laughter, "jolly singing," and frequent refreshments. She was seldom in trance, and no spiritistic implications were involved. However, her secondary personality was an exaggerated version of the medium's normally unstable, hypersensitive self, quick to rage and sulk at any slight, real or fancied. Such tantrums disrupted the séances and interfered with the systematic experimentation that Winther had planned. He therefore worked with the medium for several months, through hypnosis and other techniques, both to make her feel more at ease and to condition the secondary personality to accept his direction. He noted that this effort was successful, so that he and his associates were able to obtain some PK effects of the kinds they requested at almost every séance. But the price was a concurrent decline in the strength and variety of the phenomena.

2.2.4. The Decline of Physical Phenomena

During the 1920s the prospect appeared excellent for accumulating objective evidence that would decisively resolve the controversy over the reality of psychokinetic phenomena. Instrumental technology was increasingly adapted to preclude fraud and provide objective records of séance phenomena. Further, several mediums had given impressive performances in good light and without the persistent attempts to evade control that had marred the records of Palladino and others. The presumption appeared justified that the traditional darkness and spiritistic atmosphere were not essential to the production of physical phenomena, and consequently that objective evidence of such phenomena under fraud-proof conditions might soon be generally accepted.

But events did not work out that way. Instead, reports of investigations of physical mediums dwindled nearly to zero in the ensuing decade. Rudi Schneider, whose career ended in the early 1930s, was the last notable practitioner. Why the reports of physical séance phenomena died out just when the prospect of their validation was most promising is a complex question for historians of the field. The skeptic will insist that the phenomena died out precisely because of the improved controls against fraud. Certainly this factor thinned the ranks of mediumistic claimants; but it does not appear adequate in the light of the better investigations cited earlier. Price's denunciation of Rudi Schneider, whether justifiable or not, had a strong adverse effect. The disastrous culmination of the notorious "Margery" mediumship (Tietze, 1973a) at about the same time contributed to discrediting this type of investigation.

Probably more significant than these adverse influences, however, was the shift of fashion in psychical research that was induced by the program of statistical experiments that was begun at the Parapsychology Laboratory of Duke University in 1930.

3. The Era of Statistical Experiments: From 1930 to about 1960

3.1. The Duke University Experiments with Dice

The experiments in psychokinesis that J. B. Rhine initiated at the Parapsychology Laboratory of Duke University in 1934 (Rhine and Rhine, 1943) marked a sharp methodological departure from prior investigations of physical psi phenomena. The Duke ESP experiments (Rhine, 1934/1964), begun in 1930, had consolidated techniques that had been developing sporadically since the 1870s. The PK experiments were closely analogous to the ESP techniques in their simplicity, their dependence on undistinguished subjects, and their adaptability to statistical evaluation; but they had no antecedents. Why none of the earlier investigators of "mind reading" had reported analogous controllable tests for PK effects is not clear. The nearest approximations had been in some of the experiments in psychic photography mentioned earlier.

Rhine's approach to PK experimentation embodied several distinctive features:

1. Dependence upon cumulative low-level performance by subjects having no claims to unusual psychic powers.
2. Use of standardized tasks and apparatus (dice), with potentially complete control of the physical aspects of the experiment.
3. Simple, rigorous statistical evaluation of scores.
4. Analyses of results for position effects (principally declines).

Experiments designed on these principles offered obvious advantages. A subject who claims rare and spectacular PK ability is necessarily suspect; but performance at a low, nonobvious level is more credible, particularly if it is exhibited by a number of ordinary subjects. Science, after all, is concerned with relationships; it rejects uniqueness. Dice throwing offered the advantage of familiarity, a gamelike atmosphere of playful challenge, and simple evaluation of scores. Also, dice tests were in principle easy to control against fraud and most other sources of error.

Experimental designs were flexible. The size, material, or other characteristics of the dice, the number thrown simultaneously, the method of throwing, the number of throws in a continuous run, the target face or combination, all could be varied as the experimenter might choose, subject to certain precautions.

An inherent disadvantage of experimenting with dice is mechanical bias in the dice themselves. Imperfections in shape and homogeneity of a die have the effect of "loading" it, so that on average certain faces turn up more frequently than others. Experiments, therefore, must be designed to cancel the effects of such deviations from the ideal expectations if the results are to be unambiguous. A more fundamental disadvantage of these or other experiments that depend upon statistical evaluation is the simple fact that they do depend upon such evaluation. The ostensible psychokinetic influence does not produce a directly observable effect, such as obvious movement of a visible object or alteration of the reading of a thermometer. Its effect must be inferred from small deviations in the behavior of moving dice from that to be expected from empirical control runs or probability theory. The effect is at best an obscure change in the random motions of tumbling cubes, inevitably less convincing than motion imparted to a stationary object.

3.1.1. The Exploratory Period

Though the first dice experiments were done at Duke in 1934, none was published until the first of the accumulated reports appeared nine years later (Rhine and Rhine, 1943). Nearly all of the reports of statistical PK experiments done from 1934 to 1960 are summarized in evaluations by J. G. Pratt (1960) and Edward Girden (1962a); each includes a comprehensive bibliography. Louisa E. Rhine (1970) covers the subject at a more popular level.

It is clear from the experimental reports that Rhine and his staff deliberately conducted the early PK experiments in a rather free, casual style. They felt that any psi ability in their subjects would be facilitated by this approach, and that any resulting evidence for PK could then be confirmed by more rigorous procedures. These exploratory experiments consequently embodied various faults in designs or procedures. Precautions against dice bias were recognized to be necessary, but usually were inadequate. Subjects often were allowed to choose their targets (they preferred 6). Many tests were unwitnessed, and inadequate checks were made for recording errors. Optional stopping and other statistical faults sometimes occurred.

Subjects were almost all students who had heard of the experiments and volunteered to participate in them. This tacit screening process may have been a significant factor in the success of most of the early experiments. The subjects were there of their own volition, actively involved, not recruited for pay or incidentally to their course work. Instructions were of necessity somewhat vague. Subjects had the rationale of an experiment explained to them. They were then asked to wish for the assigned target face, or to concentrate on it and "will" it to come up. Though some subjects appeared to concentrate deeply, none showed obvious evidence of trance or other unusual state of consciousness.

Dice were thrown by hand in a few early tests, then from a cup or other receptacle. Very soon apparatus began to be devised to throw or roll the dice mechanically (e.g., Gibson, Gibson, and Rhine, 1944; Rhine, 1943; Rhine and Rhine, 1943). Two dice might be thrown for high or low combinations. Usually a single face (number) was the PK target, though the number of dice thrown simultaneously varied from 1 to 96. After each throw, the uppermost faces (or, usually, only the number of "hits" on the target) were written on a standardized record sheet. Tests usually were subdivided into "runs" of 24 trials.

Statistical evaluation of the test scores was done by conventional methods (Rhine and Rhine, 1943). Since each of the 6 faces of a die could be expected (in the absence of mechanical bias) to turn up on average in $\frac{1}{6}$ of the throws, a run of 24 throws could be expected to turn up an average of 4 hits on the target face. Slightly more complicated odds applied to combination targets, such as doubles or high dice. The theoretical standard deviation σ for a test series was calculated by the usual formula: $\sigma = \sqrt{npq}$, where n is the number of individual trials, p the probability of a hit per trial, and q the probability of a miss. The experimental deviation D is the excess of hits over the mean chance expectation $n/6$. D/σ is the critical ratio (CR), which is related to probability values by computation or the use of statistical tables.

Somewhat more complex statistical methods were required to assess the irregularities in hit distributions known as position effects. Since this type of analysis amounts to an important innovation in method, it will be dealt with later.

3.1.2. Later Experiments

The reports from the Duke laboratory of PK experiments done after 1943 indicate substantial improvements in methods and procedures. Possibly these were prompted by critical reactions to the publications of the earlier work. Systematic rotation of targets among the six die faces, to cancel effects of biased dice, was generally adopted. Improvements in dice-throwing techniques culminated in a fully automatic machine that at the push of a button would tumble the dice down an inclined chute and photograph the resulting upper faces. Recording procedures were improved, and unwitnessed experiments became rare.

Though most of the dice experiments were designed primarily to detect evidence of PK, some attempted to explore the dependence of PK scoring upon experimental variables. These will be noted in more detail later.

The experiments at Duke excited much interest and controversy. Even before they were published, others heard of them and tried similar tests (e.g., Gibson, Gibson, and Rhine, 1944; Rhine and Humphrey, 1944a). C. B. Nash (1944) independently hit on the idea of using dice in PK experiments in 1940, but tests with his biology students did not yield significant results. Publication of the Duke experiments stimulated numerous attempts to replicate them, both in America and abroad (Girden, 1962a,b; Rhine, 1970). Most of these later dice experiments, both at Duke and elsewhere, produced nonsignificant or marginally significant scores. Interest in such experiments declined during the 1950s. By 1960, reports of PK experiments with dice had almost ceased.

3.2. Variations on the Duke Experimental Model

Generally, the PK experiments with dice that were inspired by the reports from the Duke laboratory duplicated or improved upon them only in detail. A few introduced methodological innovations.

Despite the accumulated evidence for clairvoyance (cognition of a concealed target), none of the early PK experimenters attempted to test it in connection with PK. A Cambridge psychologist, Robert H. Thouless (1951) first carried out such an experiment, with himself as subject. He determined the targets by shuffling cards, and turned up each card only after the trials on it as target had been completed. Thus, any scoring success logically would have to be attributed to clairvoyant knowledge of the target plus psychokinetic influence on the dice. Karlis Osis (1953) reported on a similar blind-target procedure at Duke. A. M. J. Mitchell and G. W. Fisk (1953) in England reported some remarkable dice tests with blind targets 170 miles (274 km) from the subject. They also employed a method of differential scoring that distinguished among hits on the target face of the die, an adjacent face, or the face opposite the target, and offered evidence that this method was a more sensitive indicator of nonrandom effects than scoring on the target face alone. Another complex-target experiment was reported from the Duke laboratory by Betty M. Humphrey (1947b). She threw 6 red and 6 white dice simultaneously, with 1-faces as targets, while trying for a positive score on dice of one color and negative (i.e., misses) on the other.

Like dice throwing, coin tossing or spinning is a familiar device for demonstrating chance effects or departures from them. Coins or plain disks have been little used in PK experiments, possibly because greater care is required to insure essentially random falls than in the case of dice. Thouless (1945) reported an experiment with spinning coins. Elizabeth McMahan (1945) at Duke carried out a series of tests with children in which poker chips with differently colored faces were tumbled in a tube with baffles. S. R. Binski (1957) in Germany reported an experiment that involved hand-throwing 100 coins simultaneously. (He also used a roulette wheel in some tests.) Except for the scores of one remarkable subject discovered by Binski, the coin or disk experiments led to no strong results.

3.2.1. PK Placement Tests

During the late 1940s several experimenters adapted the basic tumbling-cube technique to what are known generally as PK placement tests because they are concerned with the final locations of the cubes rather than the orientations of their faces. The first of these was devised by W. E. Cox (1951), a North Carolina businessman who had become interested in the psi investigations at Duke University. His intention was to compare the rates of PK success in turning up target faces vs. placing the dice in target locations. His first apparatus was essentially a shallow box, the bottom of which was marked off in a checkerboard array of numbered squares. To make the placement task similar to that for face targets, each square carried the numeral 1, 2, 3, 4, 5, or 6, so arranged that no contiguous squares bore the same number. A trial consisted in tumbling 24 dice from a cup into the box. If 3, for example, was the target, then all dice that turned up 3 were counted as face hits, and all that came to rest on squares numbered 3 were placement hits. Rather than ask his subjects to strive for both face and placement targets at the same time, Cox designated one as primary and the other as secondary target for each trial. Either face or placement was primary target in half the trials.

Cox's results are worth pondering. He found no significant difference in the total scores for face and for place, but a highly significant difference between the scores for primary and secondary targets. Scores on primary targets (both face and place) were positive, while those on the secondary targets were negative.

Some of the Duke laboratory staff, feeling that the task that Cox had imposed upon his subjects was unduly complex, devised an apparatus to test placement PK alone and in only one dimension. Dice were mechanically released at the top of a ramp; they tumbled onto a horizontal surface and of course scattered and came to rest in an irregular pattern. A line along the approximate mean path of the dice divided the surface into right and left halves, either of which could be designated as the placement target: e.g., if the right side was the target, all dice stopping on that side were counted as hits. Target sides were alternated to cancel possible bias in the apparatus. This design was used successfully (Pratt, 1951; Rhine, 1951).

A Swedish engineer, Haakon Forwald, adopted the Duke placement technique about 1949 and used it with many detailed variations in experimental design in the longest and most persistent individual series of PK experiments on record. He worked almost entirely alone, devoting his efforts mainly to trying to discover consistent physical relations in the PK phenomenon. Though his variations of cube materials, methods of evaluating results, and other factors were in a sense methodological innovations, they were incidental to his quest for physical correlates of PK. His work appears in a series of reports (e.g., Forwald, 1952; Rhine, 1951) and in a comprehensive monograph (Forwald, 1969).

The success of placement tests for PK carries a theoretical implication of some interest. In principle, it had been obvious that the PK influence on dice might be effected either by an alteration in the die itself analogous to loading or by a hypothetical force that might alter the tumbling motion of the die. Either mechanism might conceivably influence the die in favor of the target face. The placement techniques, however, are insensitive to loading. If such mechanical models are relevant at all, PK in these experiments must be conceived as a transient dynamic effect.

3.3. Analyses of Position Effects

Systematic variations in scoring rates relative to positions in a repeated trial sequence had been noticed in the ESP card-guessing data at Duke. Similar tendencies were noted even in the very early PK experiments (Rhine and Rhine, 1943), appearing most obviously as a sharp decline in scoring between first and last halves of the runs. Sessions consequently were kept brief to minimize the influence of this effect on the total scores. However, it was not until 1942, eight years after the first PK tests with dice, that the Duke staff undertook a systematic analysis of position effects in all of the available PK data (Pratt, 1944; Rhine and Humphrey, 1944a,b; Rhine, Humphrey, and Pratt, 1945).

Because the present discussion is concerned with methods rather than results, the inclusion of the analyses of position effects might seem inappropriate. However, the strong and consistent patterns that they disclosed (principally a sequential decline in scoring rate) provided additional controls on dice bias and some other sources of error. Analysis of position effects thus constitutes an additional, important methodological device in the PK research.

The PK trial sequences customarily were recorded in a succession of columns on a page, from top to bottom of each column and from left to right across the page. Preliminary analyses had revealed tendencies for scoring to decline both from top to bottom and from left to right: i.e., from the earlier to the later trials. After some exploratory examinations of this kind, an analytical procedure was decided upon. Each homogeneous record page was divided into quarters by a vertical line down the middle of the page and a horizontal line through the middle of the columns. The score for each quarter on all the records of an experiment, or of a group of experiments, was computed separately. The differences among the composite scores for the four quarters were then evaluated for statistical significance.

The purpose of the analysis was to discover any position effects that might develop in an unperturbed trial sequence. This meant that any record page that included a change of subject or experimenter, or any other interruption of the psychological continuity of the trial sequence, was omitted from the analysis. Some other detailed criteria and precautions are explained in the reports cited above. The resulting study comprised analyses of 18 experiments. In 12 of these, the targets had been single die faces. The remaining 6 experiments involved combination targets for two or more dice.

The results showed remarkably consistent declines among the quarter-page composite scores. In all but two experiments, the sum of scores for the first (upper left) quarter of the page exceeded that for the last (lower right). Critical ratios of the differences ranged from .28 to 3.09, about half of them being greater than 2.00.

This decline effect has appeared repeatedly in later PK experiments. L. A. Dale (1946) found a similar tendency in her data, and Forwald (1969) noted that most of his successes occurred in the first trial of each set of five trials. In R. A. McConnell's meticulously controlled experiment, the significance of the results depended entirely upon the strong and consistent quarter-page decline effect (McConnell, Snowdon, and Powell, 1955).

The quarter-page division does not appear to be the most sensitive basis for detecting a decline effect. Scoring in the upper half of the second data column, for example, is at a lower rate than in the lower half of the first column, since it occurs later in the trial sequence. But in the quarter-division, the upper half of the second column is in the high-scoring first quarter, while the lower half of the first column is in the lower-scoring second quarter. If a consistent decline occurs, it should appear more prominently in a comparison of successive quarters of the trial sequence than in the geometrical quarters of the page.

Pratt (1946, 1947a–d) carried out detailed analyses of the trial sequences in several PK experiments. His outstanding finding was that scoring tended to rise at the end of each column, particularly the first (each column comprising one run of 24 trials), and that almost all of the significant scoring tended to occur in the first few trials of the first run.

The methodological significance of these position effects is most obvious in relation to dice bias. If, for example, six is the target for all of the trials in an experiment (as was the case in many early experiments, because of subject preference), an extra-chance score may be due to PK or to mechanical bias favoring sixes, or both. However, no plausible hypothesis has been suggested by which biased dice could produce the systematic rhythms in scoring rate that appear in the decline analyses. Similar arguments apply to the effects of recording errors and other irregularities. Further, statistically significant declines or other departures from random distribution of hits are in themselves independent evidence of anomalous influence on the dice.

3.4. Effects of Experimental Variables on PK Performance

Even in the earliest phase of the dice PK experiments, attempts were made to discover how the phenomenon might depend upon physical, physiological, or psychological variables. During the ensuing years, the few such experiments that have been reported have involved methodological weaknesses, and most have yielded only statistically marginal results at best. They must be regarded as exploratory probings; a few representative examples will be summarized briefly.

3.4.1. Physical Variables

PK implies an influence on the dice analogous to a force, so that the size or weight of the dice, or the number thrown in a single trial, might be expected to affect the experimental score. However, tests of such dependence (e.g., Hilton and Rhine, 1943; Hilton, Baer, and Rhine, 1943; Pratt, 1951; Rhine, 1944; Rhine and Humphrey, 1945) all yielded either null or inconsistent results.

The most extensive investigations of dependence of scoring upon the composition and weight of the cubes were done by Forwald (1969) in the course of his PK placement experiments. He also found inconsistent, though sometimes significant, differences that seemed to relate more to his expectations or attention than to physical factors. He has, however, reported orderly relations of a more complex kind between the composition and even nuclear properties of his cubes and the magnitude of the corresponding displacements.

Any physical influence in space ordinarily decreases with increasing distance from its source. C. B. Nash (1946; Nash and Richards, 1947) compared PK scores of several subjects at 3 ft (.9 m) and 30 ft (9.1 m) from the dice. The results of two such experiments were inconsistent but suggested better scores at the greater distance. Experiments by McConnell (1955) and by Mitchell and Fisk (1953) succeeded at distances of a few miles and 170 miles (274 km) respectively, but did not provide short-distance control tests.

In these experiments, any dependence of PK scoring upon simple physical variables clearly was masked by tendencies that exhibit little if any order. Apart from confusion of some of these exploratory results by dice bias, recording errors, or other faults, none of the experiments was designed to distinguish between physical and psychological variables. If a subject scores higher at 9.1 m than at .9 m from the dice, is that result due to an anomalous physical relation or to the subject's reaction to a challenge? Insofar as these experiments support any inferences, they suggest that alterations in results under various physical conditions were due more to incidental psychological effects on the subject (and possibly the experimenter) than to impersonal influences on the PK phenomenon.

3.4.2. Physiological Variables

Many incidental observations during PK experiments have suggested that the physiological condition of a subject, and possibly of an experimenter also, affects the results. Fatigue or illness, for example, has appeared to reduce the scoring rate. Hardly any controlled experiments on physiological variables have been reported. However, two such tests were carried out at the Duke laboratory in 1936. The first of these (Averill and Rhine, 1945) compared both authors' PK scoring with dice before and after ingestion of alcohol (gin in ginger ale). One subject was unable to retain the concoction long enough for it to be effective. The other scored at a highly significant rate before taking the mixture, but dropped slightly below chance level afterward.

A few days later three subjects tested the effect on scoring of a physiological stimulant, Coca-Cola (Rhine, Humphrey, and Averill, 1945). The results were striking. Each subject exhibited a distinct rise in scoring rate; the combined difference in scores before and after drinking was highly significant.

As the experimenters recognized, these casual tests could not distinguish between physiological effects of the drinks and effects of incidental suggestion or expectation. More sophisticated experiments under double-blind conditions would have been necessary to make such a distinction, and no such tests have been done.

3.4.3. Psychological Variables

Uncontrolled psychological variables in psi tests, as in any psychological experiments, are unavoidable. The experimenter can only try to circumvent their effects by insightful designs and hope for the best. In the PK investigations a few experimenters attempted to identify the effects on scoring of certain definable psychological variables.

Early in the PK research with dice, Humphrey (1947a) had two subjects try to influence each throw of the dice, one being assigned to "help" or "hinder" the other by trying for the same or a different target, in alternation. The scores on "help" runs proved to be highly significant, while those on "hinder" runs were not. In a comparable experiment (Price and Rhine, 1944) the experimenter tried actively to distract and discourage the subject. His scoring declined steadily from his previously established level of over 20% above chance expectation to a negative deviation. However, it is impossible to determine whether the decline resulted from the ostensible conflict of wills, or from a desire on the part of the subject to produce such an effect.

Several experiments were designed to determine whether a subject's belief or skepticism as to the possibility of PK would influence the scores with dice. L. A. Dale (1946) did such an experiment with 54 subjects, asking each before the dice trials whether he believed that PK was possible. C. B. Nash (1946) tried a similar procedure with nine subjects. Neither of these experiments showed any significant difference between believing "sheep" and skeptical "goats." R. L. Van de Castle (1958) separated his subjects into sheep, goats, and those who felt uncertain about PK. Scores of the sheep were substantially but nonsignificantly higher than those of the goats.

Van de Castle (1958) also tested for correlations between PK scoring and certain indices of personality differences. One of these was an estimate of "expansive" vs. "compressive" tendencies, judged by a subject's exhibition of freedom or inhibition in freehand drawings. This characteristic was rated on a scale of five steps for each of 31 subjects. Subsequent PK scores showed a consistent downward trend from those of the most expansive to those of the most compressive subjects, but did not reach statistical significance.

In studying these diverse attempts to test for the effects of specific variables upon PK scoring, one must be impressed by the difficulties inherent in such experiments. When the obvious sources of error—dice bias, recording errors, physical access of subject to the dice, and the like—have been eliminated, there remain subtle variables that can be only partially controlled. It is essential that the subject not know what conditions are being varied in an experiment; otherwise, it is impossible to determine whether to attribute any observed effect to direct influence of the variable or to the subject's expectation. Further, in view of the subtle communication that occurs when the experimenter is with the subject, it is obvious that the experimenter must be either absent or ignorant of the immediate test conditions. Double-blind procedures are essential; yet even subject blinds seldom were in force in the experiments mentioned above. And with all precautions one cannot entirely eliminate the nagging questions: who is influencing the dice; and how to design an experiment to be blind to ESP?

3.5. Criticisms of the Statistical PK Research

Like the Duke ESP research a decade earlier, the PK dice experiments stimulated both imitation and criticism. However, the criticism was not so vociferous or wide ranging as that of the ESP controversy, in part because some aspects that were common to both the ESP and the PK experiments already had been dealt with. Some of the earliest criticisms of the PK work came from Britain. Early efforts at replication there of the Duke dice scores failed, so that skepticism flourished. D. J. West (1945) published a critical survey of the American experiments, but concluded that the faults probably were minor and that the case for PK was strong. In a later evaluation (West, 1954) he somewhat modified this optimistic position.

S. G. Soal (1947, 1948) was severely critical of the Duke reports, particularly as to deficiencies in the experimental procedures. E. G. Boring (1955), C. W. K. Mundle (1950), and J. Fraser Nicol (1954, 1955, 1956) commented on controversial aspects of the research. C. E. M. Hansel (1966) devoted a portion of his book to criticism of the PK work. Much later, Frederick W. Knowles (1972) proposed that success in the dice experiments may have been achieved by subtle manipulative skill in positioning or throwing the dice, guided by clairvoyance and precognition.

These criticisms are not summarized here. Their principal arguments are presented in a detailed critical analysis by an American psychologist, Edward Girden (1962a). A rebuttal by psychologist Gardner Murphy (1962) followed, with a brief rejoinder by Girden (1962b). These papers were reprinted with comments by several additional authors (Girden, Murphy, Beloff, Eisenbud, Flew, Rush, Schmeidler, and Thouless, 1964).

In his analysis, Girden distinguished between the early PK experiments, done principally at or in association with the Duke laboratory, and the more sophisticated and broadly distributed studies done after the first publications of the early work in 1943. Not surprisingly, he found many faults in the first group, mainly under the headings of: loose, variable, undefined procedures; inadequate controls for dice bias; liability to recording errors; lack of empirical control tests; statistical pooling of nonhomogeneous data. He recognized that the experiments in the later group generally were better both in design and in execution; but he still found faults that in his judgment rendered the results inconclusive.

Murphy conceded that the early experiments were faulty, but noted that they were exploratory, not definitive. He charged that Girden had magnified the defects by ignoring the instances in which they had been avoided. He considered that Girden had exaggerated the value of formal empirical control tests to compare results of "wishing" with "not wishing" for the target faces. The equivalent control, Murphy noted, was achieved by comparing scoring on the target face of the dice with that on the nontarget faces in the same series of PK trials.

Girden pointed out that, if dice were biased in favor of a certain face and this face was the PK target predominantly during the early portion of an experimental sequence, a decline effect would result from the dice bias alone. He seemed to imply that this fault compromised all of the data used in the decline analyses discussed earlier; however, as Murphy noted, it was applicable to a few series only, and had been recognized and allowed for in the original analyses (Rhine and Humphrey, 1944a). Girden also termed the decline effect revealed in these analyses "a new hypothesis subject to subsequent test." As Murphy (1962) and Pratt (1963) both noted, any comparable but independent body of data meets the need for such confirmation. The first experiment to which the quarter-page analysis was applied inspired the decline hypothesis; the others, not yet analyzed, served to test and confirm it. The time order in which the experiments were done is irrelevant.

This summary indicates the principal bases of the controversy, but it cannot do justice to the complexity of the issues or to the diversity of expressions concerning them. The adverse criticisms could not dispose of the evidence for an anomalous psychologically determined effect that had been developed by the better experiments. Neither could the supportive arguments avoid the fact that the progressive "cleaning up" of experimental designs had coincided with a dwindling harvest of positive results. By 1960, the possibility that further confidence in the occurrence of psychokinesis could be gained from such experiments appeared unpromising. Interest in dice experiments waned as new ideas and techniques evolved.

3.6. Poltergeists Psychoanalyzed

Continuing interest in the rare and enigmatic poltergeist manifestations expressed itself in several new collections and analyses of case records (Carrington and Fodor, 1951; Moser, 1950; Thurston, 1954; Tizane, 1951). Tizane's work is especially interesting. It is a comparative analysis of many reports of poltergeist investigations by the French police, in which Tizane tried to discover what patterns or characteristics the unexplained cases had in common. His findings confirm the lore of such phenomena: stones fall; doors or windows open by themselves; loud noises occur; objects are moved or broken, etc. All of these works, however, were in the tradition of Barrett and other collectors of cases. Significant methodological innovations in the investigation of poltergeists came from another direction.

John Layard (1944), a Jungian psychologist in Britain, proposed that poltergeists resemble other psychological phenomena in that they serve a curative function or purpose by providing relief of psychological conflicts. The two clinical cases he offered in support of this interpretation admittedly were weak, but Layard emphasized that he was merely offering a hypothesis that ought to be investigated further. His insightful paper was denounced by most of the writers who responded.

Meanwhile Nandor Fodor, psychic investigator and psychoanalyst, had been developing a similar concept through practical experience. In a succession of cases that came to his attention (Fodor, 1948, 1958, 1959, 1964), he repeatedly found evidence that unresolved emotional tensions may be expressed in poltergeist phenomena. Sometimes he witnessed paranormal events; more often he had to rely upon testimony of others. However, he found enough evidence to convince him that at least a substantial portion of such reports was reliable, and he was more concerned with their psychiatric implications.

Fodor's cases exhibit a common pattern. Deeply repressed drives or conflicts in persons with hysteric tendencies sometimes became so intense that they produced various "conversion" symptoms, including externalization as PK phenomena. Usually these repressions concealed deep guilt or fear. Whenever he was able to take the tormented person into analytic treatment, both the paranormal and the clinical hysterical symptoms subsided as repressed material was acknowledged. In one case (Fodor, 1964, p. 177), spontaneous PK effects developed around an adolescent boy who, Fodor learned, was a potentially creative writer, but was oppressed by lack of recognition among even family and friends. When his frustration was relieved by an opportunity to write for publication, the phenomena stopped.

This psychological interpretation of poltergeist phenomena found wide acceptance in later years, so that recent investigators have looked immediately for the motivations behind their cases and have included psychiatric evaluations of the agent and his or her interpersonal situation wherever possible.

4. Old Wine in New Bottles: PK Research Since 1960

4.1. The Return of the "Stars"

Reports of physical psi phenomena produced by rare individuals declined almost to zero at about the time that the PK experiments with dice were begun at Duke University. Now, for whatever obscure reasons, we find the cycle repeating. Reports of PK experiments declined to a trickle by the early 1960s. At about the same time, the first of a series of new PK "stars" appeared, heralding a revival of interest in directly observable physical phenomena that continues today.

4.1.1. Ted Serios

Early in 1964, an unlikely meeting occurred between Jule Eisenbud of the University of Colorado and Ted Serios, an erstwhile Chicago bellhop. Serios had gained a local reputation for producing paranormal photographs by mental effort directed at a Polaroid camera. Eisenbud, psychoanalyst and experienced parapsychological investigator, brought Serios to Denver. The experiments that he and several associates conducted during the next three years are reported in a popular book and several journal articles (Eisenbud, 1967, 1972; Eisenbud and Associates, 1967, 1968, 1970a,b). During this period Ian Stevenson and J. G. Pratt (1968, 1969) of the University of Virginia also studied Serios for short periods.

It is quite impossible to summarize this work here. Hundreds of anomalous photographs were produced under widely varied conditions, and several nonphotographic experiments were reported. A few examples will be mentioned to illustrate the methods used in the investigations.

The first concern of the investigators, as always, was to exclude the possibility of fraud. The Polaroid camera offered great advantages over earlier equipment by eliminating darkroom processing and providing the result of each test within a few seconds. In most trials, an experimenter aimed the camera approximately at Serios and tripped the shutter at Serios's signal. Whenever he was within reach of the camera, Serios liked to hold a small paper or fiber cylinder against the lens. This nonsense device, dubbed by Eisenbud "the gismo," became the obvious focus for controversy; but in many tests it was eliminated as a means of fraud. For example, an anomalous picture was obtained while Serios was inside an electrically shielded room (Faraday cage) and the camera "some inches" outside the copper screen. With masking tape or an experimenter's hand over the lens, many exposures developed entirely white, as if heavily overexposed to light. Many exposures came out solid black or nearly so, as if severely underexposed; control shots (with Serios not "trying") produced normal pictures. Such effects were obtained with cameras at distances up to several miles from Serios (Eisenbud, 1967, p. 84; 1972).

Probably the strongest bit of evidence for paranormal agency concerned not photography but electronics (Eisenbud, 1972). A photocell in the camera was connected to a cathode ray oscilloscope, so that tripping the shutter in normal light produced a brief "blip" on the otherwise flat oscilloscope trace. As the shutter was tripped repeatedly, Serios gradually suppressed the blips, holding the trace down to zero level as if the shutter were not opening. He then gradually depressed the trace far *below* the zero axis. A magnet held near the oscilloscope, if opportunity offered, could shift the trace; but it could not influence it in the selective manner that was reported.

Experiments with physical variables produced no effect when Serios was separated from the camera by electrical shielding or glass opaque to X-rays. Distances of more than a few feet, or tape over the lens, inhibited pictures but not "blackies" or "whities" (yet pictures were obtained with an experimenter's hand over the lens). Cardboard in front of part of the film frame usually produced a black silhouette on the print, but sometimes this was overlapped by imagery. Frame-by-frame videotape analyses of pictures that Serios impressed on a television camera revealed details of image formation and dissolution (Eisenbud et al., 1970b). Eisenbud understandably appears to have been more intrigued by the internal peculiarities of Serios's productions than by the physical aspects. He found many features, too complex and varied to summarize here, that he felt related the pictures to ESP experiments with drawings and to broader aspects of psychology and psychoanalysis.

It is easy in retrospect to suggest that more varied physical experiments should have been done, or that control conditions should have been routinely more rigorous. However, Eisenbud's reports make clear that Serios was a creative artist in the grand tradition of Eusapia Palladino, and equally averse to stereotyped test situations. When one considers that this research was a spare-time project of a busy professional man, undertaken without institutional support, the omissions are at least understandable.

4.1.2. Nina Kulagina

About the time the work with Serios began, reports were coming from the U.S.S.R. of a woman who had demonstrated remarkable PK abilities. Nina Kulagina came to the attention of L. L. Vasiliev, late dean of Soviet parapsychologists, who helped develop and direct her capability. His reports led to widespread interest in Kulagina by both Soviet and foreign scientists. The results of their investigations, so far as they are known in the West, are summarized in an article by four authors who have observed Kulagina's phenomena (Keil, Herbert, Ullman, and Pratt, 1976).

Her demonstrations have included these effects: movements of small objects and alterations of existing motions; physiological effects; exposure effects on photographic film. She is able to rotate a compass needle, start or stop a pendulum, cause one of a group of small objects (e.g., matches) to move independently of others, or move several objects in different directions. She once changed the beat rate of a frog's heart and stopped it. Contact with her hand on several occasions produced sensations of severe heat in witnesses' arms, though a thermometer registered no change. She has produced simple exposure patterns on photographic film, and also diffuse exposure on film adjacent to objects being moved.

Kulagina has been accessible to a few Western investigators only sporadically, and then under informal conditions. However, on the basis of their observations and numerous Soviet reports, they are confident that her phenomena are paranormal.

4.1.3. Felicia Parise

A movie film of a PK demonstration by Kulagina was the direct inspiration of Felicia Parise, a research technician at Maimonides Medical Center in New York, to go and do likewise (Keil et al., 1976; Honorton, 1974). After several weeks of persistent practice, she began to move small objects (e.g., a plastic bottle) a few centimeters. Later she learned to rotate a compass needle. Charles Honorton, J. G. Pratt, Montague Ullman, and other parapsychologists observed her demonstrations under informal but carefully investigated conditions.

The climax of Parise's PK demonstrations occurred during a visit to the FRNM (Foundation for Research on the Nature of Man) parapsychology laboratory (successor to the Duke University laboratory) at Durham, N.C. (Watkins and Watkins, 1974). The test setup consisted of a magnetic compass mounted inside the coil (sensitive area) of an electronic metal detector, with sealed packets of photographic film under the metal detector and at distances up to 3 m from it. Sitting immediately in front of this apparatus, Parise was able after some effort to deflect the compass. It moved slowly 15 degrees and remained there. Meanwhile, the audible signal from the metal detector changed in a way that normally was consistent with the introduction of several pounds of metal into the exploring coil.

At this point, Parise moved to a far corner of the room; but the compass deflection did not change, nor was the needle responsive to a magnet brought near it. When moved 4 ft. (1.2 m) from the point of concentration, the needle slowly returned to normal behavior. When returned to the original location, the needle again was deflected 15 degrees and became insensitive to the magnet. This procedure was repeated several times, while during approximately 25 minutes the needle gradually returned to normal behavior at the original location. The film at the test location was strongly exposed, and decreasingly so at successive distances from it.

This promising case ended when Parise decided that the demands on her time and energy of keeping in practice for PK demonstrations were becoming excessive.

4.1.4. Uri Geller

By all odds, the most noted claimant to psychokinetic powers among the new generation of stars is the Israeli entertainer, Uri Geller. Many reports of informal demonstrations have attested to his abilities. Harold Puthoff and Russell Targ (1974) recorded variations in output signal voltage from a precision balance that implied anomalous forces under Geller's influence in excess of 1 g weight. They also observed full-scale (.3 gauss) deflections of a magnetometer when Geller brought his hands near the measuring probe.

A. R. G. Owen (1974b) reported paranormal bending of keys and other metal objects by Geller under what he considered reliable conditions. W. E. Cox (1974) observed key bending under Geller's influence, and also the starting of a watch that Cox had stopped by blocking the balance wheel with a bit of foil. A physicist, Wilbur Franklin (1975), used a scanning electron microscope to examine the metallic structure in a platinum ring that broke spontaneously in Geller's presence. He reported several different microscopic structures, similar to those produced by such varied agencies as fracture at very low temperature and melting at very high temperature, all in close proximity in the fractured area. These and other observations appear in Panati (1976).

Unfortunately for parapsychology, Geller has shown little interest in research, preferring the role of public showman. Consequently, few serious experiments with him have been reported, and none of the sustained investigations that are necessary for confidence and insight.

4.1.5. Two British Stars

A British investigator, Benson Herbert (1973), reported experiments in which the subject, Suzanne Padfield, demonstrated an anomalous effect upon the intensity of a beam of plane-polarized light. It was determined that the effect was not accomplished by rotating the plane of polarization.

Matthew Manning (1974) was the focus of poltergeist disturbances briefly during his childhood in England. When he was about age 15, the phenomena resumed chronically, and he learned to control them voluntarily. He found that he could suppress the PK effects by engaging in automatic writing or painting. After hearing of Geller's reputed metal-bending feats, Manning found that he could produce similar effects, as he demonstrated to a conference in Canada (A. R. G. Owen, 1974a, 1975). Electroencephalograph records revealed anomalous characteristics during such performances (Whitton, 1974).

4.1.6. Ingo Swann

This New York artist has served as agent in three notable experiments that attest to remarkable PK capability. At his suggestion, Gertrude Schmeidler (1973) designed an experiment to test his ability to modify the temperature registered by an electronic sensor (thermistor). Three thermistors in various locations in the experimental room were connected to a chart recorder. One thermistor was designated the target. According to a prepared schedule, Swann was instructed on each trial to make the target thermistor either hotter or colder. Strongly significant results were obtained, together with differences among the target and accessory thermistors that implied a high degree of selectivity in the PK process.

Puthoff and Targ (1974, 1975) invited Swann to try to influence a research magnetometer located underground inside a superconducting shield that was impervious to normal external disturbances. When Swann tried to "see" the inside of the instrument, and when he then tried to perturb it, strong fluctuations appeared in the normally stable chart record.

Edwin C. May and Charles Honorton (1976) reported tests with Swann on a special PK testing machine. His task essentially was to alter the generation of electronic noise in a circuit. Results were nonsignificant while Swann was in the room with the apparatus, but improved significantly when he was in another room.

4.1.7. The New Look: An Evaluation

The contrast between this new generation of PK stars and those of an earlier day could hardly be greater. Gone are the last remnants of the spiritistic séance. All of the PK agents mentioned in this section have worked customarily in normal light; none has exhibited a "spirit control" or even a secondary trance personality. For that matter, none has gone into trance to produce PK effects, though some alterations of state of consciousness have been evident. Yet striking differences appear in their methods. Some—Kulagina, Parise, Serios—have worked themselves into physiological states of strong arousal. Others, notably Geller and Swann, have shown little indication of stress.

A second contrast with the investigations of the mediumistic period is in the sophisticated instrumentation that is currently used. Polaroid cameras, television cameras and videotape recording, sensitive electronic recording instruments, and other laboratory resources now are commonplace. These serve a dual function, in making fraud more difficult and in providing quantitative measurements of a broad range of PK effects (though it should not be overlooked that the feat that has gained by far the most contemporary fame is the bending of spoons and door keys).

Complex test measurements, however, introduce a serious methodological disadvantage into the investigations. If a spoon is bent by paranormal means, one can with some confidence assume that the elusive agency has acted directly upon the spoon. But, when a chart recorder indicates an anomalous perturbation of a thermistor or magnetometer circuit, the locus of the PK influence is ambiguous. The temperature of the thermistor may have changed, or the electrical properties of some component in the circuit; or the recording pen may have been commandeered directly. Targ (Firsoff, 1975, p. 126) mentioned a drastic demonstration of this perplexing flexibility of the PK agency. He suggested that Geller alter the motion of a pendulum, explaining that the effect would appear on the chart recorder trace. Geller cracked his knuckles, and the recorder pens immediately ran off scale. A postmortem check disclosed that both recorder amplifiers had burned out.

The PK demonstrations by current star performers, even granting the validity of all of them, have not advanced scientific understanding of the phenomena very much. Of those mentioned, only Serios and Kulagina have been amenable to sustained investigation, and the latter only to Soviet scientists whose available reports are meager. Much evidence suggests that outstanding PK agents are necessarily creative personalities, readily bored by repetitive procedures, and, in some cases, upset by the professionally distrustful surveillance of their every movement. Further, no test has yet reliably disclosed any dependence of these PK phenomena upon identifiable physical variables, though a decline with distance is suggested in some cases. Again and again, the effects appear to relate primarily if not solely to the intent or "will" of the agent. At this point, probably the greatest gain from the emergence of the new stars has been the widespread revival of interest in macroscopic physical phenomena, particularly among physicists.

4.2. Poltergeist Investigations: RSPK

The elusive poltergeist phenomena continued to inspire collections and analyses of eyewitness reports. Cox (1961) carried out a comparative analysis of several such cases. George Zorab (1964) published a similar collection of cases from continental Europe. A. R. G. Owen (1964) produced the most comprehensive collection of poltergeist cases to date, including some he personally had investigated. His case of the "Sauchie Poltergeist" merits attention as one of the best examples of the methods and possibilities of field investigations that depend upon the testimony of witnesses.

The phenomena were associated with an 11-year-old girl, Virginia Campbell, who because of an economically disrupted home situation had been brought from her Irish home to live with an older brother and his family in Sauchie, a small town in Scotland. Apparently she was well treated (a striking aspect of the case is the sensitivity and good sense shown toward the child by all of those principally concerned). But she had suffered abrupt separation from everything familiar to her, and Owen surmised that the resulting emotional stress caused the poltergeist outbreak late in November, 1960. The phenomena were of the types usual in such cases: movements of objects, various noises, and speech in apparent trance.

By the time Owen learned of the occurrences and visited Sauchie in mid-January, 1961, the manifestations had almost ceased. He based his report of the case on interviews with seven witnesses of various aspects of it. These were a minister, three physicians, Virginia's teacher, and the brother and his wife with whom Virginia was staying. Their testimony was supplemented by a letter from the headmaster of Virginia's school. These witnesses appear to have been unusually intelligent and well informed. The resulting report must stand as one of the strongest such case studies in the literature. Nevertheless, it is subject to the limitations inherent in any investigation of testimony after the fact.

Several investigators have reported direct observations of poltergeist manifestations. The most active and persistent have been Hans Bender in West Germany and William G. Roll in the United States, who introduced the term *recurrent spontaneous psychokinesis* (RSPK) for poltergeist phenomena. Roll's work, reported in a series of papers (e.g., Pratt and Roll, 1958; Roll, 1968; Roll and Stump, 1971), is summarized in a book (Roll, 1972/1976). The best example of the application of his methods is afforded by his Miami, Florida, case (Roll and Pratt, 1971; Roll, Burdick, and Joines, 1973).

The first essential in the methodology of RSPK investigation is publicity. To be effective, the investigator must be informed of an outbreak almost immediately. He therefore needs to be widely and favorably known as a competent and sympathetically interested professional in such matters. In the Miami case, an employee in the import warehouse where the phenomena were occurring heard Susy Smith, a popular writer on psychic topics, in a radio interview. She phoned Smith, who phoned Roll. After surveying the situation, Roll brought Pratt into the investigation. The involvement of two investigators provided for more thorough observation and strengthened the credibility of the resulting report.

The phenomena consisted principally of an almost monotonous series of falls or flights of novelty items, mostly glass or ceramic, from open shelves in the warehouse. The events were associated almost immediately with a 19-year-old employee, Julio.

Roll and Pratt were able to move inconspicuously among the tiers of shelves, meanwhile noting the locations and movements of the several employees on their tape recorders. When an object was heard to fall, all "froze" as instructed until their locations could be verified and recorded. The original location of the object and its impact point were noted on a diagram of the room, and other details were recorded. By such means, the investigators were able in a substantial number of instances to conclude that no one had been in a position to move the object. Noting that objects moved repeatedly from certain locations on the shelves, they tried "baiting" these target areas with similar objects and keeping them under close surveillance. In ten instances, the target object fell or flew from the shelf under test conditions.

Analyses of the locations and movements of objects relative to the location of the agent, Julio, at the time of each event (Roll et al., 1973) revealed significant correlations among several variables. The frequency of events declined sharply with the distance of the initial location of the object from the agent (though the data do not appear to justify the authors' inference of an exponential decline). About 80% of events occurred behind the agent; and a similar majority moved clockwise (viewed from above) relative to the agent. A tentative theoretical "energy beam" model was derived from these and earlier observations of similar effects.

Hans Bender has earned a reputation as the leading poltergeist investigator in Europe. Of the active cases he has seen, one that occurred in a law office at Rosenheim, Bavaria, affords the best example of the application of technical investigative methods (Bender, 1968, 1971a,b, 1974). The RSPK effects, associated with a 19-year-old woman employee, included movement of a heavy cabinet and other objects. Photographs were made of violently swinging light fixtures and of a picture rotating on its hanger.

The most interesting and prevalent phenomena involved interferences with the electric and telephone services in the office. Light bulbs exploded, circuit breakers cut out without reason, telephones rang or calls were dialed without hands. Technicians from the power company and the post office (telephone) authority could find no cause for the disturbances, though they monitored the circuits with various instruments. In fact, they found that the voltage-monitoring instrument was tracing anomalous records that were not attributable to line-voltage fluctuations. Two physicists (Karger and Zicha, 1968, 1971) were baffled. They considered the instrumental methods valid, and recognized also the diversity and intelligence of the paranormal agency.

Both Roll and Bender have given much attention to motivational and psychiatric aspects of their cases. In the Rosenheim case, Bender noted that, as the lawyer turned from skepticism to conviction, the PK phenomena increased. In the Pursruck case (Bender, 1974), two young girl agents were encouraged to sing and dance to relieve their anxiety, and to interrogate the "rapper." This active, positive approach coincided with decline of the physical phenomena.

Roll (1968) combined his physical investigation with a psychological study of a 12-year-old boy agent. His report developed in detail the evidence that the RSPK phenomena were projections of repressed needs and hostilities on the part of the boy. A similar study of Julio, the agent in the Miami case, revealed much conflict and tension, not surprising in a young refugee who had left his mother in Cuba.

4.3. Developmental Séance Experiments: Poltergeists to Order

During the heyday of spiritualism, amateur séances were common. A group of believers sat in dim light or darkness and witnessed marvels. Tables and other objects were moved and levitated; lights, cold breezes, touches, and other physical phenomena were reported. Usually, these effects were attributed to spirits, who communicated through rappings or the trance speech of a member of the circle. This pattern of events resembled that of poltergeist episodes, and was as little believed by critical-minded people.

Claims of physical séance phenomena declined as investigative methods became increasingly strict. Some evidence has suggested that the skeptical, professionally suspicious scientific approach, with its primary emphasis on detecting fraud rather than nurturing a temperamental function, may have abolished genuine PK phenomena along with the fraudulent. This possibility led an English psychologist, K. J. Batcheldor (1966), to test a bold hypothesis. He conjectured that PK ability is not a rare "gift," but merely unusual human behavior that can be elicited in ordinary people under favorable conditions. His theoretical ideas, unfortunately, are not set forth in his report, but are summarized and elaborated in later work by Colin Brookes-Smith (1973; Brookes-Smith and Hunt, 1970).

Batcheldor held that in ordinary circumstances two psychological factors block PK expression. "Witness inhibition" is the initial reaction of shock or fear if one directly witnesses a paranormal event, a reaction that Batcheldor believed tended to block further manifestations. "Ownership resistance" implies a similar effect if one feels personally responsible for a PK event.

To circumvent these obstacles and facilitate the emergence of any latent PK ability, Batcheldor reverted to the amateur séance type of experiment. Darkness, he reasoned, minimizes the witness reaction; and participation in an indiscriminate group allows each sitter to attribute any disturbing phenomena to the others. (Many people can work a ouija board in pairs; few can work it alone.) Apprehension was further allayed by a lighthearted approach to the sittings, with casual talk, laughter, and sometimes singing to distract attention and discourage dwelling on the implications of the experiment. No religious or spiritistic trappings were used, nor did anyone go into trance. The work was approached in a matter-of-fact attitude of objective inquiry.

Confidence and plausibility were further enhanced by approaching the paranormal gradually. Sessions were held in an ordinary room, with attention focused initially on an ordinary table rather than an unfamiliar instrument. Requests for specific effects were addressed to the table rather than to the sitters directly; the table thus served as a scapegoat for the onus of responsibility. In early sittings, simple rocking and tilting of the table, readily attributable to familiar automatism, were called for; then greater tilting, sliding, or hopping. If these went well, levitation often followed as group acceptance and confidence mounted.

Batcheldor's regular sitters were himself, another man, and a woman. Others were present at some sittings. He notes that, despite their ostensible expectations, they were shocked by the first levitation (which occurred at the eleventh, and first fully dark, session). The next session was a riot of levitations and other activity; the next blank! Batcheldor surmised that the preceding session's violent activity had aroused anxiety in the participants.

Inspired by Batcheldor's report, Brookes-Smith and D. W. Hunt (1970) carried out a similar experiment in which Hunt sat with two other men and a woman; a fourth man was added later. They followed procedures similar to those advocated by Batcheldor, with one remarkable exception: their first, highly successful, series of sittings was conducted in normal light. They reported results comparable to Batcheldor's: levitations and other strong effects, plus actuation of a light switch consistently on command. Brookes-Smith (1973) reported a third such experimental series that was designed primarily to test the feasibility of instrumenting the séance table with strain gauges and other devices and recording their readings and a soundtrack continuously on magnetic data tape. The readings could be translated later into chart-recorder traces for analysis. By this means, forces and other variables that could not be directly observed became accessible in accurate time-register with voiced comments and other sounds. Further, Brookes-Smith believed that the inhibiting effect of measuring and recording instruments so often noted would be reduced by the tape-recording procedure, which was inconspicuous and did not confront the participants with immediate evidence of the paranormal. Strong PK phenomena were obtained, and enough success in the data-tape recording technique to justify it as a promising methodological device.

A novel feature of Brookes-Smith's experiment was the secret designation in some sessions of one participant to "assist" the initiation of levitation by normal lifting of the table edge. The purpose was to evoke paranormal levitation by raising the confidence and expectations of the other participants. The tape record showed clearly when such intervention was occurring.

Further testimony to the efficacy of Batcheldor's methods appeared in the experience of a Toronto group (I. M. Owen, 1975; Owen and Sparrow, 1974, 1976). They decided to "invent" a traditional spirit with a tragic background and try to have him manifest in a séance situation. For a year they met weekly and soberly meditated on their "ghost"; but nothing happened. Then they learned of Batcheldor's experiments and changed to a similar procedure, with songs, laughter, and a generally lively approach. Almost immediately they began to get raps and table movements, with small levitations, in good light. A second Toronto group, using the same principles, also reported success.

A promising beginning toward physical analysis of the rapping sounds familiar in the lore of séances was made by J. L. Whitton (1975). He succeeded in measuring the individual durations of raps made by the Owen group's synthetic ghost and of normally produced raps of similar loudness. The PK raps lasted about .16 second, only a third as long as a normal rap.

Many clues suggest that Batcheldor's methodological approach may be a valuable alternative to the experimenter-and-subject tradition of the laboratory. Instruments capable of measuring and recording many aspects of physical phenomena are now commonplace. By suitable designs, such instrumentation can circumvent fraud, even in a dark séance.

Yet some apparent inconsistencies remain to be clarified. Allaying witness inhibition by suppressing immediate evidence of paranormal effects is contrary to an increasing emphasis by various experimenters (e.g., Tart, 1976) upon the value of immediate or continuous feedback of results to a subject. Further, despite Batcheldor's confidence that almost anyone can develop PK abilities, his phenomena depended on the presence of one particular sitter (the other man); and Hunt's successful sessions ended when the one woman member dropped out of the circle. Whether the other groups similarly depended upon particular individuals is not clear. Notwithstanding Batcheldor's optimistic interpretation, it remains an open question whether his procedure is really a training method, or simply the traditional device for discovering psychically gifted persons.

4.4. Paranormal Voices on Tape

New technology repeatedly has been followed by reports of PK manifestations that make use of it. In the 1950s reports began to appear of paranormal voices and other sounds on magnetic recording tape. This is a modern variant of what, in the earlier literature, was termed "direct voice." See Bayless (1976b) for a survey. Raymond Bayless, a Los Angeles painter (Bayless, 1959; Rogo, 1976), reported experiments with a voice medium, Attila von Sealay (or Szalay), in which a microphone and amplifier–recorder were placed inside a dark cabinet while Bayless and the medium remained outside it in full light. Voices were heard through a loudspeaker and recorded on tape.

A Swedish filmmaker, Friedrich Jürgenson, found anomalous voices on some recordings of bird songs that he had made. He experimented with these and published two books about them (1964, 1967). Later Bender (1972) investigated Jürgenson's phenomena and became convinced that they were paranormal. In one experiment, Bender obtained a clear taped voice through only one microphone and recording channel of a stereo pair.

By far the best known claimant to taped voices was the late Konstantin Raudive (1971), a Latvian who learned of Jürgenson's experiments and spent the rest of his life in similar studies. He recorded through a microphone in a relatively quiet room or, preferably, through a radio tuned between stations. The sounds that he interpreted as paranormal voices usually were faint, very brief words or phrases in several languages.

As critics have pointed out (e.g., Ellis, 1974, 1975; Smith, 1972/1974), Raudive's procedures were not well controlled. His favored radio recording method was shown sometimes to pick up weak, transient radio voices. Interpretation of the voices was strained and tedious work, requiring typically several hours of repeated listening to tease out a few disjointed phrases from a few minutes of recording. Under such conditions, anyone tends to hear voices or music in random noise. Although Raudive had some of his recordings "verified" by others, apparently he showed each listener his transcription first, thus preventing independent verification.

In a variation on the taped-voice experiments, Bayless (1976a) has reported detecting ordinarily inaudible "microraps" and other sounds by placing the microphone of his tape recorder on a tabletop or other soundboard.

This area of PK research clearly is in an unsatisfactory state. Nearly 20 years since the first publications on tape-recorded voices, only a handful of reports have appeared; and most of these are methodologically weak. Yet, further efforts would appear justified, for effective controls can easily be devised for such experiments.

4.5. Advances in Statistical PK Experiments

The foregoing topics all have dealt with PK effects that can be directly observed (though Schmeidler's experiment with Swann was marginal in this respect). By contrast, experiments such as dice tests that usually yield low-level results must be evaluated statistically over many trials to identify any anomalous scoring. Since 1960, dice experiments have declined in favor as investigators have sought more efficient and convincing methods for statistical experimentation.

Cox reported tests of several mechanical and electromechanical devices in PK experiments. In one of these (1971b), the task was to increase or decrease the amplitude of a pendulum stroke, as measured by a photocell or a magnetic switch. In another (1965), PK influence on either a cascade of electrical relays or on an electrolytic cell (either device involving quasi-random events) could influence the electric pulse that was recorded. A third device (1973), entirely mechanical, provided for comparison of individual trial and "majority vote" scoring procedures for any PK effects on steel balls rolled down chutes.

But the dominant trend has been toward electronic instrumentation because of its flexibility and easily attained precision. Schmeidler's thermistor experiment with Swann required statistical evaluation, because the observed temperature changes were small and easily confused with normal drift. She reported a second, partially successful, experiment of this type with 22 volunteer subjects (Schmeidler, Mitchell, and Sondow, 1975). Brian Millar (1976), of the University of Edinburgh, criticized Schmeidler's experiments, alleging that her use of a thermos bottle to enclose the target thermistor introduced thermal transients that could simulate the intended PK effects. His attempted replication with a modified design and 20 subjects was unsuccessful.

Meanwhile, several experimenters had tried to develop electronic equivalents of dice or coin tossing for PK testing, to avoid the slowness, uncertain randomness, and difficulties of control that plagued the dice experiments. The most elegantly random process known to physics is the decay of a radioactive atom. Its occurrence is not merely unpredictable; it is theoretically indeterminate. John Beloff and Leonard Evans (1961) at the University of Edinburgh set up a radiation counter adjacent to a bit of a uranium compound and asked their subjects to try to alter the count rate. They liked the natural randomness of the process and believed that its inherently noncausal character might make it more susceptible to PK influence than a causal process would be. However, their results were not significant. A similar experiment at Cambridge (Wadhams and Farrelly, 1968) also failed; but two French experimenters (Chauvin and Genthon, 1967) obtained very high scores by two of their child subjects in a radiation-counting experiment.

It remained for Helmut Schmidt, an industrial physicist who joined the staff of the FRNM at Durham, to incorporate the radiation counter into a flexible, highly sophisticated random-number generator (RNG) for psi experiments. His circuit (1970d) is essentially a square-wave oscillator that is stopped when the counter registers an atomic disintegration. The oscillator is an electronic switch or flip-flop that alternates its output voltage between positive and negative polarities at rapid, regular intervals. When, at a random time, an atomic disintegration actuates the counter, the oscillator is stopped momentarily and its polarity tested. The resulting positive or negative indication is transferred to the output terminals of the machine, thus supplying a random series of binary plus-or-minus, yes-or-no, heads-or-tails signals that can be used for any desired purpose. The sequence is simultaneously registered on counters, and can be recorded on tape or stored in a computer. Schmidt (1970c) showed by theoretical analysis that the output is highly random. In practice, the randomicity is checked frequently to detect any malfunction.

In adapting his RNG to a PK experiment, Schmidt (1970b) considered how best to present the task to a subject. A request to influence the counter readings, or the radioactive process directly, he felt would be unappealing; it appeared too technical and complex. Instead, he presented to the subject a remotely connected display consisting of nine small light bulbs arranged in a circle. One was lighted initially. The first binary signal from the RNG would turn that light off and light the adjacent one in either the clockwise or the counterclockwise direction, depending on the polarity of the binary signal. Each signal from the RNG would repeat this operation, so that the successive lights executed a "random walk" along the circle, making little progress in either direction. The PK task presented to the subject was simply to make the lights progress in one prescribed direction. Significant results were obtained with this procedure.

The RNG apparatus, essentially an "electronic coin tosser," offers distinct advantages over coins, dice, or other mechanical devices. It affords speed, flexibility of application, reliable randomization of targets, adaptability for subject appeal and feedback, immunity to sensory leakage and subject fraud, and adaptability to automatic recording or processing of data. However, like all complex PK apparatus, it probably facilitates cheating by an experimenter, and it makes the locus of PK influence ambiguous.

Schmidt's PK apparatus exemplifies a fundamental concept to which he subscribes: namely, that psi is "goal oriented" and indifferent to intermediate means and complexities. For that reason, he felt that it was more important to present the subject with a psychologically simple and appealing task than to have him concentrate on the randomization process directly. The goal-oriented character of psi is supported by much incidental evidence. Schmidt (1974) tested the concept directly by arranging a PK experiment in which trials alternated randomly between the RNG circuit described above and a substantially more complex circuit. The subject was not told that two different machines were involved. Scores were significant, but differed only insignificantly between the two modes. However, a comparison of significant PK scores on attempts to influence audible binary signals presented at rates of 30 and 300 per second showed significantly higher scoring at the lower rate (Schmidt, 1973).

Attempts to use the RNG to explore distinctions between PK and precognition have led to an acute awareness of the ambiguity that is inherent in these concepts. Recognizing the provisional character of such categories, Schmidt and Lee Pantas (1972) nevertheless arranged the circuitry to compare ostensibly precognitive trials with others that logically required PK, while subjects were under the impression that the entire procedure was precognitive. Again, scores were significant, but without significant difference between precognitive and PK scores.

Schmidt's most intriguing experiments (1975a, 1976) involve retroactive PK, the psychokinetic analogue of precognition. They test the hypothesis that a conscious intention developed today can influence a sequence of events that happened yesterday. Omitting details of several variations on this experiment, the essential procedure was to compare PK scoring on currently generated RNG targets with scores of current trials on magnetic tape records of similar RNG sequences that had been generated and recorded several days earlier and selected by an impersonal procedure. Nontarget tape records later were evaluated as controls. No one examined these tape records until the target tapes had been presented to the subjects. Under these conditions, significant scores were obtained on both contemporary and prerecorded target sequences. When a prerecorded tape was used as target four times (without subjects' knowledge), scores improved.

It is evident that Schmidt's contributions to PK methodology are not limited to sophisticated devices. He has employed variations of the RNG to explore analytically various aspects of PK effects, guided in part by a provisional theoretical model of psi processes that he developed (1975b).

4.6. PK Effects on Biological Systems: Animal PK

The concept of psychokinetic influence of one person upon the behavior of another is clearly ambiguous. Telepathy is an alternative concept, depending upon whether the influence of the agent is seen as coercive or suggestive. PK influence upon another's physiological condition also is ambiguous, in view of the known possibilities of such influence through psychosomatic mechanisms. PK influence of a human upon a mouse or a growing seedling appears to be generally accepted as an unambiguous concept; however, this assurance would seem to rest more upon conceit than logic. So, with full awareness of the artificiality that is involved, all of the alleged psi influences of humans upon the physiological conditions of humans or other organisms, or upon the behavior of nonhuman organisms, will be treated provisionally as PK effects.

4.6.1. The Enigma of Healing

Like all psi phenomena, biological PK effects have roots in folklore: in witchcraft and sorcery, and particularly in paranormal healing. Though claims of such healing powers still persist, they are as difficult as poltergeists to investigate clinically. The efficacy of a conventional medical treatment is difficult enough to establish because of uncertainties in diagnosis and prognosis, psychosomatic influences, and other variables. To establish reliable data on sporadic cases of apparent paranormal healing is doubly difficult, so much so that no consistent or satisfactory methodology for such investigations has developed. Some efforts, however, have been made in that direction.

The first such approach is that traditional in parapsychology, the collection and study of records of individual cases. Of various such efforts, two are worth citing here as examples of the method and its shortcomings. For more than a century miraculous cures have been reported from the shrine at Lourdes, France. These cures have received probably more sustained attention by physicians and other investigators than any other such body of data.

Physicians François Leuret and Henri Bon (1957) and British parapsychological investigator D. J. West (1957) published evaluations of some of the more impressive cases from Lourdes. Leuret and Bon wrote from the standpoint of sympathetic Catholics (Leuret had been President of the Medical Bureau at Lourdes). Despite their efforts to review the evidence objectively, they—as West and other critics pointed out—omitted some significant information and in other ways gave the impression of tacitly supporting a preconceived position. West examined all of the available records of 11 cases, noting inconclusive diagnoses, primitive examination facilities at the shrine, and other serious methodological defects in the medical evaluations. He concluded that none of the cases presented satisfactory evidence of paranormal healing.

Under the direction of Hans Bender, Freiburg University conducted a detailed clinical study of 538 patients who came for treatment by a reputed healer, Kurt Trampler (Strauch, 1963). Each patient was examined by physicians and psychologists before treatment and in a followup program for a year or longer. Diagnostic examinations, however, appear not to have been thorough. Emphasis was primarily upon the patients' personality types, expectations, and reactions to the treatments. Substantial improvements were found in many cases, but they were functional and attributable to suggestion rather than organic changes.

4.6.1a. Experiments Relevant to Healing. Some investigators have tried to approach the issue of paranormal healing through experiments that involved physiological effects but were susceptible to laboratory methods and controls. Bernard Grad, psychiatrist at McGill University, and associates (Grad, 1965; Grad, Cadoret, and Paul, 1961), tried a direct approach. They cut the skin from small areas of the backs of 300 mice. Then by frequent measurements of wound areas they compared rates of healing for 100 mice that were "treated" by a professed healer, 100 that were handled similarly by ordinary persons, and 100 controls that were not handled. Randomization and blinds were used to avoid preferential treatment with respect to housing, handling, or other variables. The treated wounds healed more rapidly than those of the other two groups, to a marginally significant degree.

Grad (1963, 1964, 1965) then tried experiments on plant growth. In a series of exploratory tests with the same healer, he determined that significant effects could be obtained by having the healer handle only a container of water to be used on the plants and that the anomalous effects were greater on plants that were deprived of optimum growth conditions. Accordingly, he carried out several experiments in which barley seeds were planted in pots of soil under standardized conditions and divided into experimental and control groups. Under randomized and double-blind conditions, each experimental plant was initially watered with a stoppered bottle of 1% saline solution that had been handled for 30 minutes by the healer. Controls were initially watered with identical solution that had not been so handled. Significant differences developed between the two groups of plants as to sprouting rate, height, and weight, the experimental plants being superior in these respects.

In a similar experiment, Grad (1967) compared the effects of untreated sterile saline solution with samples handled by a normal person, a depressed neurotic patient, and a depressed psychotic. The solution handled by the normal person produced significantly taller plants than did the other three categories. (The neurotic patient produced better growth than the control; interest in the experiment had temporarily relieved her depression!)

Grad noted that his experiments hold serious implications for therapy and for experiments that involve the handling of living organisms. Also, his procedure with plants affords great advantages over direct handling of the experimental organisms by the healer. Double-blind conditions are much easier to maintain, the organisms are less disturbed, and fraud is more difficult. Further, the observations suggest that the healer's treatment does something to the solution itself that might be detectable by analytical techniques. Grad found no significant differences between treated and control saline samples in salt content, pH, or spectral transmission.

Several experimenters have tried to test the healing influence in various biological situations, particularly in processes more elementary than those used by Grad. These include: recovery of mice from ether anesthesia (Watkins and Watkins, 1971; Wells and Klein, 1972); "electrical activity" of plant leaves (Brier, 1969); evolution of carbon dioxide by a yeast culture (Nash and Nash, 1967); growth of fungus colonies (Barry, 1968); reactivity of enzymes (Smith, 1973); hemoglobin content of blood in humans (Krieger, 1975); and infrared absorption properties of water (Dean, 1975). In all of these diverse situations, significant alterations have been achieved by the literal or figurative "laying on of hands."

4.6.2. Behavioral Experiments

A few experiments have been directed, not to influencing the metabolic processes of organisms, but to modifying their behavior. In the first of these, Nigel Richmond (1952) in England tried to influence the movements of single-celled animals (paramecia) while viewing them in the field of a microscope. He divided the field into quadrants and randomly assigned one quadrant as target for each 15-second trial. Working only with individuals that appeared "undecided" and almost stationary, setting the center of the visual field over the animal at the start of each trial, he "willed" it to move into the target quadrant. In control trials, he did not try to influence the animal, and he determined the target quadrant only after each such trial. He obtained strong positive results.

"L. Metta" (pseudonym), a zoologist at the Sorbonne (1972), reported a similar experiment on small caterpillars, in which one of three agents exhibited significant negative scoring.

4.6.3. Animal PK

All of the foregoing experiments have involved humans as psychokinetic agents. A quite different task is to determine whether nonhuman organisms can produce PK effects in their environments. Helmut Schmidt (1970a) wondered whether a cat's love of warmth could motivate it to effective PK activity. The cat was left in a cold room with a cushion under a 200-watt lamp that was controlled by the RNG described earlier. Once each second the RNG delivered an "on" or "off" signal, so that the lamp was on or off in a random sequence. In five 30-minute sessions with the cat, the lamp was on consistently and significantly more often than not.

In a second experiment, Schmidt (1970a) similarly exposed cockroaches to electric shocks controlled by the RNG, expecting that their aversion to shocks might reduce their exposure to them. Instead, he found that the frequency of shocks increased by 2.4%. This curious result dramatizes the fundamental ambiguity in all attempts to test for PK effects by animals. Do cockroaches like being shocked? Were they demonstrating psi-missing? Or was the experimenter unconsciously expressing his feelings about cockroaches?

In a similar experiment, Graham Watkins (1972) exposed small lizards in a cool cage to an RNG-controlled heater. Highly significant scores in positive or negative directions on different days indicated that the animals' need for heat in the test situation was dominated by barometric pressure, being greater when pressure was low and evaporative cooling of the lizards' bodies more effective.

4.7. Process-Oriented Research

Most parapsychological experimentation has sought primarily to demonstrate that significant manifestations can be obtained with varied experimental techniques and procedures. Only a few experiments have been designed to explore the PK process by controlled tests of psychological or physical variables. Yet, the literature of RSPK field studies and of mediumistic phenomena affords many suggestive indications that physical and psychological variables significantly influence PK performance. Roll (1972/1976) found in several RSPK cases consistent declines in frequency of disturbances with increasing distance from the agent, and dependence of RSPK upon repressed emotional conflicts in the agent is generally acknowledged. Mediumistic phenomena have appeared to decline sharply with distance and usually to be inhibited by light. Many incidental observations in controlled experiments suggest dependence of scoring upon personality type, mood, physiological condition, motivation, and other attributes of both subject and experimenter.

4.7.1. Physical Variables

Explorations of physical variables have been sparse. Two of Schmidt's experiments (1973, 1974), described earlier, indicated indifference of PK scoring to complexity of the target-generating apparatus, but some degree of dependence on the rate at which targets were presented.

Cox (1971a) reported an experiment designed to compare PK effects on lead and celluloid dice thrown simultaneously. The dice were colored, and machine-thrown in such a way that the different masses did not produce noticeably different behavior. Neither the subjects nor the assistants who conducted the tests knew that the dice were not uniform. Results indicated marginally significant scoring about equally on both materials, but positive on the celluloid dice and negative on the lead. No further experiments to test the generality of this result have been reported.

The nearest approximation to a controlled test of PK at varied distances was reported by physical scientists Robert N. Miller and Philip

B. Reinhart (1975). At Agnes Scott College in Atlanta, Georgia, they tested the influence of a healer, Olga Worrall, on a cloud chamber. This device ordinarily is used to trace high-energy atomic particles, whose tracks are marked by the formation of fog droplets. When the healer placed a hand at each side of the chamber, a broad wavelike fog pattern appeared. It was entirely different from that ordinarily caused by ionizing particles. Two months later, Worrall at her home about 600 miles (966 km) distant tried at a prearranged time to influence the cloud chamber. Three minutes later the experimenters observed again the anomalous wavelike cloud formation. The test was repeated successfully the same evening.

Eisenbud, in his photographic experiments with Serios, obtained abnormal "blackies" and "whities" at distances up to several miles between Serios and the camera; but he did not get anomalous imagery beyond a few feet (Eisenbud, 1972). He also tried optically shielding portions of the film in the camera with cardboard, with inconsistent results. However, Serios was normally aware of the conditions in these experiments, so that no clear physical inference is justified.

Definitely the most intriguing test of a physical parameter in PK phenomena is Schmidt's (1976) experiment with retroactive PK. This experiment, which appears to have been well controlled, probes nearer than any other to the ineffable aspects of the physical world.

4.7.2. Psychological Variables

Several experiments have been designed to test definable variations in certain psychological conditions. Sara R. Feather and her mother, Louisa E. Rhine (1969), participated as experimenter–subjects in a PK dice test in which they tried sometimes for different targets, sometimes for the same target. Neither knew during a trial which condition applied. All faces were used equally as targets, and the experimenters' roles were entirely symmetrical. The scores in 2304 trials showed a marginally significant difference between the two conditions but not in the expected direction. Deviations were negative in the trials for a common target but positive when targets were competitive.

An additional series by the same procedure when Sara Feather was in a "bad" mood (depressed, irritable) resulted in nonsignificant scores on common targets, but a significant difference related to mood. During bad-mood sessions both experimenters scored negatively. During good-mood sessions they scored positively to about the same degree. Despite the care taken to insure symmetrical roles in the experiment, the highly unsymmetrical mother–daughter relation dictates caution in generalizing from the results.

Charles Honorton and Warren Barksdale (1972), at Maimonides Medical Center, tested their subjects on an RNG apparatus, comparing conditions of muscular tension versus relaxation, and also active concentration versus passive attention to the target. In the first series, conducted by Honorton, the six subjects worked as a group to influence the machine. Before one-half of the runs they were given waking suggestions to induce relaxation; before the other half, suggestions were for sustained muscular tension. Scores in the relaxed state were nonsignificant; those under tension were highly significant. The significant scoring was concentrated in the trials that involved muscle tension with passive attention to the task.

In the second series, which Barksdale conducted, 10 subjects tried individually under the same conditions to influence the RNG. Scores were nonsignificant. Honorton then ran a third series as sole subject, under the conditions of muscle tension versus relaxation only; Barksdale served as experimenter. The score under each condition was highly significant, that under tension being positive and that in relaxation almost equally negative.

This experiment dramatizes the difficulties in trying to replicate psi experiments or to establish consistent relationships. The second series ostensibly was a replication of the first. However, the experimenter and subjects were different persons; and—possibly a crucial point—the subjects worked individually, not as a concerted group. Much diverse evidence, some of which has been mentioned, suggests that clear responsibility for PK manifestations may inhibit them. Honorton's remarkable success in the third series raises the most vexing ambiguity of all, the covert role of the experimenter.

Two fairly distinct modes of mental functioning have become recognized in recent years (Ornstein, 1974). The linear mode is characterized by analytical, sequential thinking and perception. The holistic mode includes visual imagery and space perception, musical and artistic awareness, and intuitive insight; some evidence suggests that it may be the favored mode for psi experience. William G. Braud, Gary Smith, Ken Andrew, and Sue Willis (1976; Andrew, 1975), at the University of Houston, devised an experiment to investigate this possibility. In each of three series of tests, separate groups of subjects were assigned to holistic and to linear mental activities during their PK trials on an RNG. Each subject before and during the trials listened to a tape recording that was designed to induce the appropriate mental mode. The first two series yielded scores differing significantly in the expected direction: i.e., positive in holistic mode, negative or nonsignificant in linear. Scores in the third series were nonsignificant.

The experimenter in the first series knew in which mode each subject was working; that in the third was uninformed. Whether the second experimenter knew the mode in use was not stated. The results therefore suggest that experimenter expectation may have been a factor in evoking the diverse results in the three series.

A somewhat related experimental concept was explored by a Dutch graduate student, Bjorn J. Steilberg (1975). Each of his 10 subjects tried to influence dice while either actively concentrating on making the target face appear or passively visualizing the target. Scores were marginally significant, being slightly positive during visualization and significantly negative during active concentration.

All of the preceding experiments have attempted to compare the effects of various psychological conditions or states of consciousness. In a similar investigation, Rex G. Stanford (1969) combined such a test with a personality factor as an additional variable. Each of his 20 subjects tried to influence dice under two conditions. In the first the subject was asked to visualize the tumbling die stopping with the target face up. In the second condition, termed "associative activation of the unconscious," each subject was asked for two minutes to give all the free associations he could to the next target number. Then, during the trials, he was to distract his attention by reading or other extraneous activity. Scores relative to these conditions were equal and nonsignificant.

Following the PK trials, each subject was tested to determine whether he tended to think in terms of visual imagery. Average scores of "imagers" were found to be significantly higher in visualization than in the activation-of-consciousness condition. Nonimagers did better in the activation condition.

These few essays in process-oriented PK experimentation convey a vivid impression of the multiplicity of variables that they involve. Many variables, including probably the more sensitive, can be controlled only statistically by comparing results obtained with many subjects and experimenters. A substantial number of replications of each experimental procedure clearly is required if there is to be any hope of extracting generally valid principles from the tangle of varied and even contradictory results.

4.8. Interactions between Psi and Sensorimotor Processes

Scientific demonstration of the occurrence of psi phenomena has required that they be isolated from sensory and motor (sensorimotor) processes. This approach has encouraged a concept of psi experiences as rare, extraordinary intrusions in the normal course of sensorimotor functioning. Yet, in everyday life, psi and sensorimotor functions are free to interact, and many considerations suggest that they do so in a complementary relation (Rush, 1964).

As to PK effects particularly, Kulagina (Keil et al., 1976) and Parise (Honorton, 1974) used forceful gestures that simulated the PK movements they were trying to evoke. Forwald (1969) released his cubes while holding a mental image of the behavior he wanted. Brookes-Smith (1973) had one participant secretly lift the edge of the séance table to encourage the onset of levitation. Stanley Krippner (1976, p. 58) mentioned a matter-of-fact application of this reinforcement principle by Soviet scientists to develop a person's PK ability. RSPK phenomena appear to express aggressive urges that the agent cannot acknowledge consciously. Eugen Herrigel (1953) related experiences in ritualistic Zen archery that strongly suggest a fusion of sensorimotor and psi functioning. Eisenbud (1963, 1966–67), on the basis of his clinical and other observations, explored the motivations for psi-facilitated interplay among human as well as animal species.

These and many other observations suggest a hypothesis of "lead-in and frustration" (Rush, 1964, p. 31): if strongly motivated sensorimotor activities are frustrated in their convergence toward a goal, then complementary psi activity is facilitated. Many spontaneous incidents suggest that such facilitation, illustrated in the above examples, may be commonplace in ordinary activities.

4.8.1. Experimental Interactions: PMIR

Recently Stanford has undertaken the challenging task of detecting such an everyday psi component, which he has termed *psi-mediated instrumental response* (PMIR), despite its involvement with complex sensorimotor behavior. In two comprehensive papers (1974a,b), he reviewed the background of anecdotal and experimental evidence that supports the hypothesis of psi mediation in ordinary activities. He then proposed a formal hypothesis of PMIR, too extensive for adequate summary here, which in essence holds that a human or other organism employs ESP and PK capabilities, usually unconsciously, to realize desires and satisfy needs. With respect to PK particularly, the model assumes that a PMIR incident can involve extrasensory information input and consequent advantageous psychokinetic action without conscious awareness of either the information or the related action.

In an experiment designed to test this hypothesis (Stanford, Zenhausern, Taylor, and Dwyer, 1975), each of 40 subjects was given a conscious PK test on an RNG. Each then was assigned a dull, boring task from which he could escape by scoring 7 out of any block of 10 trials on the RNG, which was running continuously in another room. However, the subject was not told of this contingency; the purpose was to see whether he would unconsciously use it to his advantage. Eight subjects (a significant number) escaped the boring task before the 45-minute limit.

4.8.2. Implications for PK Methodology: Experimenter Effect

If covert and unintentional psi intervention occurs, the most immediate situation in which to look for it is a psi experiment. Yet, almost all experimental designs have implicitly ignored the implications of the phenomena they are intended to investigate. They have done so by assuming that only the person designated as subject (i.e., the one who will not write the paper) will use psi, and then only as directed! This assumption is made despite all the evidence that psi operates usually outside conscious direction or awareness. The experiment is open to complex psi interactions among all those concerned in it, and possibly still others.

Like all other experiments with persons as subjects, parapsychological experiments involve unintentional "normal" communication by manner, verbal suggestions, and other cues. Psychical researchers recognized very early that certain persons by their mere presence seemed to inhibit psi phenomena, while others enhanced them. Similar "experimenter effects" were soon noticed in the statistical experiments at the Duke University laboratory; but, at first, they were attributed solely to psychologically familiar interactions between experimenters and subjects. More complex and diversified experiments, however, have yielded abundant evidence that inadvertent psi interactions also occur. Some instances of such effects have been apparent in experiments discussed earlier.

This evidence and its implications have been reviewed and analyzed recently in three landmark papers. Rhea A. White (1976a,b) has assembled a great number of experiments that directly or implicitly illuminate covert psi interactions. She demonstrates that evidence for such communication between experimenter and subject is commonplace, and that in many instances significant scoring anomalies are inescapably related to persons in such incidental roles as preparing target material or checking results. Her conclusion is that no limits can be assumed to the range of such extraneous influences on a psi experiment (or other human situation), and that the traditional experimenter–subject dichotomy must give way to a holistic assessment of the entire experimental ensemble.

J. E. Kennedy and Judith L. Taddonio (1976) deal more specifically with the relations of experimenter and subject. They note that, ironically, the experimenter usually is more involved and more highly motivated for success than is the subject, and thus presumably is more likely to influence the scoring successfully. In terms of the conditions for covert psi set forth in Stanford's PMIR model, the experimenter is better qualified than the subject. In their extensive review of the pertinent literature, the authors find much evidence of psi influence by experimenters.

Because no clear causal relations have been established, psi research is plagued by ambiguities. Is foreknowledge of an event precognition, or PK? Is agent influence on another person PK or telepathy? Experiments to test PK ability in animals (Schmidt, 1970a; Watkins, 1972) expose further ambiguity: is the animal or the experimenter the effective PK agent? Kennedy, Taddonio, and White have undertaken to generalize from such considerations and to assess the implications for parapsychological research. Clearly, the methodology that will be required for deeper understanding of psychokinesis and of extrasensory phenomena must be increasingly complex and subtle.

Yet, in a larger sense, it may become simpler. The analytical approach, expressed in terms of experimenters and subjects, of telepathy and clairvoyance, ESP and PK, precognition and retrocognition, is derived from the causal concepts of prequantum physics; but in parapsychology it has revealed no causal chains and, consequently, has become mired in ambiguities. As the above authors note, the subtleties of recent research point increasingly to psi as an inclusive, holistic attribute of a group of organisms, and to a crucial role of conscious cognition in the determination of "random" events—even events that in ordinary terms have already happened.

5. References

Andrew, K. Psychokinetic influences on an electromechanical random number generator during evocation of "left-hemispheric" vs. "right-hemispheric" functioning. In J. D. Morris, W. G. Roll, and R. L. Morris (Eds.), *Research in parapsychology 1974*. Metuchen, N.J.: Scarecrow Press, 1975, pp. 58–61.

Averill, R. L., and Rhine, J. B. The effect of alcohol upon performance in PK tests. *Journal of Parapsychology*, 1945, *9*, 32–41.

Barlow, F., and Rampling-Rose, W. Report of an investigation into spirit-photography. *Proceedings of the Society for Psychical Research*, 1933, *41*, 121–138.

Barrett, W. F. Poltergeists, old and new. *Proceedings of the Society for Psychical Research*, 1911, *25*, 377–412.

Barry, J. General and comparative study of the psychokinetic effect on a fungus culture. *Journal of Parapsychology*, 1968, *32*, 237–243.

Batcheldor, K. J. Report on a case of table levitation and associated phenomena. *Journal of the Society for Psychical Research*, 1966, *43*, 339–356.

Bayless, R. Letter. *Journal of the American Society for Psychical Research*, 1959, *53*, 35–38.

Bayless, R. Tape-recording of paranormally generated acoustical raps. *New Horizons*, 1976, *2*(2), June, 12–17. (a)

Bayless, R. *Voices from beyond*. Secaucus, N.J.: University Books, 1976. (b)

Beloff, J., and Evans, L. A radioactivity test of psychokinesis. *Journal of the Society for Psychical Research*, 1961, *41*, 41–46.

Bender, H. Der Rosenheimer Spuk–ein Fall spontaner Psychokinese. *Zeitschrift für Parapsychologie und Grenzgebiete der Psychologie*, 1968, *11*, 104–112.

Bender, H. An investigation of "poltergeist" occurrences. In W. G. Roll, R. L. Morris, and J. D. Morris (Eds.), *Proceedings of the Parapsychological Association No. 5,1968*. Durham, N.C.: Parapsychological Association, 1971, pp. 31–33. (a)

Bender, H. New developments in poltergeist research. In W. G. Roll, R. L. Morris, and J. D. Morris (Eds.), *Proceedings of the Parapsychological Association No. 6,1969*. Durham, N.C.: Parapsychological Association, 1971, pp. 81–102. (b)

Bender, H. The phenomena of Freidrich Jürgenson. *Journal of Paraphysics*, 1972, *6*, 65–75.

Bender, H. Modern poltergeist research. In J. Beloff (Ed.), *New directions is parapsychology*. London: Elek Science, 1974.

Besterman, T. The mediumship of Rudi Schneider. *Proceedings of the Society for Psychical Research*, 1932, *40*, 428–436.

Binski, S. R. Report on two exploratory PK series. *Journal of Parapsychology*, 1957, *21*, 284–295.

Bjerre, P. *Spökerier*. Stockholm: Centrum, 1947.

Boring, E. G. The present status of parapsychology. *American Scientist*, 1955, *43*, 108–117.

Braud, W. G., Smith, G., Andrew, K., and Willis, S. Psychokinetic influences on random number generators during evocation of "analytic" vs. "nonanalytic" modes of information processing. In J. D. Morris, W. G. Roll, and R. L. Morris (Eds.), *Research in parapsychology 1975*. Metuchen, N.J.: Scarecrow Press, 1976, pp. 85–88.

Brier, R. M. PK on a bio-electrical system. *Journal of Parapsychology*, 1969, *33*, 187–205.

Brookes-Smith, C. Cromwell Varley's electrical tests. *Journal of the Society for Psychical Research*, 1965, *43*, 26–31.

Brookes-Smith, C. Data-tape recorded experimental PK phenomena. *Journal of the Society for Psychical Research*, 1973, *47*, 69–89.

Brookes-Smith, C., and Hunt, D. W. Some experiments in psychokinesis. *Journal of the Society for Psychical Research*, 1970, *45*, 265–281.

Carrington, H. *The physical phenomena of spiritualism.* Boston: H. B. Turner, 1907.

Carrington, H. *Eusapia Palladino and her phenomena.* New York: B. W. Dodge, 1909.

Carrington, H. *Laboratory investigations into psychic phenomena.* New York: Arno Press, 1975. (Originally published, 1939.)

Carrington, H. *The American séances with Eusapia Palladino.* New York: Garrett Publications, 1954.

Carrington, H., and Fodor, N. *Haunted people: the story of the poltergeist down the centuries.* New York: Dutton, 1951.

Chauvin, R., and Genthon, J. P. An investigation of the possibility of PK experiments with uranium and a Geiger counter. *Journal of Parapsychology*, 1967, *31*, 168. (Abstract)

Cook, C. H. Experiments in psychic photography. *Journal of the American Society for Psychical Research*, 1916, *10*, 1–114.

Cox, W. E. The effect of PK on the placement of falling objects. *Journal of Parapsychology*, 1951, *15*, 40–48.

Cox, W. E. Introductory comparative analysis of some poltergeist cases. *Journal of the American Society for Psychical Research*, 1961, *55*, 47–72.

Cox, W. E. Effect of PK on electromechanical systems. *Journal of Parapsychology*, 1965, *29*, 165–175.

Cox, W. E. A comparison of different densities of dice in a PK task. *Journal of Parapsychology*, 1971, *35*, 108–119. (a)

Cox, W. E. The use of pendulums in PK measurement. In W. G. Roll, R. L. Morris, and J. D. Morris (Eds.), *Proceedings of the Parapsychological Association No. 6, 1969.* Durham, N.C.: Parapsychological Association, 1971, pp. 45–46. (b)

Cox, W. E. PK measurement with balls in a 32-channel machine. In W. G. Roll, R. L. Morris, and J. D. Morris (Eds.), *Research in parapsychology 1972.* Metuchen, N.J.: Scarecrow Press, 1973, pp. 60–62.

Cox, W. E. Note on some experiments with Uri Geller. *Journal of Parapsychology*, 1974, *38*, 408–411.

Crookes, W. *Researches in the phenomena of spiritualism.* London: J. Burns, 1874.

Dale, L. A. The psychokinetic effect: The first A.S.P.R. experiment. *Journal of the American Society for Psychical Research*, 1946, *40*, 123–151.

Dale, L. A., and Woodruff, J. L. The psychokinetic effect: Further A.S.P.R. experiments. *Journal of the American Society for Psychical Research*, 1947, *41*, 65–82.

Dean, D. The effects of healers on biologically significant molecules. *New Horizons*, 1975, *1*(5), 215–219.

Eisenbud, J. Two approaches to spontaneous case material. *Journal of the American Society for Psychical Research*, 1963, *57*, 118–135.

Eisenbud, J. Why psi? *Psychoanalytic Review*, 1966–67, *53*(4), 147–163.

Eisenbud, J. *The world of Ted Serios.* New York: William Morrow, 1967.

Eisenbud, J. The Serios "blackies" and related phenomena. *Journal of the American Society for Psychical Research*, 1972, *66*, 180–192.

Eisenbud, J., and Associates. Some unusual data from a session with Ted Serios. *Journal of the American Society for Psychical Research*, 1967, *61*, 241–253.

Eisenbud, J., and Associates. Two experiments with Ted Serios. *Journal of the American Society for Psychical Research*, 1968, *62*, 309–320.

Eisenbud, J., and Associates. An archaeological *tour de force* with Ted Serios. *Journal of the American Society for Psychical Research*, 1970, *64*, 40–52. (a)

Eisenbud, J., and Associates. Two camera and television experiments with Ted Serios. *Journal of the American Society for Psychical Research*, 1970, *64*, 261–276. (b)

Ellis, D. Tape recordings from the dead? *Psychic*, 1974, *5*(3), 44–49.

Ellis, D. Listening to the "Raudive Voices." *Journal of the Society for Psychical Research*, 1975, *48*, 31–42.

Feather, S. R., and Rhine, L. E. PK experiments with same and different targets. *Journal of Parapsychology*, 1969, *33*, 213–227.

Feilding, E. *Sittings with Eusapia Palladino and other studies.* New Hyde Park, N.Y.: University Books, 1963.

Feilding, E., Baggally, W. W., and Carrington, H. Report on a series of sittings with Eusapia Palladino. *Proceedings of the Society for Psychical Research*, 1909, *23*, 306–569.

Firsoff, V. A. Life and quantum mechanics. In Laura Oteri (Ed.), *Quantum physics and parapsychology.* New York: Parapsychology Foundation, 1975.

Fodor, N. The poltergeist psychoanalyzed. *Psychiatric Quarterly*, 1948, *22*, 195–203.

Fodor, N. *On the trail of the poltergeist.* New York: Citadel Press, 1958.

Fodor, N. *The haunted mind.* New York: Garrett Publications, 1959.

Fodor, N. *Between two worlds.* West Nyack, N.Y.: Parker Publishing, 1964.

Forwald, H. A further study of the PK placement effect. *Journal of Parapsychology*, 1952, *16*, 59–67.

Forwald, H. *Mind, matter, and gravitation: A theoretical and experimental study (Parapsychological monographs No. 11).* New York: Parapsychology Foundation, 1969.

Franklin, W. Fracture surface physics indicating teleneural interaction. *New Horizons*, 1975, *2*(1), 8–13.

Fukurai, T. *Clairvoyance and thoughtography.* New York: Arno Press, 1975. (Originally published, 1931.)

Gauld, A. *The founders of psychical research.* London: Routledge & Kegan Paul, 1968.

Geley, G. *Clairvoyance and materialization.* New York: Arno Press, 1975. (Originally published, 1927.)

Gibson, E. P., Gibson, L. H., and Rhine, J. B. The PK effect: Mechanical throwing of three dice. *Journal of Parapsychology*, 1944, *8*, 95–109.

Girden, E. A review of psychokinesis (PK). *Psychological Bulletin*, 1962, *59*, 353–388. (a)

Girden, E. A postscript to "A review of psychokinesis (PK)." *Psychological Bulletin*, 1962, *59*, 529–531. (b)

Girden, E., Murphy, G., Beloff, J., Eisenbud, J., Flew, A., Rush, J. H., Schmeidler, G., and Thouless, R. H. A discussion of psychokinesis (PK). *International Journal of Parapsychology*, 1964, *6*, 26–137.

Grad, B. A telekinetic effect on plant growth. *International Journal of Parapsychology*, 1963, *5*, 117–133.

Grad, B. A telekinetic effect on plant growth, II. *International Journal of Parapsychology*, 1964, *6*, 473–498.

Grad, B. Some biological effects of the "laying on of hands": A review of experiments with animals and plants. *Journal of the American Society for Psychical Research*, 1965, *59*, 95–129.

Grad, B. The "laying on of hands": Implications for psychotherapy, gentling, and the placebo effect. *Journal of the American Society for Psychical Research*, 1967, *61*, 287–305.

Grad, B., Cadoret, R. J., and Paul, G. I. The influence of an unorthodox method of treatment on wound healing in mice. *International Journal of Parapsychology*, 1961, *3*(2), 5–24.

Gregory, A. The physical mediumship of Rudi Schneider. In W. G. Roll, R. L. Morris, and J. D. Morris (Eds.), *Proceedings of the Parapsychological Association No. 5, 1968*. Durham, N.C.: Parapsychological Association, 1971, pp. 19–21.

Gregory, A. Ethics and psychical research. *Journal of the Society for Psychical Research*, 1974, *47*, 283–305.

Gurney, E., Myers, F. W. H., and Podmore, F. *Phantasms of the living*. (2 vols.) Gainesville, Fla.: Scholars' Facsimiles, 1970. (Originally published, 1886.)

Hansel, C. E. M. *ESP: A scientific evaluation*. New York: Charles Scribner's Sons, 1966.

Herbert, B. Suzanne Padfield. *Journal of Paraphysics*, 1973, *7*, Supplement to No. 5, 9–11.

Herrigel, E. *Zen in the art of archery*. New York: Pantheon, 1953.

Hilton, H., Jr., and Rhine, J. B. A second comparison of three sizes of dice in PK tests. *Journal of Parapsychology*, 1943, *7*, 191–206.

Hilton, H., Jr., Baer, G., and Rhine, J. B. A comparison of three sizes of dice in PK tests. *Journal of Parapsychology*, 1943, *7*, 172–190.

Hodgson, R. Mr. Davey's imitations by conjuring of phenomena sometimes attributed to spirit agency. *Proceedings of the Society for Psychical Research*, 1892, *8*, 253–310.

Hodgson, R., and Davey, S. J. The possibilities of mal-observation and lapse of memory from a practical point of view. *Proceedings of the Society for Psychical Research*, 1887, *4*, 381–495.

Honorton, C. Apparent psychokinesis on static objects by a "gifted" subject. In W. G. Roll, R. L. Morris, and J. D. Morris (Eds.), *Research in parapsychology 1973*. Metuchen, N.J.: Scarecrow Press, 1974, pp. 128–131.

Honorton, C., and Barksdale, W. PK performance with waking suggestions for muscle tension versus relaxation. *Journal of the American Society for Psychical Research*, 1972, *66*, 208–214.

Hope, C., et al. Report of a series of sittings with Rudi Schneider. *Proceedings of the Society for Psychical Research*, 1933, *41*, 255–330.

Humphrey, B. M. Help–hinder comparison in PK tests. *Journal of Parapsychology*, 1947, *11*, 4–13. (a)

Humphrey, B. M. Simultaneous high and low aim in PK tests. *Journal of Parapsychology*, 1947, *11*, 160–174. (b)

Jürgenson, F. *Rösterna from Rymden*. Stockholm: Faxon & Lindstrom, 1964.

Jürgenson, F. *Sprechfunk mit Verstorbenen*. Freiburg, W. Germany, Verlag Hermann Bauer, 1967.

Karger, F., and Zicha, G. Physikalische Untersuchung des Spukfalles in Rosenheim 1967. *Zeitschrift für Parapsychologie und Grenzgebiete der Psychologie*, 1968, *11*(2), 104–112.

Karger, F., and Zicha, G. Physical investigation of psychokinetic phenomena in Rosenheim, Germany, 1967. In W. G. Roll, R. L. Morris, and J. D. Morris (Eds.), *Proceedings of the Parapsychological Association No. 5, 1968.* Durham, N.C.: Parapsychological Association, 1971, pp. 33–35.

Keil, H. H. J., Herbert, B., Ullman, M., and Pratt, J. G. Directly observable voluntary PK effects. *Proceedings of the Society for Psychical Research,* 1976, *56,* 197–235.

Kennedy, J. E., and Taddonio, J. L. Experimenter effects in parapsychological research. *Journal of Parapsychology,* 1976, *40,* 1–33.

Knowles, F. W. Correspondence. *Journal of the Society for Psychical Research,* 1972, *46,* 99–100.

Krieger, D. Therapeutic touch: The imprimatur of nursing. *American Journal of Nursing,* 1975, *75,* 784–787.

Krippner, S. Interview. *Psychic,* 1976, *6*(6), 48–58.

Layard, J. Psi phenomena and poltergeists. *Proceedings of the Society for Psychical Research,* 1944, *47,* 237–247.

Leuret, F., and Bon, H. *Modern miraculous cures.* New York: Farrar, Strauss, and Cudahy; London: Peter Davies, 1957.

Manning, M. *The link.* New York: Holt, Rinehart, & Winston, 1974.

May, E. C., and Honorton, C. A dynamic PK experiment with Ingo Swann. In J. D. Morris, W. G. Roll, and R. L. Morris (Eds.), *Research in parapsychology 1975.* Metuchen, N.J.: Scarecrow Press, 1976, pp. 88–89.

McComas, H. C. *Ghosts I have talked with.* Baltimore: Williams and Wilkins, 1935.

McConnell, R. A. Remote night tests for PK. *Journal of the American Society for Psychical Research,* 1955, *49,* 99–108.

McConnell, R. A., Snowdon, R. J., and Powell, K. F. Wishing with dice. *Journal of Experimental Psychology,* 1955, *50,* 269–275.

McMahan, E. PK experiments with two-sided objects. *Journal of Parapsychology,* 1945, *9,* 249–263.

Medhurst, R. G., and Goldney, K. M. William Crookes and the physical phenomena of mediumship. *Proceedings of the Society for Psychical Research,* 1964, *54,* 25–156.

Metta, L. Psychokinesis of lepidopterous larvae. *Journal of Parapsychology,* 1972, *36,* 213–221.

Millar, B. Thermistor PK. In J. D. Morris, W. G. Roll, and R. L. Morris (Eds.), *Research in parapsychology 1975.* Metuchen, N.J.: Scarecrow Press, 1976, pp. 71–73.

Miller, R. N., and Reinhart, P. B. Measuring psychic energy. *Psychic,* 1975, *6*(2), 46–47.

Mitchell, A. M. J., and Fisk, G. W. The application of differential scoring methods to PK tests. *Journal of the Society for Psychical Research,* 1953, *37,* 45–60.

Moser, F. *Spuk. Irrglaube oder Wahrglaube?* Baden bei Zurich: Gyr-Verlag, 1950.

Mundle, C. W. K. The experimental evidence for PK and precognition. *Proceedings of the Society for Psychical Research,* 1950, *49,* 61–78.

Murphy, G. Report on paper by Edward Girden on psychokinesis. *Psychological Bulletin,* 1962, *59,* 520–528.

Nash, C. B. PK tests of a large population. *Journal of Parapsychology,* 1944, *8,* 304–310.

Nash, C. B. Position effects in PK tests with twenty-four dice. *Journal of Parapsychology,* 1946, *10,* 51—57.

Nash, C. B., and Nash, C. S. The effect of paranormally conditioned solution on yeast fermentation. *Journal of Parapsychology,* 1967, *31,* 314. (Abstract)

Nash, C. B., and Richards, A. Comparison of two distances in PK tests. *Journal of Parapsychology,* 1947, *11,* 269—282.

Nicol, J. F. The design of experiments in psychokinesis. *Journal of the Society for Psychical Research,* 1954, *37,* 355—357.

Nicol, J. F. Randomness: The background and some new investigations. *Journal of the Society for Psychical Research,* 1955, *38,* 71—87.

Nicol, J. F. Remarks. In G. E. W. Wolstenholme and E. C. P. Millar (Eds.), *Ciba Foundation Symposium on extrasensory perception.* Boston: Little, Brown, 1956.

Ornstein, R. *The nature of human consciousness.* New York: Viking, 1974.

Osis, K. A test of the relationship between ESP and PK. *Journal of Parapsychology,* 1953, *17,* 298—309.

Osty, E., and Osty, M. Les Pouvoirs inconnus de l'esprit sur la matière. *Revue Métapsychique,* 1931, No. 6, 393—427, and 1932, No. 1, 1—59.

Osty, E., and Osty, M. *Les pouvoirs inconnus sur la matière; premières étapes d'une recherche.* Paris: Felix Alcan, 1932.

Owen, A. R. G. *Can we explain the poltergeist?* New York: Garrett Publications, 1964.

Owen, A. R. G. A preliminary report on Matthew Manning's physical phenomena. *New Horizons,* 1974, *1*(4), 172—173. (a)

Owen, A. R. G. Uri Geller's metal phenomena: an eyewitness account. *New Horizons,* 1974, *1*(4), 164—171. (b)

Owen, A. R. G. The evidence for psychokinesis. *New Horizons,* 1975, *1*(5), 196—200.

Owen, I. M. The making of a ghost. *Psychic,* 1975, *6*(3), 27—31.

Owen, I. M., and Sparrow, M. H. Generation of paranormal phenomena in connection with an imaginary communicator. *New Horizons,* 1974, *1*(3), 6—13.

Owen, I. M., with Sparrow, M. H. *Conjuring up Philip: An adventure in psychokinesis.* New York: Harper & Row, 1976.

Panati, C. *The Geller papers.* Boston: Houghton-Mifflin, 1976.

Podmore, F. *Mediums of the nineteenth century.* (2 vols.) New Hyde Park, N.Y.: University Books, 1963. (Originally published under title *Modern Spiritualism,* 1902.)

Podmore, F. The report on Eusapia Palladino. *Journal of the Society for Psychical Research,* 1909, *14,* 172—176.

Podmore, F. *The newer spiritualism.* New York: Arno Press, 1975. (Originally published, 1910.)

Pratt, J. G. A reinvestigation of the quarter distribution of the (PK) page. *Journal of Parapsychology,* 1944, *8,* 61—63.

Pratt, J. G. Lawfulness of position effects in the Gibson cup PK series. *Journal of Parapsychology,* 1946, *10,* 243—268.

Pratt, J. G. Restricted areas of success in PK tests. *Journal of Parapsychology,* 1947, *11,* 191—207. (a)

Pratt, J. G. Rhythms of success in PK test data. *Journal of Parapsychology,* 1947, *11,* 90—110. (b)

Pratt, J. G. Target preference in PK tests with dice. *Journal of Parapsychology*, 1947, *11*, 26–45. (c)

Pratt, J. G. Trial-by-trial grouping of success and failure in psi tests. *Journal of Parapsychology*, 1947, *11*, 254–268. (d)

Pratt, J. G. The Cormack placement PK experiments. *Journal of Parapsychology*, 1951, *15*, 57–73.

Pratt, J. G. The case for psychokinesis. *Journal of Parapsychology*, 1960, *24*, 171–188.

Pratt, J. G. The Girden–Murphy papers on PK. *Journal of Parapsychology*, 1963, *27*, 199–209.

Pratt, J. G., and Roll, W. G. The Seaford disturbances. *Journal of Parapsychology*, 1958, *22*, 79–124.

Price, H. *Stella C.: An account of some original experiments in psychical research*. London: Souvenir Press, 1973. (Originally published, 1925.)

Price, H. *Rudi Schneider: A scientific examination of his mediumship*. London: Methuen, 1930.

Price, H. *Confessions of a ghost hunter*. London: Putnam, 1936.

Price, M. M., and Rhine, J. B. The subject–experimenter relation in the PK test. *Journal of Parapsychology*, 1944, *8*, 177–186.

Puthoff, H., and Targ, R. PK experiments with Uri Geller and Ingo Swann. In W. G. Roll, R. L. Morris, and J. D. Morris (Eds.), *Research in parapsychology 1973*. Metuchen, N.J.: Scarecrow Press, 1974, pp. 125–128.

Puthoff, H., and Targ, R. Physics, entropy, and psychokinesis. In Laura Oteri (Ed.), *Quantum physics and parapsychology*. New York: Parapsychology Foundation, 1975.

Raudive, K. *Breakthrough*. New York: Taplinger, 1971.

Rayleigh, Lord. On a method of silhouette photography by infra-red rays for use in mediumistic investigation. *Proceedings of the Society for Psychical Research*, 1933, *41*, 89–98.

Rhine, J. B. *Extra-sensory perception*. Boston: Humphries, 1964. (Originally published, 1934.)

Rhine, J. B. Dice thrown by cup and machine in PK tests. *Journal of Parapsychology*, 1943, *7*, 207–217.

Rhine, J. B. The PK effect: early singles tests. *Journal of Parapsychology*, 1944, *8*, 287–303.

Rhine, J. B. The Forwald experiments with placement PK. *Journal of Parapsychology*, 1951, *15*, 49–56.

Rhine, J. B., and Humphrey, B. M. The PK effect: Special evidence from hit patterns. I. Quarter distributions of the page. *Journal of Parapsychology*, 1944, *8*, 18–60. (a)

Rhine, J. B., and Humphrey, B. M. The PK effect: Special evidence from hit patterns. II. Quarter distributions of the set. *Journal of Parapsychology*, 1944, *8*, 254–271. (b)

Rhine, J. B., and Humphrey, B. M. The PK effect with sixty dice per throw. *Journal of Parapsychology*, 1945, *9*, 203–218.

Rhine, J. B., Humphrey, B. M., and Averill, R. L. An exploratory experiment on the effect of caffeine upon performance in PK tests. *Journal of Parapsychology*, 1945, *9*, 80–91.

Rhine, J. B., Humphrey, B. M., and Pratt, J. G. The PK effect: Special evidence from hit patterns. III. Quarter distributions of the half-set. *Journal of Parapsychology*, 1945, *9*, 150–168.

Rhine, L. E. Placement PK tests with three types of objects. *Journal of Parapsychology*, 1951, *15*, 132–138.

Rhine, L. E. *Mind over matter*. New York: Macmillan, 1970.

Rhine, L. E., and Rhine, J. B. The psychokinetic effect: I. The first experiments. *Journal of Parapsychology*, 1943, *7*, 20–43.

Richet, C. *Thirty years of psychical research*. New York: Macmillan, 1923.

Richmond, N. Two series of PK tests on paramecia. *Journal of the Society for Psychical Research*, 1952, *36*, 577–588.

Rogo, D. S. *In search of the unknown*. New York: Taplinger, 1976.

Roll, W. G. Some physical and psychological aspects of a series of poltergeist phenomena. *Journal of the American Society for Psychical Research*, 1968, *62*, 264–308.

Roll, W. G. Poltergeist phenomena and interpersonal relations. *Journal of the American Society for Psychical Research*, 1970, *64*, 66–99.

Roll, W. G. *The poltergeist*. Metuchen, N.J.: Scarecrow Press, 1976. (Originally published, 1972.)

Roll, W. G., and Pratt, J. G. The Miami disturbances. *Journal of the American Society for Psychical Research*, 1971, *65*, 409–454.

Roll, W. G., and Stump, J. P. The Olive Hill poltergeist. In W. G. Roll, R. L. Morris, and J. D. Morris (Eds.), *Proceedings of the Parapsychological Association No. 6, 1969*. Durham, N.C.: Parapsychological Association, 1971, pp. 57–58.

Roll, W. G., Burdick, D. S., and Joines, W. T. Radial and tangential forces in the Miami poltergeist. *Journal of the American Society for Psychical Research*, 1973, *67*, 267–281.

Rush, J. H. *New directions in parapsychological research (Parapsychological monographs No. 4.)* New York: Parapsychology Foundation, 1964.

Schmeidler, G. R. PK effects upon continuously recorded temperature. *Journal of the American Society for Psychical Research*, 1973, *67*, 325–340.

Schmeidler, G., Mitchell, J., and Sondow, N. Further investigation of PK with temperature records. In J. D. Morris, W. G. Roll, and R. L. Morris (Eds.), *Research in parapsychology 1974*. Metuchen, N.J.: Scarecrow Press, 1975, pp. 71–73.

Schmidt, H. PK experiments with animals as subjects. *Journal of Parapsychology*, 1970, *34*, 255–261. (a)

Schmidt, H. A PK test with electronic equipment. *Journal of Parapsychology*, 1970, *34*, 175–181. (b)

Schmidt, H. Quantum-mechanical random-number generator. *Journal of Applied Physics*, 1970, *41*, 462–468. (c)

Schmidt, H. A quantum mechanical random number generator for psi tests. *Journal of Parapsychology*, 1970, *34*, 219–224. (d)

Schmidt, H. PK tests with a high-speed random number generator. *Journal of Parapsychology*, 1973, *37*, 105–118.

Schmidt, H. Comparison of PK action on two different random number generators. *Journal of Parapsychology*, 1974, *38*, 47–55.

Schmidt, H. Observation of subconscious PK effects with and without time displacement. In J. D. Morris, W. G. Roll, and R. L. Morris (Eds.), *Research in parapsychology 1974.* Metuchen, N.J.: Scarecrow Press, 1975, pp. 116–121. (a)

Schmidt, H. Toward a mathematical theory of psi. *Journal of the American Society for Psychical Research,* 1975, *69,* 301–319. (b)

Schmidt, H. PK effect on pre-recorded targets. *Journal of the American Society for Psychical Research,* 1976, *70,* 267–292.

Schmidt, H., and Pantas, L. Psi tests with internally different machines. *Journal of Parapsychology,* 1972, *36,* 222–232.

Sidgwick, Mrs. H. On spirit photography: A reply to Mr. A. R. Wallace. *Proceedings of the Society for Psychical Research,* 1891, *7,* 268–289.

Smith, E. L. The Raudive voices–objective or subjective? *Journal of the American Society for Psychical Research,* 1974, *68,* 91–100. (Reprinted from *Journal of the Society for Psychical Research,* 1972, *46.*)

Smith, M. J. The influence of enzyme growth by the "laying on of hands." In *The dimensions of healing: a symposium.* Los Altos, Calif.: Academy of Psychology and Medicine, 1973.

Soal, S. G. The experimental situation in psychical research. (*Ninth Myers memorial lecture.*) London: Society for Psychical Research, 1947.

Soal, S. G. Review of *The reach of the mind* by J. B. Rhine. *Journal of the Society for Psychical Research,* 1948, *34,* 183–185.

Stanford, R. G. "Associative activation of the unconscious" and "visualization" as methods for influencing the PK target. *Journal of the American Society for Psychical Research,* 1969, *63,* 338–351.

Stanford, R. G. An experimentally testable model for spontaneous psi events. I. Extrasensory events. *Journal of the American Society for Psychical Research,* 1974, *68,* 34–57. (a)

Stanford, R. G. An experimentally testable model for spontaneous psi events. iI. Psychokinetic events. *Journal of the American Society for Psychical Research,* 1974, *68,* 321–356. (b)

Stanford, R. G., Zenhausern, R., Taylor, A., and Dwyer, M. Psychokinesis as psi-mediated instrumental response. *Journal of the American Society for Psychical Research,* 1975, *69,* 127–134.

Steilberg, B. J. "Conscious concentration" versus "visualization" in PK tests. *Journal of Parapsychology,* 1975, *39,* 12–20.

Stevenson, I., and Pratt, J. G. Exploratory investigations of the psychic photography of Ted Serios. *Journal of the American Society for Psychical Research,* 1968, *62,* 103–129.

Stevenson, I., and Pratt, J. G. Further investigations of the psychic photography of Ted Serios. *Journal of the American Society for Psychical Research,* 1969, *63,* 352–365.

Strauch, I. Medical aspects of "mental" healing. *International Journal of Parapsychology,* 1963, *5,* 135–165.

Tart, C. T. *Learning to use extrasensory perception.* Chicago: University of Chicago Press, 1976.

Thouless, R. H. Some experiments on PK effects in coin spinning. *Journal of Parapsychology,* 1945, *9,* 169–175.

Thouless, R. H. A report on an experiment in psycho-kinesis with dice, and a discussion on psychological factors favouring success. *Proceedings of the Society for Psychical Research*, 1951, *49*, 107–130.

Thurston, H. *Ghosts and poltergeists*. Chicago: Henry Regnery, 1954.

Tietze, T. R. *Margery*. New York: Harper & Row, 1973. (a)

Tietze, T. R. The mystery of Rudi Schneider. *Psychic*, 1973, *4*(4), 38–43. (b)

Tizane, E. *Sur la piste de l'homme inconnu. Les phénomènes de hantise et de possession*. Paris: Amiot-Dumont, 1951.

Van de Castle, R. L. An exploratory study of some personality correlates associated with PK performance. *Journal of the American Society for Psychical Research*, 1958, *52*, 134–150.

Wadhams, P., and Farrelly, B. The investigation of psychokinesis using beta particles. *Journal of the Society for Psychical Research*, 1968, *44*, 281–288.

Warrick, F. W. *Experiments in psychics*. New York: Dutton, 1939.

Watkins, G. K. Possible PK in the lizard *Anolis sagrei*. In W. G. Roll, R. L. Morris, and J. D. Morris (Eds.), *Proceedings of the Parapsychological Association No. 8, 1971*. Durham, N.C.: Parapsychological Association, 1972, pp. 23–25.

Watkins, G. K., and Watkins, A. M. Possible PK influence on the resuscitation of anesthetized mice. *Journal of Parapsychology*, 1971, *35*, 257–272.

Watkins, G. K., and Watkins, A. M. Apparent psychokinesis on static objects by a "gifted" subject: A laboratory demonstration. In W. G. Roll, R. L. Morris, and J. D. Morris (Eds.), *Research in parapsychology 1973*. Metuchen, N.J.: Scarecrow Press, 1974, pp. 132–134.

Wells, R., and Klein, J. A replication of a "psychic healing" paradigm. *Journal of Parapsychology*, 1972, *36*, 144–149.

West, D. J. A critical survey of the American PK research. *Proceedings of the Society for Psychical Research*, 1945, *47*, 281–290.

West, D. J. *Psychical research today*. London: Duckworth, 1954.

West, D. J. *Eleven Lourdes miracles*. New York: Garrett Publications, 1957.

White, R. A. The influence of persons other than the experimenter on the subject's scores on psi experiments. *Journal of the American Society for Psychical Research*, 1976, *70*, 133–166. (a)

White, R. A. The limits of experimenter influence on psi test results: Can any be set? *Journal of the American Society for Psychical Research*, 1976, *70*, 333–370. (b)

Whitton, J. L. "Ramp functions" in EEG power spectra during actual or attempted paranormal events. *New Horizons*, 1974, *1*(4), 173–186.

Whitton, J. L. Qualitative time-domain analysis of acoustic envelopes of psychokinetic table rappings. *New Horizons*, 1975, *2*(1), 21–24.

Wijk, H. Karin: an experimental study of spontaneous rappings. *Annals of Psychical Science*, 1905, *2*, 143–180.

Winther, C. Experimental inquiries into telekinesis. *Journal of the American Society for Psychical Research*, 1928, *22*, 25–31, 82–99, 164–180, 230–239, 278–290.

Zöllner, J. C. F. *Transcendental physics*. Boston: Colby & Rich, 1881.

Zorab, G. A further comparative analysis of some poltergeist phenomena: cases from continental Europe. *Journal of the American Society for Psychical Research*, 1964, *58*, 105–127.

Research Findings in Psychokinesis   2

Gertrude R. Schmeidler

1. *Problems, Problems!*

When a chapter is supposed to cover research findings, how much should it include? The results of experiments, of course—but experiments are not the only proper kind of research. Careful observations made under controlled conditions surely belong in the chapter, too; and astronomy shows us that if such observations are quantitative, they can be the basis for sound science. When we look for careful, fully specified reports, however, we find that they shade by almost imperceptible degrees into those that are weakly controlled and do not tell us about relevant surrounding conditions. When should we omit a set of statements because they seem little more than an observer's personal guess about what happened, instead of giving them the dignity of a research finding?

This is one set of problems. Another whole set arises with the last word of the assigned topic: psychokinesis. How wide an umbrella is it? What do we mean by it?

In the introductory section that follows I will give, and try to defend, the broad directives I have hammered out for myself about the ground this chapter will cover. The next section is a quick survey of history, to show the picture in the large. In the following sections, I will try to summarize what seem to me the major research findings and the generalizations to which they point, under these headings: Controlled Laboratory Research, Documented Surveys, Attempts to Control Séance Room Phenomena, Studies of Special Individuals Not in a Séance, Poltergeists, and Isolated Instances. (The headings may seem to make

Gertrude R. Schmeidler · Psychology Department, City College of the City University of New York, New York.

clear differentiations, but unfortunately they do not. To cite one example, a laboratory experiment on a gifted individual could equally well be put in the first category or the fourth. There is considerable overlap among the groups.)

2. What the Chapter Covers

A proper definition of psychokinesis is not easy to find. It should describe current usage, which makes older definitions useless. My 1927 *Webster's Dictionary,* for example, equates psychokinesis with the medical term "psychokinesia: A fit of violent temporary insanity or maniacal action, due to defective inhibition." It has interesting implications, but clearly it does not speak to our topic.

The other standard dictionary we have at home is the *American Heritage,* published in 1969. It uses the word in the current sense which the Rhines introduced (L. E. Rhine and J. B. Rhine, 1943) and have made familiar, but this does not seem fully adequate to me. Its definition is: "The production of motion, especially in inanimate or remote objects, by the exercise of psychic powers." Here psychokinetic effects are unduly limited to motion. What of a change in color? A chemical change? A change in a photograph? The materialization of something claimed not to have existed earlier? If we stretch the idea of motion far beyond its ordinary meaning, to include intramolecular motion, for example (and if we accept the vague term "psychic powers"), the definition can stand; but it is not ideally clear.

The last source I will cite is the Glossary published in each issue of the *Journal of Parapsychology.* This is the one that should provide our best definition, both because it is in a technical journal and this is a technical topic, and also because the Rhines, who originated the term, are on the journal's editorial staff. It defines psychokinesis (listed under its convenient acronym, PK) as "The extramotor aspect of psi; a direct (i.e., mental but nonmuscular) influence exerted by the subject on an external physical process, condition, or object."

This resolves one difficulty mentioned above by including what we ordinarily think of as static effects, but it seems to me to introduce two others (and to dodge a third). In the first place, it does not exclude enough. It properly specifies that psychokinetic effects should be nonmuscular. But what of physical effects due to other body processes, such as chemical secretions, or electrical changes, or heat variations? Surely they should be excluded too. If for semantic convenience we make a distinction between mind and body, these all belong on the body or physiological side, along with muscular action. We are on safer ground if we enlarge the "nonmuscular" in the definition to some broader term for body activity. Thus, we should exclude from psychokinetic effects not only those due to muscles, but also any due to odors caused by body change, to changes in body heat, to electrical change in the body, etc. On this basis, we should exclude the effects reported in studies of Kirlian photography, since there is good reason to think they result directly from the physiological change in the subject, probably chiefly the variations in autonomic nervous system activity.

Another problem raised by the definition in the *Journal of Parapsychology* is that when it specifies that psychokinetic changes must be external to the subject it does not seem to include enough. The question of what is external is not easy, and demands delicate distinctions. Where does the outside begin? Would an abrupt change in the subject's hair tips or the ends of his fingernails be called external or internal? In the length of his arms and legs? In levitation of his whole body? Most parapsychologists would, I think, prefer to put levitation under the rubric of PK, and the definition should be enlarged to include it and probably some other body changes also.

One major gray area remains. If a subject tries to direct his or her psychokinetic powers to another individual, human or animal, and if that other individual responds as the first person hoped, is this psychokinesis? For some such effects the answer would ordinarily be yes; the prime example here is a physiological change in the second person, as studied in psychic healing or psychic hurting. Others are ambiguous. What if our psychokinetic subject tries to make someone scratch his ear, or turn around, and the other person does so? Should such movement be attributed to the first person's PK, like a change in the movement of a falling die? Or should it be attributed to a telepathic message which the second person received, and then voluntarily acted upon? Still a third class belongs here theoretically: the cases in which our subject tries to transmit a message, and the other individual responds with that message. This is ordinarily considered ESP rather than PK, but it could easily be conceptualized as a PK alteration in the brain processes of the percipient, who then makes the conscious response dictated by the change in his brain.

And there may even be a fourth class. When an apparition is reported by independent observers, might it represent an external change in the physical world, i.e., a PK change, rather than being a purely mental effect? Or to put it another way, could a person's or group's prior thoughts create some external effect which is then observable by others? This too has been suggested (see for example, Maher and Schmeidler, 1975; Owen and Sparrow, 1976).

All four of these groups pose the same problem. In all of them, even the psychic healing or hurting, the effect (if there is one) may be due to a mental change in the other person which then stimulates his brain or other body processes to changed activity, or it may be due to a direct psychokinetic effect which is then mirrored in consciousness. Since I do not know how to resolve the problem, I will follow in this chapter the conventional line of including what is classed as psychic healing or hurting under the topic of PK (although if it occurs it may be only an indirect effect of telepathic messages) but of excluding apparitions and conscious report from the topic of PK (even though they may represent direct physical changes in the external world or the brain). For overt behavior, where there is no conventional line, I will waver.

And now for the other set of initial difficulties. What is research? When does it produce a finding? Since I am a psychologist, I will follow here the general directives of my own field. Psychology texts ordinarily describe with approval a variety of research methods. Usually, they begin with naturalistic observations, such as those of the ethologists who watch animal behavior or the anthropologists who report what they see in various societies. At the weaker end, obviously, such observations shade off into traveler's tales and are unreliable. It is unfortunate—even embarrassing—that there is no clear line of demarcation between the accounts colored by the reporter's imagination or observed too narrowly so that important context is omitted, and the ones that should be accepted as fully accurate. Perhaps the only way to cope with this embarrassment is to recognize that it exists, and make our own subjective judgments: to class any particular account in the pejorative category of an anecdote or in the prestigious category of a field report according to what evidence we have of the care and the accuracy of the reporter.

Other types of acceptable research make up a long list. There are case studies and field surveys, public opinion polls, questionnaire responses, formal tests (e.g., of intelligence or personality) often correlated with other behavioral measures, and there are experiments in which all relevant conditions are controlled except for the independent variables that are manipulated by the experimenter. But for all these, we meet with the same need for judgment as with field reports or spontaneous cases. Not all accounts are sufficiently detailed, with enough description of prior or concomitant conditions, to justify confidence. Further, a research worker who describes a "significant" finding will often mean that the odds are one in twenty that the outcome was due to chance; and this may not seem to us strong enough to give much confidence in its validity.

In short, no matter what kind of research we consider, we run into trouble when we try to specify a finding. Not every firm statement can be accepted. Some are outright lies; others are self-delusions. Still others, though they are literally true, are useless because they omit essential details of stage props or accomplices, or lapses of the observer's attention, or equipment failures, or selection of data, etc. We dare not reject even the most implausible merely because of what it claims; we do not want to fall into the classical error of disregarding descriptions of meteorites because we have made up our minds in advance that it is impossible for stones to fall from the sky. On the other hand, we must look carefully for possible sources of error in the statements, even the experimental statements, that come our way.

Without being content about it, I therefore propose that we tentatively consider or even accept some unsupported naturalistic observations as if they represent research findings. And at the other extreme, I suggest that we be equally tentative in considering or accepting some of the findings of laboratory research, whether they be null or affirmative, unless a full report of the conditions is included and unless similar, confirming data are obtained in other laboratories.

But where does this leave us? Hundreds of articles in technical journals and many books have been published on psychokinesis. It would be tedious and unprofitable to review them all; and I shall not attempt to do so. No single clear criterion for omission or exclusion seems appropriate; and with multiple criteria the selection process is fuzzy. My own reasons for deciding what to include, as well as I can state them, are these. One is chronological: there will be more of the recent reports, and fewer of the early ones. Another is the research approach: there will be many of the two hundred or so laboratory observations, and relatively few of the more numerous other descriptions. Another is my subjective impression of the quality of the report. And a fourth will be even more subjective: the criterion of meaningfulness, of material which is process-oriented, or which seems to relate psychokinetic functioning to the functioning of other abilities, or to physical theory.

3. History

3.1. Prehistory

If we accept reports that are vouched for by the authorities of their day, a survey of psychokinetic findings would start with the dawn of history, where the miracles that are part of religious lore describe how God or the divinely gifted made bushes burn without being consumed, or staffs turn into serpents, or a wall tumble down on command. If we limit our acceptance to firsthand reports, we begin no earlier than written records; and here also there are many accounts and from many cultures (although Dodds [1971] tells us that they are rare among the Greeks and Romans). Some are considered miracles of God or the gods; others, like poltergeists, were thought of as the work of evil spirits. Many are associated with holiness, such as the saintly blood that liquefies repeatedly, or the ability of St. Joseph of Cupertino to float in the air while at prayer, or the ability of holy men especially in India and Tibet to levitate, to withstand fire, burial, or piercing of the skin, and to create objects by willing them to exist; or the ability of anointed kings and of medicine men to perform psychic healing. (See, for example, David-Neel, 1959; Dingwall, 1947; Evans-Wentz, 1966.) The range of phenomena is enormous, but only a few are described in enough detail to fit into the category of research. Let us pass quickly from these fascinating periods to more recent times.

3.2. Early History

In the nineteenth century, and especially in England after the spiritualistic phenomena of the Fox sisters and D. D. Home commanded popular attention, psychokinetic claims began to be investigated scientifically; and a few scientists, like Crookes and Galton, rendered affirmative reports on some of the claims (e.g., see Crookes, 1874). When the Society for Psychical Research was founded in 1882, its members made many careful investigations, exposed some claims as false, and described others that seemed to be valid. Most such reports were studies of physical mediums or of poltergeists. Since poltergeists had to be studied in their natural setting, and mediums like Palladino demanded special testing conditions which usually interfered with careful observation, full control of all relevant variables was seldom possible. A summary statement (S[alter], 1952) is that

> When . . . conditions were formulated that would effectively exclude deception, great difficulty was experienced in finding mediums willing to accept them. In consequence the field of investigation into physical phenomena has proved disappointingly barren, and there are few records of positive results obtained by competent researchers under good conditions. (p. 642)

It might seem to you and me that even a few records obtained under good conditions of psychokinetic movement of heavy tables or psychokinetic changes in light and electricity would be striking enough to justify further intensive research. Typically, however, the follow-up consisted of offering alternative explanations months or even decades after the project was completed, so that no one could test the counterexplanations. An extreme example is a review ninety years later (Broad, 1964) of Varley's 1874 report about electrical changes apparently produced by PK, followed in 1966 (Stephenson) by an article suggesting additional controls that the 1874 work should have employed. The pattern was the reporting of odd events, but then merely discussing them rather than trying to establish their generality and the conditions under which they could reliably occur. The research following the reports was historical rather than scientific. Representative examples of the best of this kind of work will be mentioned briefly in later sections; modern work, though usually less spectacular, will be described in more detail.

3.3. Recent History (1943–1959)

Studies along the earlier lines continued in the 1940s and 1950s, but a major innovation by J. B. Rhine altered the entire field. Its story begins with a visit from a professional gambler to Rhine's Parapsychology Laboratory at Duke University. The gambler claimed that he could sometimes use psychic influence to make dice fall the way he wanted; Rhine decided to test the possibility that such effects could occur. He and his associates at the laboratory made extensive tests under increasingly well-controlled conditions, using themselves as subjects and anyone else who was at hand. Their findings were affirmative.

In 1943, L. E. Rhine and J. B. Rhine published the first formal report of their research and introduced the term psychokinesis to describe the effect. The report was quickly followed by others. The findings stimulated research workers elsewhere, who followed the Rhines' basic approach and also introduced refinements of method or novel variations. One alternative method, for example, used in the Duke laboratory (Cox, 1951) and elsewhere (Forwald, 1952) was the "placement" technique, the attempt to influence by wishing the location to which an object would fall rather than the side of it that fell uppermost.

By the end of the 1950s, so many parapsychologists had reported so many data consistent with the hypothesis that PK occurred that an outsider, Girden, undertook to make a full-scale analysis of the work. In 1962, he published a critical article surveying the experimental publications through 1959, and demonstrating more or less serious flaws in much of the material. His review was preceded and followed by others (Beloff, 1964; Eisenbud, 1964; Flew, 1964; Murphy, 1962; Pratt, 1960;

Rush, 1964; Schmeidler, 1964; Thouless, 1964), almost all of which defended the conclusion that PK had been demonstrated. The experimental work of this period and the subsequent critique of it will be summarized in the first unit after this history.

3.4. The 1960s to 1977

Since 1959 (and through the year of 1976) further experiments have used the same basic method of releasing small objects and hoping they would fall a certain way; and there have also been continuations of the earlier studies. But, in addition, two markedly different lines of research have been increasingly emphasized.

One investigation followed a technical advance largely due to the work of a physicist, Schmidt (1969), who developed and distributed a machine called a Random Number Generator (RNG). The machine selects random ESP targets or shows PK effects by the discharge of radioactive particles, and can automatically record targets, calls, and hits. The machine can be adapted to study many forms of ESP and PK, and it provides a research technique that is appealing to both subjects and experimenters. It offers an interesting task, quick feedback of results, the potential of rapidly gathering a large amount of data, and automatic recording, all of which simplify the experimenters' chores. The fact that the machine is available has stimulated research, and Schmidt's analysis of how PK can relate to radioactive emissions has stimulated theory.

The other recent change has come with the appearance of a large number of subjects who seem to have strong PK ability, some of whom permit themselves to be tested under laboratory conditions. Many subjects have shown striking effects there, and analysis of their massive changes encourages theory, which in turn leads to further research.

3.5. Summary

Any attempt to bring history up to date is hazardous, but I shall try. The research pattern seems to me to be like a line which bifurcated in 1943, and in which the two branches first grew apart, but are now tending toward each other instead of diverging further. Rhine's dice tests, in which the results depended on statistical evaluation of small, erratic effects, were an important and influential break with the earlier tradition of studying only spectacular phenomena. At first, the two methods of study seemed qualitatively different. Increasingly, however, there are attempts to make quantitative measurements and to introduce

sophisticated controls even with the phenomena that appear spontaneously, such as poltergeists, or the erratic displays of gifted subjects. And,
increasingly, with the cooperation of some of these gifted subjects and
with better understanding of the necessary psychological conditions for
PK, there are attempts to elicit and investigate massive phenomena in the
laboratory. The lines have not met; but research workers are trying to
effect a junction.

4. Controlled Laboratory Research

4.1. Changes of Objects in Motion: 1943–1959

In February, 1934, J. B. and L. E. Rhine began exploratory studies
of whether it was possible to influence by wishing which side of a falling
die would fall uppermost; and in March, 1943, they published their
"First Experiment" reporting affirmative findings. Their initial rather
weak controls and the later more stringent ones have been covered in
chapter 1.

In the first experiment, as in later ones, individuals and sessions
varied, but there was a preponderance of successes over the number
expected by chance. Sometimes a single experiment, and always the
pooled results of many experiments, gave cumulative results significantly
higher than chance expectation. This in itself seemed to provide evidence
for PK.

Even stronger evidence came first from a retrospective analysis of
early work, then from confirmatory studies. This line of evidence was a
variation of the decline effect and was known as the "quarter distribution" or QD (Rhine and Humphrey, 1944). Within a series or
subseries of releases, PK scores were found to be better at the beginning
and worse at the end. In the method that eventually became standard,
each page of the record sheet required 24 releases for the same die face,
and successive pages required that the subject try for a different die face,
until all six faces had been the target. Subjects typically grew bored as
they made the 24 repetitive tries, but felt refreshed and remotivated for
the new page when the target changed. Analysis of the pattern of hits
on the page showed more hits in the first quarter and fewer later, so that
the difference between the first and last quarter was highly significant.
The significance values for the decline effect were repeatedly orders of
magnitude greater than for the differences between total successes and
mean chance expectation.

The quarter distribution of hits on a 24-item page thus seemed especially strong evidence for PK, not only because its results were so striking, but also because it indicated that the psychological factor of lively initial interest, contrasted with later boredom, was a key to PK success. Further, it was impressive that a similar decline effect was often found in ESP results and in many psychological or everyday repetitive tasks (Pratt, 1949). The research seemed to have uncovered a process common to both paranormal and normal functioning. Experimenters began to plan routinely to score any PK data obtained by this method both for critical ratio of successes and for QD.

Among the many experiments performed in the Rhine laboratory at Duke University and elsewhere in this period, several other problems were examined, although none were replicated often enough to make us sure of the generality of the findings. As we look back at them now, the most important is an issue raised by Humphrey (1947): when a subject releases the dice and hopes for a certain number, and the experimenter, eagerly watching, also hopes for that number, and the scores show extrachance success, was the success due to the PK of the subject or of the experimenter? Or both? Humphrey (1947) reported that when two subjects hoped for either the same face or different faces, the scores were significantly higher in the "help" condition than in the "hinder" condition. Although this does not answer the initial question, it shows that the question is worth attention.

A great deal of the research was directed toward comparison of different objects: cubes vs. balls, disks vs. dice, coin spinning, different numbers of dice released at a single throw, etc. Since neither attitude nor ability of the subjects was controlled, no clear conclusions emerged. However, the trend of the data, along with the experimenters' comments about their subjects, seemed to show that what the subjects liked best, they scored best with.

Data from four other laboratories were of special interest. In England, Mitchell and Fisk (1953) did a pilot study in which they found a conscientious and cooperative subject, Dr. Blundun, who seemed especially gifted at PK. In subsequent experiments (Fisk and West, 1958), Dr. Blundun threw dice while hoping they would turn up as specified by a concealed target. She recorded her own throws, but since she did not know the target, her scores were blind. She achieved highly significant successes. The method is straightforward and provides a clear control for biased recording; it seems curious that more experimenters did not adopt it. One exception was Osis (1953), who after the Mitchell and Fisk report used a method that was similar except that targets were given to the subjects in unsealed envelopes.

Another method with blind scoring was used by McConnell (1955) and McConnell, Snowdon, and Powell (1955) at Pittsburgh. Dice were photographed after they fell, and the photographs scored blind. It had been stated in advance that data would be scored for both hits and QD. The results were significant, in the anticipated direction, for QD scores but not for total deviation.

The most striking data were obtained by Forwald, a Swedish engineer, when he used himself as a subject. He published a long series of experiments which, with subsequent work, are summarized in a later monograph (1969). The method he preferred was a placement test in which a release mechanism dropped the objects while he hoped they would fall to one or the other side of a table. His scores were extremely high, especially at the beginning of a series, even with full counterbalancing for the two sides; and he maintained those high scores when the falls were independently recorded by a witness at the Duke laboratory (Pratt and Forwald, 1958). He also showed an idiosyncratic pattern of scores in relation to atomic weight (Forwald, 1969).

With Blundun and Forwald producing such high scores, and with laboratory lore telling of certain subjects who were good at PK but of others who were not, systematic research on individual differences seemed in order. Further support for the importance of individual differences came from Dale at the American Society for Psychical Research, who found in a first experiment (1946), though not in a later one (Dale and Woodruff, 1947), that her subjects were self-consistent. The first experiment yielded a significantly large number of hits, with 54 subjects; and a correlation of the subjects' scores on odd-numbered and even-numbered tries gave a significant split-half reliability.

But only two experimenters showed much concern with this issue. One was Fahler (1959), who correctly predicted for eight of his nine subjects whether their scores would be above or below mean chance expectation when they pushed a release button at the usual close distance. He was also correct for seven of the same subjects when they pushed the release button in a distant room, about 27 yards from where the cubes fell. Since his predictions were made in advance of the tests, the data may reflect his clinical skills, but may, of course, be only another example of the Humphrey help—hinder effect.

The most provocative findings of this period have not yet had adequate follow-up. Van de Castle (1958), in exploratory work with 31 subjects drawn from a college sample, found higher PK scores in those who were more expansive, more spontaneous, better adjusted, and more ready to accept falling rather than to resist the pull of gravitation. Few of his differences were significant; but all have such high face validity that further study seems justified.

Now, let us turn to the surveys of the more than 70 PK experimental reports of this period. Girden (1962a) pointed out that many had procedural flaws. He considered unworthy of examination any results in which the effects of imperfect dice or mechanical imperfection in placement tests had not been completely controlled by counterbalancing. This is a sound criticism, although some of the data where counterbalancing was present but incomplete may be retrieved by appropriate statistical weighting. He also dismissed out of hand any experiments performed by students and any with optional stopping. Many would sympathize with his criteria but would disagree on his blanket dismissals.

These three criteria for serious consideration markedly reduced the number of reports, and a fourth criterion cut the number even more. Girden disallowed experiments in which an unwitnessed experimenter recorded the data. He tended to dismiss even those in which two observers, both of whom knew the target, checked each others' records. (He also, for some reason that is not clear to me, dismissed Blundun's blind recording, calling the absence of witnesses and of another independent record "irreparably basic defects." This seems odd. Ordinarily a blind record is considered properly controlled.) His general requirement of blind scoring is certainly desirable, although it is an unexpected one from a psychologist of his period, where data of perception and learning experiments were seldom recorded blind. However, the question of whether to disregard completely all data without blind recording is not easy to resolve, and Girden in some cases seemed to approve nonblind data, especially where they yielded null results.

Girden accepted some of the work, either because the recording was blind or because the independent witnessing seemed satisfactory. When he examined these reports, he dismissed those in which replication did not give consistently significant results. This also is a more stringent criterion than psychologists apply to psychological research, and many of his colleagues criticized him for it. It is improper for two reasons. One, neatly set forth in a theoretical article on statistics (Tversky and Kahneman, 1971), deals with the meaning of statistical significance. It does not, as Girden seemed to think, let us predict the finding of any particular replication; rather it describes the range within which the data of most replications will fall. The second reason is that a replication will either have different subjects or else less naive subjects; it is also likely to have somewhat different conditions. Because of this, failure to confirm a prior finding needs to be investigated further, to discover if the subject or procedural differences were important.

A third level of Girden's criticism has to do with basic methodology rather than details of method. He presents two arguments. One is that PK data should not be compared with mean chance expectation; instead the data should be compared with a control series in which no one wished for any outcome. Mathematically, this is invalid: comparison with mean chance expectation is considered correct. Psychologically, the argument is naive because the absence of wishing for an outcome is as near to an impossibility as we can get. An experimenter who runs a control series will almost surely wish for scores that conform to mean chance expectation, and if he is able to use PK may find data like those of Scarne (1956), whose long series of dice throws comes out almost exactly at the chance predicted values.

The other argument is that research should follow the pattern of controlled experiments in which conditions are manipulated and compared with each other. This is sound; we learn more by such comparisons than by simple tabulation of extrachance data. However, the argument does not bear on the validity of prior research; it merely proposes a more profitable direction for future studies.

Girden's summary statement of whether PK occurs was "a Scottish verdict: *not proven*" (1962b, p. 531). The parapsychologists who made their own evaluations accepted some of his points but disallowed others. The general purport of their summaries was that extremely strong data supporting the PK hypothesis had been obtained in research in which conditions were reasonably well but not impeccably controlled; that strong evidence for PK had in some cases also been obtained under excellent conditions with blind recording; and that some interesting patterns of individual differences had been found which implied that PK could readily be assimilated into our understanding of psychological functioning. Their verdict thus, on the whole, was that the PK research through 1959 showed that PK occurred, and that it needed further study. What did the next years bring?

4.2. Changes of Objects in Motion: After 1959

It is surprising that Girden's strong criticisms of PK methodology had little or no effect upon the research that followed. This is in part because research workers had already recognized by the time he wrote that optional stopping was a weak technique, and that they needed fully counterbalanced conditions to control for instrument bias. His criticism of nonblind scoring, however, seemed to have no impact; the same practice continued.

Later experiments tend to fall into two categories. One large group examined different physical arrangements or scoring methods. Cox, for example, published a series of reports of significant PK data on subjects using ingenious devices he invented, such as a bubble producer with which the subject is to wish that the bubbles will drift to one side or the other (Cox, 1976). He also developed methods for grouping scores, both by a "majority vote" technique and also by using pretests to predict which subgroup of scores will be higher (1977). Other mechanical novelties were introduced, e.g., by Knowles (1967), who described a device employing a container that held two kinds of objects which the subject would shake while hoping that the objects would be segregated or be mixed. Both Forwald and Cox examined objects made of different substances; Cox found higher scores with cubes made of celluloid than of lead (1971) and Forwald (1969) a relation between scoring and atomic weight. In neither research was there any control for the effect of experimenter or subject expectation.

The other category of study was that of psychological variables. The results are interesting but have not been independently replicated in other laboratories, so that we do not know if they will be found generally true. Greene (1960) described an elegantly simple relationship: subjects who report that they are generally lucky in games of chance tend to score higher at PK than subjects who report themselves unlucky. This observation has such clear face validity and is so easy to examine that it seems remarkable other experimenters do not routinely incorporate a question about it into their procedures. The value of a playful, gamelike mood was suggested by data of Ratte (1960), following work in collaboration with Greene when they tested a PK baseball game, and later by Tart, Boisen, Lopez, and Maddock (1972) in reporting data on spinning a silver dollar. Feather and L. E. Rhine (1969), acting as a subject—experimenter team, were not able to replicate the "help—hinder" effect, but instead found Feather's mood a key factor in the direction of PK scores. Rubin and Honorton (1972) found, as they had anticipated, that subjects' acceptance of the *I Ching* related positively to success in throwing for it. Mischo (1971) made an intensive study of two gifted teenagers, and reported that, compared to population norms, they were more labile and irritable, also they were given to short bursts of displaced aggression, and to showing conflict between efficiency and frustration. The data have only partial overlap with Van de Castle's study of a different population, but tie in well with descriptions of the central figures in the poltergeist cases discussed in Section 8.

One unreplicated experiment is outstanding in its careful internal controls and meaningful findings. Stanford (1969) required subjects to try for PK success by visualizing the desired face of the die on half their trials, and by associating words or ideas to the desired number on the other half. He recorded the data, but since his hypothesis dealt with individual differences between subjects and he had not yet tested for these differences, his scoring should be considered blind. He then gave subjects a test of their tendency to visualize or to make verbal associations. As predicted, there was a significant positive correlation between visualizing score and PK success in the visualizing condition, and also between associative score and PK success in the associating condition. Thus, his experiment found a meaningful relation between cognitive styles and conditions for PK success, and it demonstrated the differential effect of test conditions that has so often been reported in ESP research (Rao, 1965).

One report made an interesting use of PK with moving objects as part of a study of a gifted individual, Bill Delmore, who was then a law student (Kelly and Kanthamani, 1972). He had originally displayed what seemed to be remarkable psi ability in informal, playful groups where he varied spontaneously what he did. Typical were card tricks in which someone else would shuffle cards after he had predicted the order they would come in, or in which he would let drop from a deck one concealed card that corresponded to what someone else had predicted. These might, of course, have been sleight of hand or collusion (though many informal tests indicated they were not); if valid, they might have been due to ESP, to PK, or to a combination of the two. Kelly and Kanthamani's later formal laboratory testing found that under excellent control of conditions he had not only phenomenally high ESP scores but also phenomenally high PK scores, both with machines which determined the outcome by radioactive emissions and also with dice tumblers and a machine which registered how quickly the sand in an hourglass would fall. His high success with a variety of methods implied that PK functioned similarly for macroscopic objects and subatomic particles, and also implied, as does much other work, a commonality between PK and ESP.

4.3. Causing Movement in Static Objects

Perhaps the first formal PK experiment made by an established scientist was performed by Crookes (1874), working with D. D. Home as subject. Home had repeatedly, in good light, and with no props, been reported to levitate, to elongate his body, to handle burning coals without signs of injury, to persuade others to handle the burning coals and show that they also were uninjured, to carry the coals in a borrowed handkerchief without scorching it, and on occasion to do other special feats. To test Home's power over inanimate matter, Crookes arranged a lever so that it would record its position on smoked paper mounted on a revolving drum. He covered the apparatus so that air currents would not affect it and checked that it did not register street or house vibrations. He then had Home stand before it and command it to move. The tracing showed the expected straight line without Home's command, but clear, large deflections with the command.

Many others tried to produce similar effects and failed, so that it stood alone as an example of an affirmative finding from controlled research until Green (1971), a physicist at the Menninger Foundation, secured the cooperation of an Indian adept named Swami Rama. Swami Rama said that his master in India could make an object move both toward him or away, but that he himself would be able to produce only one or the other type of motion. Green asked him to move an object toward him. The swami prepared by fasting, "purifying" himself, and meditation. Green prepared the test object: a knitting needle, mounted on a pivot with a strong spring. On the appointed day, with other scientists assembled to watch, Swami Rama put on a face mask constructed to prevent inhalation of dangerous air particles, so that he could not be accused of causing motion by blowing or inhalation; sat in the lotus position some feet from the knitting needle; and three times "gave the word of command." On two of the three times, the needle rotated toward him through about ten degrees of arc.

With only two such reports attested by trained scientists under laboratory conditions, the reader may be torn between two or even three opinions. One would be to wait and see if there are more such cases before accepting them. A second might be to remember James's dictum that the rule "All crows are black" must be set aside with the discovery of even a single white crow. The third might be to consider that these careful studies fit well with the less formal field reports of Kulagina's and Parise's abilities (described below) and with mediumistic or poltergeist observations and some spontaneous cases. From this third point of view, the corpus of observations has already become substantial. We could, in my opinion, well defend the statement that an exceptionally gifted individual can use PK to make a static object move over a short distance.

4.4. *Physical Changes with Subatomic Particles*

Since some data had suggested that PK is more effective on light targets than on heavy ones, Beloff and Evans (1961) tested PK with beta particles as the target. They found null results; but Wadhams and Farrelly (1968) with a similar method report suggestively positive data. Chauvin and Genthon (1967), in a preliminary report in which the decay of uranium nitrate was to be influenced by PK, described promising data which reached the level of significance for two of their seven subjects; and Chauvin (1968) reported two later series which confirmed the PK effect. Chauvin also reported the control series which Girden had felt was needed for work with dice: when the instrument continued recording during a control period when no subject was present, its output of radioactive decay processes was significantly different from the output when subjects hoped for a change.

A great upswing in research with this method came when Schmidt (1970a) introduced his Random Number Generator (RNG). This was an adaptation of his basic instrument (Schmidt, 1969) in which electrons emitted by strontium-90 decay trigger a switch. As arranged for PK, in this first study, a two-position switch was used. Careful pretesting showed that under control conditions the output of the two positions was random. The subject was instructed to try to make the output register what was equivalent to faster (or slower) electron emission; automatic recording showed the scores. Schmidt made the instrument available to other investigators; and he reported such strong data and raised such interesting theoretical questions that many others have eagerly used it, both to try to answer his questions and to work on problems of their own.

One of his basic, and perhaps unanswerable, theoretical questions had arisen earlier and has been asked (with different examples) by others. Consider his other instrument when it was arranged for precognition. The subject's pressing a button registered a call; the machine's next switch choice was the target; recording was automatic; scores were extrachance. The question here is: were the extrachance scores due to the subject's precognition of the next target, or rather to his PK acting upon the electron flow and thus determining the target? Schmidt now raises the mirror-image question. Were his subjects' significant psi-missing scores on the PK machine due to PK influence on the machine, or rather to the subjects (or the experimenter) starting the series at the moment when precognition told that the subsequent electron output would be appropriate? Interpretation of extrachance RNG data should be that they are due to psi, but they may at the interpreter's option be more specifically interpreted as either PK or ESP.

The easy way to make a distinction between a PK and an ESP experiment would seem to be procedural. If the subjects are told to outguess the machine, it is ESP; if they are told to influence the machine, it is PK. But is there a difference, even here? An especially ingenious experiment by Schmidt and Pantas (1972) indicates there may not be. They used two RNGs with different internal circuitry, one for precognition and one for PK. The subjects' instructions oriented them toward either precognition or PK, and they began their trials with the appropriate machine. In front of the subject were the buttons to be pushed and the lights that gave feedback for success; the machine was in another room. Midway through each subject's trials, the experimenter secretly flipped a switch that connected their buttons and feedback lights to the other type of machine. The subjects made similar significantly high scores both before and after the change.

This was a striking finding. The subjects' task changed without their knowing it, and their scores on the new task stayed at the same level as on the old one. Apparently the ability which let them predict output also let them influence output. It is reminiscent of the findings in research with the alpha waves generated by the brain, in which subjects who could identify when they were producing alpha were also able to change their alpha output at will (Kamiya and Nowlis, 1970).

A more recent experiment (Schmidt, 1976) presents us with a related but more difficult problem. Schmidt prerecorded PK data and presented them to his subjects, interspersed with data that were momentarily generated. The prerecorded data were presented (without the subject's knowing this) four times; the momentarily generated data only once. Scoring was significantly high on both, but significantly higher on the prerecorded data. This suggested to Schmidt that repeated tries were more effective than single tries, and also that the subjects' PK responses worked backward in time to influence the data that had been recorded earlier, i.e., that PK influenced past events. Both Schmidt and others (e.g., Donald and Martin, 1976) considered that this backward causation was consistent with the theory of quantum physics.

Schmidt alternatively suggested that he, as experimenter, might have caused the PK effect when the data were recorded, although, of course, he did not intend to do so. Could he have made such a PK change without a conscious wish? This raises again the question posed by Humphrey's help—hinder research, of the relation between conscious wishes and PK effects. Let us consider what data we have on this issue.

Is volition necessary for PK? The question might seem to be answered in the negative by some poltergeist cases, in which everyone involved has the conscious wish that the phenomena will stop. But here, of course, depth psychologists could argue that to the key person, the poltergeist effects were unconsciously gratifying. Data from the laboratory are ambiguous. Kuyper et al. (1972) arranged their RNG output so that it would make a disagreeable noise unless there was PK success. Subjects who were told they could turn off the noise by PK succeeded significantly; but the noise stayed on for subjects who went through the same procedure without information or else with the false information that it was a telepathy test. Camstra (1973), in a pilot study, used a similar procedure and found that subjects who were told it was a PK task (but who were not asked to concentrate) succeeded, as did subjects who were falsely told it was a telepathy task. However, subjects who were told it was PK and asked to concentrate did not succeed. In a second confirmatory series Camstra's results were null for all groups. Stanford, Zenhausern, Taylor, and Dwyer (1975), in an elaborate experiment with two experimenters and 40 subjects, arranged that the subjects first be unaware that a PK test was going on, and then that their scores on the PK would, if they were high, result in their being given an interesting task, and if they were low, a dull one. The subjects next took a conventional PK test. For one of the experimenters, PK scores were near the chance level for both PK conditions; for the other, both sets of scores were significantly high. Neither conscious wishing nor reward thus seems a sufficient or a necessary condition for high PK scores.

Changes of score within a session or between sessions have been analyzed by many experimenters in following up the QD findings, but the reports seldom give enough detail about length of session, rest periods, tempo, or experimenter's encouragements and challenges to let us judge how the session seemed from the subject's point of view. Some experimenters report a strong decline, some a weak decline, some no decline, and some a U curve. (U curves are generally taken to show declining motivation but with a spurt in scoring at the very end.) Even an incline within a session or between sessions is sometimes found, but usually only for a gifted subject who feels challenged by his first low scores.

The influence of the experimenter, suggested by the old help—hinder research, is a recurrent theme in PK studies. One well-designed series which brings out this point (Braud, Smith, Andrew, and Willis, 1976) began by playing one of two tapes to the subjects. The tape either engaged the subjects in imagery and music, or else engaged them in logical, mathematical, and verbal thinking. PK scores after the music and imaging tape were significantly better than PK scores after the logical one, in two series. But in a third series the experimenter was blind to the hypothesis, and did not know which group it was hoped would give better scores; with a blind experimenter, scores were the same for both conditions.

A similar interpretation seems reasonable for the findings of Stanford et al. (1975) described above, and for data reported by Honorton and Barksdale (1972). In their first series, Honorton gave waking instructions, similar to hypnotic ones except that he did not induce a hypnotic trance, for muscle tension or relaxation, and for active or passive concentration on the PK task. Scores were significantly high for only the condition of passive concentration with muscle tension. In a replication, Barksdale tested other subjects and found scores near chance for all conditions. In a third series, Honorton acted as his own subject and found tension scores were significantly higher than relaxation scores. The data may perhaps be best interpreted as showing a difference between Honorton and Barksdale as regards their effects on PK. A similar but even stronger argument for the importance of experimenter effects is presented by Millar and Broughton (1977) after describing a series of null results (including a failure to replicate Schmidt's experiment with prerecorded data) from their laboratory at Edinburgh University.

Even research with nonhuman subjects may reflect the experimenter's attitude. Schmidt, who disliked cockroaches, arranged his RNG so that it would deliver an electric shock when cockroaches had low PK scores, and the cockroaches showed significant psi-missing (1970b); but with brine shrimp he found psi-hitting (1974). Braud (1976), on the other hand, used fighting fish as his subjects, gave them the reward of being able to see themselves in a mirror when they succeeded at PK, and found that they made a significantly high number of successes. We may wonder if the psi-hitting reflects Schmidt's sympathy with brine shrimp and Brand's sympathy with fighting fish. It is possible that in all these cases it was the experimenter, not the subjects, who influenced the machine.

One report, in which internal differences within the data are consistent with the animals' rather than the experimenter's motivational patterns, shows how careful analysis can help us arrive at a reasonable answer to the question of whose PK produced extrachance scores. Watkins (1972) put lizards into a chamber partially filled with ice and water and arranged an RNG so that PK success would turn on a light which warmed the chamber. He found in both a pilot and a confirmatory series that PK scores were significantly higher on rainy days than on clear days. Analysis also showed significantly higher scores when humidity or pressure was low; that females and dominant males made high scores but submissive male lizards did not; and that success was greater from animals kept in mixed sex cages than in cages of all males or all females. Since it was the lizards rather than the human experimenter who would be expected to be responsive to these determining conditions, the implication is that it was the lizards who used PK.

What of individual differences among human subjects, comparable to those between dominant and submissive male lizards? Mischo and Weis (1973) used the ingenious method of administering a personality test to their subjects and scoring it against two sets of PK runs: one set under normal conditions and one set after the subjects had been frustrated by trying to solve a problem which looked easy but was extremely difficult. PK scores did not correlate with personality scores under normal conditions, either here or in later research by Houtkooper (1977): but after frustration the PK scores correlated positively with calm, or sociability; and they correlated negatively with depression, neuroticism, or inhibition. The results seem meaningful, but have not been replicated; we do not know if they will recur with a different population of subjects.

Four experiments used special subjects expected to produce high scores. One with "healers" (Bierman and Hout, 1977) gave null overall results, with a hint of psi-missing; but perhaps we should not expect healers to mobilize optimal motivation when they are working with an RNG rather than a human who needs help. There were three experiments with meditators. Matas and Pantas (1972) found that 25 subjects who had practiced some form of meditation scored significantly better than chance, but that 25 control subjects scored below chance, but not significantly. The difference between the two groups was significant. Honorton (1977) found promising data with a single practitioner of transcendental meditation, whose scores after (but not before or during) meditation were significantly high for half his trials. A follow-up by Winnett and Honorton (1977) with practitioners of Ajapa yoga showed psi-missing before meditation and null results during and after.

4.5. Chemical, Electromagnetic, and Temperature Changes

An isolated experiment that has radical implications for human affairs was conducted by a chemist, Smith, with Estebany, a "healer," as subject (1972). Estebany, who was not a chemist, presumably did not know the molecular structure of enzymes. Smith prepared enzymes, asked Estebany to influence certain ones, and found faster change in those than in the control samples. The implications for a mechanism of psychic healing are striking, especially if considered in conjunction with the data of Schmidt and Pantas (1972). They imply that neither a healer nor a PK subject needs to know the details of the change he hopes to produce by PK; that his directing his wishes toward the general goal of success may produce the change he wants. However, these are only implications. An attempted replication of Smith's work by Kief (1973) with an unspecified subject gave null results.

An impressive report came from Puthoff and Targ (1974) working with a gifted subject, Ingo Swann. He was asked to influence a magnetometer which had previously been found to be extremely well-shielded and which was showing a periodic curve of the decay of a magnetic field. Swann asked where and what the apparatus was; was told to find out for himself; tried to use ESP to do so; reported success and gave a description of it which the listening physicists accepted as accurate—and at the moment he reported finding the apparatus, the previously regular decay curve flattened out. As Swann's attention turned to the group, the decay curve became regular again. An observer then asked Swann to try to increase the decay rate; and for another short interval, the decay rate became much faster.

Just prior to this, Swann had given results equally impressive in a temperature experiment (Schmeidler, 1973). A shielded thermistor was set at distances varying from a few feet to 25 feet away from him, and he was asked to make it hotter or colder in a predetermined, counterbalanced sequence. Computations from the recordings showed highly significant successes. (In a follow-up experiment, Schmeidler, Mitchell, and Sondow [1975] found a substantial number of other subjects able to produce significant temperature changes with this method, but Schmeidler, Gambale, and Mitchell [1976] found only a few subjects able to do so, and Millar [1976], with a generally similar procedure, reported null results.)

4.6. Changes in Plants

Highly publicized but inadequately controlled experiments have been interpreted to mean that plants responded to the thoughts of an experimenter or of other organisms. This led Brier (1969) to design a PK experiment in which his subjects tried to influence the electrical activity in one of two plants in front of them. Blind scoring of the records showed more changes in the plants the subjects tried to influence than in the others. Thus, Brier's data suggested that changes in plant physiology which occur when a person's attitude changes may be attributed to PK from the person.

Grad (1963, 1964) conducted a series of experiments to investigate PK effects on plant growth. He initially worked with the healer, Estebany, and pilot work showed no effect on healthy plants or seedlings. Grad, therefore, ingeniously injured the seeds by treating them with a mild saline solution; further preliminary work showed that Estebany seemed, as it were, able to heal the injured plants. In subsequent formal tests, Grad (1964) described identical treatment of seeds randomly drawn from the same population, except for one difference: Estebany held the flask of saline solution which was to be poured on some seeds but did not hold the flask for others. Blind measurements showed significantly better growth for plants watered from the flask Estebany had held. In four confirmatory studies with a procedure similar except that the flask was sealed before Estebany held it, similar results were found and were significant in each of three of the series.

An interesting variant (Grad, 1967) used three different subjects: a man thought to have a "green thumb," a depressive neurotic, and a depressive psychotic. The neurotic reacted to the procedure with interest and pleasure and cradled the bottle as a mother would a child. Plants watered from the flask held by the man with the "green thumb" grew much faster than control plants; those from the neurotic, slightly faster; and those from the psychotic, slower.

Somewhat similar results have been reported by others. Perhaps the most impressive come from Pauli (1974), who describes seven series in which groups hoped that plants would grow well. There were significant differences (all in the predicted direction) for five of the series, including experiments in which the subjects were three to ten kilometers from the plants.

A recent report asked two "healers," Olga Worrall and Dean Kraft, to try to influence seedling growth. Worrall's plants grew faster; Kraft's grew slower; and this, taken in conjunction with Grad's data, suggested that PK can affect plant growth but that the subject's attitude is an interacting variable (MacDonald, Hickman, and Dakin, 1977).

Four experiments with fungi have all reported significant PK effects. In Canada Grad found that PK could cause fermentation increase in yeast (1965). Nash and Nash in the United States found fermentation decrease in yeast after the sealed bottles containing the yeast had been held by psychotics (1967). Barry in France found that subjects told to try to inhibit the growth of a fungus by PK were able to do so (1968). Haraldsson (1973) in Iceland found significant increase in yeast growth from the pooled PK data of seven subjects, but further analysis showed that the positive effects came from the three subjects classed as healers (two "mental healers" and a physician), whereas the other four subjects had only chance scores. This series of consistently affirmative results from four different laboratories may be unparalleled in parapsychology, and the pattern of personality differences indicates that it is meaningful.

4.7. Changes in the Behavior of Infrahuman Animals

When the RNG is the target for PK changes, and the experimenter hopes that animals will influence the RNG output, there is some question as to whether the animal subjects or the experimenter are the source of significant changes. This may be the case with the four RNG experiments with animals cited in Section 4.5.

When a human experimenter tries to change animal behavior, a different question arises. This was discussed in the introductory section, but will be reintroduced here, taking as an example a series of experiments by the great physiologist, Bekhterev (see Vasiliev, 1963). Bekhterev used trained circus dogs and later his own dog as subjects and tried to give them mental commands to perform various acts. His later trials were so carefully controlled that he considered no sensory cues were present; the animals repeatedly did what his mental orders had commanded. If we assume that this experienced research worker did indeed control sensory cues and sequence effects, do we interpret his data to mean that by PK he influenced the animals' behavior? Or do we rather interpret the results to mean that the dogs received his telepathic messages and "voluntarily" did what he commanded? It seems to me that we have a free choice here. And because I prefer the latter explanation, many later experiments that follow the same pattern will be omitted. In general, when the experimenter could expect the animal to obey a verbal or gestural command, and especially if the animal was a pet, I will tentatively consider the results to show ESP rather than PK.

Five experiments remain: two with protozoa, two with insects, and one with mammals. The earliest was by Richmond (1952), who tried to influence the swimming direction of paramecia into a quadrant randomly selected. He scored a success if the paramecium, at the end of 15 seconds, was in either the selected quadrant or the diametrically opposite one. As a control, he observed paramecia for 15 seconds without willing them to swim in any direction and scored successes according to a concealed list. He reported results that were significantly positive for the willing series and significantly below chance expectation for the control series. Randall (1970), using a basically similar procedure but a different protozoan, *Styloinchia mytilus,* did not obtain significant results either with Richmond's scoring method or a different one.

Two experiments with insects gave provocative or extrachance results. Randall (1971) reported that of the 12 schoolboys who completed his specified number of attempts to influence the direction in which woodlice would crawl, three obtained significant results, two psi-hitting and one psi-missing. Metta (1972) had two subjects who tried systematically to influence the crawling direction of caterpillars; one obtained significant psi-missing results (i.e., below mean chance expectation).

An experiment with the same basic method is reported by Randall (1972), using gerbils. Schoolboys tried to make the gerbils move into a randomly selected target area; the findings were similar to those with woodlice in that some of the schoolboys scored significantly.

4.8. Changes in the Body Processes of Infrahuman Animals

All the experiments in this section report attempts to find if psychic healing is effective with infrahuman animals. The first and most important were done by Grad, using mice as the experimental animals and initially using Estebany as the healer. (See Grad, 1976, for a summary report.)

In his first experiments, Grad induced goiters in mice, divided them into equivalent groups, and had Estebany put his hands on the outside of a cage that held the experimental group. This "laying on of hands" lasted for 15 minutes, and was done 10 or 11 times a week. Control mice were put into a similar holding cage but the cage was not held. For another group the holding cage of the control animals was warmed by electro-thermal tapes so that the heat was equivalent to the heat from Estebany's hands. At the end of 20 days of Estebany's treatment, an assistant (also believed to be a healer) continued in Estebany's role for another 20 days. In still another pair of series, the control mice were provided a bed of wool and cotton cuttings not touched by Estebany. The experimental mice were provided with similar cuttings which Estebany had held three times, for 15 minutes a time. Grad reports that goiters developed significantly faster in the control mice than in the experimental ones, for each of the important comparisons.

In later series, Grad chose a different method to induce a need for healing in animals. Rather than instigating goiters, he anesthetized mice and inflicted surgical wounds, then examined the speed of healing. As before, mice with equivalent initial treatment were put into experimental and control groups. The animals that Estebany tried to heal recovered more quickly than the control animals; the difference seemed especially marked on the fifteenth day after wounding. By the twentieth day, recovery was all but complete for all animals.

This led to a collaborative experiment with excellent controls (Grad, Cadoret, and Paul, 1961). Mice were wounded as before, then divided into three groups, and carefully matched for size of wounds. The housing of the mice was also carefully matched for temperature, humidity, and so on. Normal handling was blind; measurement seems also to have been blind. Animals from one of the groups were put into a holding cage which was held by Estebany. Those from a second group were put into a holding cage which was held for a similar length of time by a succession of skeptical medical students. Those from a third group were put into a holding cage for an equivalent length of time, but the cage was not held. Size of wound was measured for 20 days after surgery.

One further control was instituted. Because of the possibility that some unknown chemical from Estebany's breath or hands had produced his prior successes in healing, half of each group had their cages enclosed in heavy paper bags which were stapled shut, and then held only from the outside. For the other half, the cages were enclosed in paper bags which were left open; and treatment consisted in placing one hand below and the other above the cage.

Perhaps because of the heat inside the stapled bag, animals in the closed-bag condition were excited, and no significant differences between groups were found. For the animals in the open bags, results on the fifteenth and sixteenth days were significantly different for the three groups. Mice in the cages held by Estebany showed more healing than in the other groups; those in cages held by the skeptical medical students showed less. Thus, in a subgroup of the data, there seems strong evidence for the beneficial effect of a psychic healer and for harmful effects from those with an antagonistic attitude.

No other research is so impressive. Elguin, for example, (reported by Onetto and Elguin, 1966) studied attempts to help and to hurt tumorigenic mice, which had been inoculated with a tumoral suspension. The mice were divided randomly into three groups: one a control, one in which PK was directed toward increasing tumor growth, and one in which PK was directed toward retarding tumor growth. The report states that there was no difference between the control group and the mice in which attempts were made to increase tumor size, but there was significantly less tumor growth in the group in which an attempt was made to retard tumor growth than in the control group. Since the summary statement suggests that the research be continued under double-blind conditions, we may assume that it was not double blind here, and thus should consider it interesting but inconclusive.

Similarly inconclusive work was initiated by Watkins and Watkins (1971). They anesthetized two pairs of mice, then asked a subject to try to make one recover quickly from the anesthesia. Significantly faster recovery was reported both here and in a follow-up experiment (Wells and Klein, 1972), but timing of recovery was not blind, and other contaminating factors, e.g., the method of deciding which was to be the experimental mouse, may also have been present.

Wells and Watkins (1975) report another project issuing from this work. The abstract, in which the procedure was not described in detail, states that after a "healer" sent healing messages to an anesthetized mouse placed in one location, the healer left the building. Two more mice were then anesthetized, one placed on the healing location, the other elsewhere. The mice put on the spot to which the healer had previously directed healing thoughts recovered from the anesthesia faster than the control mice. Wells and Watkins suggest that this "linger effect" is similar to other linger effects observed in PK work with gifted subjects and also reported in poltergeist studies.

Do these experiments show that psychic healing occurs with animals as subjects? Certainly they suggest it. But when we examine them critically, we find only one series in which it appears that neither methodological flaws nor physical effects could have influenced the results: the closed bag subseries of Grad, Cadoret, and Paul. Here, perhaps because of the side effects of excessive heat, there were null data. In the other subseries of this excellent research, significantly better results from the healer could be attributed to chemical changes from the healer's body processes—except that in other work where the same healer tried to influence plants, his beneficial effects were as strong when he handled sealed flasks as when he handled unsealed ones. If we consider that the finding with plants shows that lack of sealing was unimportant, we can claim that psychic healing with animals has been demonstrated; but the chain of reasoning is elaborate rather than straightforward. Probably our evaluation should be that the data are suggestive and interesting and are moderately but not conclusively strong.

4.9. Healing of Humans

Joyce and Welldon (1965) performed a properly double-blind experiment on psychic healing with human subjects and found a slight but not a significant difference between the subjects to whom healing messages were sent and the other subjects.

The only other experimental research which I know of on this topic is perhaps inappropriate here, because the response measure was taken from verbal reports and might therefore be classed as ESP rather than PK. This was an experiment performed by Goodrich (1976) in an examination of synchronous versus nonsynchronous healing attempts. Subjects reported their feelings after periods when they thought a distant healer had been sending them healing messages; the healers also reported their feelings when they sent the healing messages. Neither healers nor subjects knew that on half these occasions, the healer's messages were sent at a time when the subject did not expect them. Three blind judges scored all the data; the results of two out of the three judges showed significantly more positive reactions for the synchronous than for the nonsynchronous periods. We must regret that there were no physiological measures to show if the subjective feelings of betterment coincided with a change in body processes.

5. Documented Surveys

Four investigators have collected large bodies of spontaneous data that bear on the possibility of a PK effect. One ingenious study by Cox (1957) was based on the assumption that parents who had had four children of the same sex would hope that their fifth child would be of the opposite sex. Cox tabulated data from many sources of genealogical material, discarded all records in which birth dates were not given or in which the name of the child left sex doubtful, and found 661 cases where four children of the same sex were followed by a fifth child. In families with four boys, the fifth child was a boy for 207 and was a girl for 201. In families with four girls, the fifth child was a girl for only 109, but was a boy for 144. Cox suggested that because of the higher prestige of boys, the balance between boys and girls in families with four earlier sons was understandable, but that the marked surplus of boys in families with four earlier girls was due to parental yearnings. The data are of interest, although a chi square is not significant; but they are weakened because the report does not give evidence of independent or blind tabulation of the records.

West (1957) examined eleven cases of healing at Lourdes which ecclesiastical authorities considered miraculous. West's meticulously careful analysis casts doubt on the diagnoses or the progress of the cures so that his conclusion is that none of these cases clearly demonstrates psychic healing.

Recently, Stevenson (1966, 1974, 1975) has been examining cases suggestive of reincarnation. Although the evidence in most such cases is only verbal, he has in the course of his extensive investigations in many societies been recording what may be a PK effect: birthmarks or other bodily evidence which might relate to the claims (e.g., Stevenson, 1974, 1975). One of his most interesting findings has been cultural diversity. In some societies, for example, all or almost all the children he studied claim to have been the same sex in their previous lives, while in other societies many claim a change of sex. For birthmarks and deformities there is similar variability: some but not all societies use them as an important indicator of whether the dead person was reborn in the new child, and it is in these societies that more of his birthmarks were found.

Stevenson's initial survey (1966, but see, revised edition, 1974) describes some cases in which children had birthmarks in the same body location as wounds or lesions on the body of the previous personality. Later investigations adduce more such cases. One case, for example, states that an old man told a young woman he would be reborn as her child; and the child born to her after his death had body marks resembling his. A reincarnation hypothesis would take this as body change produced by the incoming spirit. A super-psi hypothesis would take it (if such events seemed beyond coincidence) as evidence of PK working on the embryo to produce the anticipated evidence of rebirth. A skeptic would ask for independent confirmation with double-blind recording.

Roll and Gearhart (1974) report a relation between poltergeist cases and geomagnetic disturbances. The geomagnetic readings were recorded by local stations and published in standard handbooks; they were classified as quiet, average, or unusually disturbed. The onset of 30 poltergeist cases was identified. It was found that though the day of onset showed insignificantly more disturbance than the yearly average, the day after inception had significantly more geomagnetic disturbance than the day preceding poltergeist activity. The interpretation is not clear; but, if the relationship is confirmed, it may have important implications for theory.

Since none of these findings has been replicated independently, they must be considered tentative. The various affirmative claims are so provocative that we can hope replications will be performed to tell us whether or not to view them with confidence.

6. Attempts to Control Séance Room Phenomena

6.1. Special Subjects

In the nineteenth century, many individuals claimed to be "mediums" through which the spirit world could make itself manifest to the world of the flesh (Podmore, 1902). The Fox sisters and D. D. Home astounded Americans and then Europeans by making tables, trumpets, harmonicas, and a variety of other objects move without any apparent cause; by having forms purporting to be spirits of the dead appear and sometimes show themselves as solid, fully materialized persons; by making objects appear from nowhere; and by other wonders. Many other such mediums followed them. Many were found to be tricksters, and controversy has continued ever since about whether all the effects were fraudulent.

Several of the keenest observers and most distinguished scientists of this early period, extending into the twentieth century, investigated the effects. Some became convinced that certain of the effects were genuine. Their reports still make impressive reading. Sir Francis Galton, for example, writing to his cousin, Charles Darwin, comments that "Home *encourages* going under the table and peering everywhere. (I did so and held his feet while the table moved.)" (Quoted in Medhurst and Goldney, 1964, p. 42.) In a similar report from an equally keen and trustworthy observer, with Eusapia Palladino as the medium, Richet (1923) tells of being at sittings held in good light in which a table floated while one of the investigators looked underneath and saw that no one was touching it, as other investigators watched from above.

Many, though not all, of the mediums required that they be in a cabinet which was fully enclosed, or have such a cabinet behind them, to concentrate the spirit power. Many, though not all, insisted on darkness or semidarkness. Many insisted on having associates with them. Obviously, these three conditions give generous opportunities for collusion and fakery. Controls in the early days before infrared photography usually included having one investigator hold the medium's left hand and foot, while another held the right hand and foot. But the medium's writhings sometimes resulted in both investigators holding the same foot by hand, or even each others', or holding an empty shoe from which the medium's foot had been removed.

The most extraordinary of the varied effects in semidarkness was the extrusion from the medium's body of a pale substance called "ectoplasm." It sometimes emanated as a cloud, or rope, or amorphous shape, then often formed into shapes like hands, rods, faces, or whole bodies. Mediums typically claimed that a sitter's touching it would result in dreadful injury to the medium. Some sitters nevertheless touched it and occasionally even retained a piece of it, which on later analysis turned out to be cheesecloth or some other mundane substance, and in one famous case gave evidence, on chemical analysis, of having been concealed in the vagina. On other occasions it was described as hard and viscous. Sometimes the medium permitted touching it, and reports then included descriptions of how it felt like a hand that terminated at the wrist, or how it felt solid when first grasped but then vanished, as no cloth or other substance could do. The ectoplasm sometimes was seen to hold or push objects and move them around, and sometimes it was found that the movements were produced by rods that a fraudulent medium was holding. Other claims are of movements that came from behind the medium, in a cabinet which was closed and held no accomplice, or otherwise occurred where no medium could have reached.

Magicians often succeeded in duplicating these effects, but sitters frequently claimed that the magicians' tricks were readily discovered or could not be performed under the conditions required of the medium. This leaves open two possibilities. One is that clever mediums used tricks which investigators, confused by razzle-dazzle and blinded by the will to believe, were unable to see—even though the same investigators, made skeptical by the presence of a known trickster, could find from where the trickery came. The other possibility is that the investigators were initially skeptical and retained their skepticism; that they were sophisticated and keenly observant; that the mediums were less trained, less intelligent, and, in general, no match for them intellectually; and that when these able investigators reported that phenomena were genuine, the phenomena were genuine.

It seems impossible to decide in retrospect between these alternatives. I will summarize here only one of the many reports and will choose the most recent of the more impressive cases of long-term physical phenomena from a medium in the séance room. These are the studies made of Rudi Schneider.

Rudi was the younger brother of a well-known physical medium, Willi Schneider, who had been carefully studied by the Baron von Schrenck-Notzing with controls that included a physical examination before the sitting, being sewn into a tight coverall with luminous bracelets and pins on it so that movement could be seen in the dark, and having three observers hold his hands and feet during the sitting. As Rudi began to show his abilities, Schrenck-Notzing studied him with the same controls. Rudi went from Austria to England where he was studied by Harry Price with still further controls: special gloves and shoes for all participants, wired so that if the hands and feet were out of contact with the neighbors, a signal light would flash. He was further extensively studied by Osty in France (1933) and less extensively by others (see Besterman, Goldney, Gregory, and Hope, 1958, for a retrospective summary).

It was the findings of Osty's (1933) research with novel instrumentation that was of most interest. Previously, the events that Rudi, and to a lesser extent Willi Schneider, had produced followed the general pattern reported in other sittings with powerful mediums: unexplained raps, movement of static objects, including complete levitations, and even some apparent materializations, e.g., of a fog that emanated from him and moved across the room, so dense that it fully obscured what was behind it, or of a handlike shape which manipulated objects.

Osty's investigations used many of the earlier controls but added a new one: two beams of infrared light arranged to detect fraudulent manipulation. If any solid object, such as a surreptitiously freed arm or leg, crossed either of the beams, this interruption would be recorded and would change the resistance of a photoelectric cell on which the infrared light was focused. It would then both activate an alarm bell and trigger a camera which would take a picture of what had interrupted the beam and would show the location of each person in the room.

The beam was interrupted, sometimes completely and sometimes partially. The partial interruptions are especially curious: they imply that a substance more tenuous than a part of the body was present, and they varied rhythmically, which implies that the density of the substance was changing. This is not inconsistent with the hypothesis of ectoplasm. The complete interruptions were extremely interesting, too, because the camera flashes which they triggered showed nothing which could have intervened to break the beam. This implied that the beam had been changed by PK. Schneider often was able to predict when the beam would be obscured.

Further observations of Osty seem worth attention, although no theory has accounted for them. Rudi Schneider's breathing was recorded and found to approximate the normal rate, about 15 breaths per minute, while he was not in trance, but to reach extraordinary rates up to 300 breaths per minute in trance. Recordings of the infrared beam showed that it fluctuated at about twice the rate of the breathing, which would correspond to one fluctuation for each inhalation and one for each exhalation.

Like all other mediums who have been tested repeatedly, Schneider's sessions were sometimes impressive, sometimes weak, and sometimes without effects. As the years passed, his effects diminished. Critics suggested that this was because testing conditions were becoming more rigorous. Few accusations of fraud were leveled at him, and these were countered, for example, by examining a photograph which claimed to show his arm moving an object, and finding indications that the photograph was a double exposure (consistent with the thesis that his arm moved at one time but the object moved at another). It was suggested that his sitters, especially his relatives, or his investigators were fraudulent, although he was not, but so far as I know this was left as a vague, unspecified accusation.

The reports as they stand are extraordinary. They have been criticized (Price, 1939) and, as in any other case of unreplicated observations, it is impossible to judge with certainty whether it is the accusations or the observations that were false.

6.2. Informal Groups of Sitters

Two contemporary series of séance-type effects have been coming from England and Canada. Neither centers around a single gifted subject, and it is therefore possible for others elsewhere to try to replicate what they describe, and investigate the effects further.

Batcheldor (1966), a psychologist, and then Brookes-Smith (1973, 1975), an engineer who worked both with Batcheldor and independently, described lively activity of a table which occasionally levitated five or six feet off the floor, moved without contact, and behaved in unexpected ways. On one remarkable occasion it traveled fast and far, finally crashing onto a container of developer and fixer fluid which spilled over the floor and over one member of the group (Brookes-Smith and Hunt, 1970).

The general thesis of Batcheldor and Brookes-Smith is that a lively, light-hearted atmosphere is conducive to these effects and that fear or "deadly doubt" destroys them. To maintain the casual atmosphere, a typical procedure is to have members of the group draw cards, one of which is a joker. The person who draws the joker surreptitiously puts his hands under the table around which the group is sitting and makes it obey the group's commands to move. Since the others know that someone is to do this, no one has an eerie feeling when movement occurs. The group exhorts the table to move with singing, stamping, and other encouragement. When the table responds, the lively mood is maintained. Later, the joker stops his deliberate manipulation, but the group does not know this; the mood, therefore, is unchanged with the occurrence of genuine phenomena.

Tape under the table top records the periods when the holder or the joker puts pressure on the lower surface; another instrument records table height from the floor. The interesting occasions are when the tape records show no normal pressure, but the other record shows levitation.

The technique is clever and theoretically clean. In practice, however, the tape below the table has been applied so that it covers only a narrow strip of the undersurface. Thus, a joker who tried to carry the joke even further than the investigator wished could exert pressure at places where the tape was not present. This is as it should be, according to the Batcheldor and Brookes-Smith thesis. A trickproof method might awe the participants and therefore destroy the mood which these experimenters consider essential for authentic paranormal effects. For us to interpret the data as paranormal, however, demands that we have faith in the honesty of all participants.

Batcheldor and Brookes-Smith give many other recommendations for inducing table activity, such as beginning the sittings in darkness so that it is easy for the sitters to assume that any effects are trickery. Then, gradually, as familiarity makes the whole affair less threatening, the investigator introduces dim light and increasingly brighter light. They also give many recommendations for developing the appropriate free, light-hearted, and even boisterous mood.

Their results are so interesting that we can hope the line of research will be continued; and some of us hope that it will be continued with even more stringent final controls. Mitchell and Perskari (1977) describe the construction of a somewhat different table which registers pressure anywhere beneath its top surface and thus permits the trickproof recordings which Brookes-Smith warns against.

Reports from Batcheldor and Brookes-Smith stimulated another group to begin similar sittings. The group first sat around a table and told it to move or give them messages, but this seemed absurd to them. They decided that it would be more comfortable to address themselves to a person instead of an object, then hit on the clever device of inventing an imaginary person, a suitable recipient (Owen and Sparrow, 1976). They jointly constructed a glamorous account of an imaginary ghost, Philip, a seventeenth-century English nobleman for whom they invented a sad and romantic history. They reported that Philip, their imaginary ghost, communicated with them through raps and other sounds which cannot be duplicated normally, that he showed ESP ability by giving them veridical information which they could not have known, that he moved the table, and that he produced other PK effects such as bending metal. They interpreted all these as manifestations of a thought form jointly produced by members of the group, and considered the Philip fantasy to serve the function that Brookes-Smith attributed to his joker's activity: it created a playful, free atmosphere in which inhibitions were lowered and in which psychic events could occur. They also reported spin-off groups that invented other imaginary figures and claimed similar results.

The PK claims of the group seem to fall into three major categories. One is table movements. These (so far as I can judge from the reports) occur only when group members are in contact with the table and may therefore be only a result of normal but unconscious muscle pressure. The second is odd noises, which will be described in more detail in Section 6.3. The third is metal bending, to be described in Section 7.1.

6.3. Acoustic Effects

Early séance accounts claimed paranormal production of raps, voices, and other sounds, such as those from musical instruments, often coming from locations where no one could normally have produced them. Since human auditory localization is notoriously imperfect and no instruments were used as direction finders, we are left with the possibility that the observers were mistaken about the source of the sounds. A common normal interpretation of raps is that they are made by the cracking of finger or toe joints, or by other surreptitious movements, or by accomplices. Musical sounds can be ascribed to sleight of hand or to accomplices. Although some mediumistic sittings with "direct voice" phenomena describe a voice which is uniquely that of the person whose spirit claims to be communicating, a skeptic who has heard clever mimics can question the identification. By now, the earlier claims are so fogged by counterexplanations that either accepting or rejecting them is an act of faith.

Currently, however, strong claims are being made that acoustic recording and analysis show that raps and other sounds are paranormal in origin. Bayless (1976) describes tape recordings of raps and vocal sounds under conditions which seem to preclude a normal origin because of his close observations. Whitton (1976) continues a series of acoustic analyses of normally produced raps and compares them with analyses of raps produced by Philip and other imaginary ghosts. He claims that the acoustic envelopes are so markedly different as to confirm that some are paranormal (or "paramorphic").

Somewhat earlier claims, also strongly made, seem by now to be discredited. Raudive (1971) tuned a radio between stations, turned on a tape recorder, then heard and recorded sounds which he interpreted as voices of the dead. They gave messages in various languages which he could recognize but sometimes so rapidly that the recording had to be replayed and slowed down before recognition. The messages, which were typically very brief, consisted of a name, or a word, or a few phrases and sometimes seemed to shift in midmessage from one language to another. A typical confirmation procedure consisted of replaying the messages, each at the speed that seemed most appropriate, and suggesting to auditors before they heard the recording what the message said.

Some of the parapsychologists he quoted in confirmation have since reported that they were convinced of his sincerity but not convinced that the sounds were authentic messages. Critics quickly suggested that accidents of radio-wave transmission could account normally for scraps of words received between nearby stations, and that static could account for some wordlike sounds. Other criticisms, such as the effect of prior suggestion on recognition, were also made. The coup de grace seems to have been given by Ellis (1975), who began a formal investigation with the expectation that well-controlled research would support Raudive's conclusions, but ended it by attributing all the effects to a combination of sounds (including speech) from those who were present when the recordings were made, or normal radio transmission erratically received, or even static, all interpreted by guesswork and suggestion. Ellis considered that the data appear to be of interest only by selection of favorable cases or by weak control of normal conditions.

7. Studies of Special Individuals Not in a Séance

7.1. Changes in Physical Objects

Among those for whom PK has been claimed in the preceding century or in this one, D. D. Home is outstanding for the strength and the range of the effects. Some of these claims have already been reported, but there are many others equally remarkable, such as making a recording thermometer change six degrees or, for example, holding a glass of brandy over his head, having an observer then report that the glass became inexplicably empty, but that when the observer held his hand over the glass, brandy fell over the observer's fingers and trickled into the glass again (Myers, 1903). We may wonder in this last example if earlier intake of brandy might have influenced the observer, but other observations equally extraordinary were often repeated and seem well-attested.

No feats comparable to Home's were observed outside the séance room for many years, but recently a series of individuals have come forward who appear also to produce physical changes of a massive, easily observable kind. Three will be described in some detail. The best publicized and most controversial is Uri Geller, whose most frequently repeated acts are the bending of metal objects, such as spoons and keys, and making stopped watches start—if no parts are missing. Geller is a professional stage magician and seldom lets himself be tested under adequately controlled conditions. Other magicians claim to be able to produce his effects by using stage tricks and to have observed him cheating. Parapsychologists, however, are likely to remember Eusapia Palladino, who frankly admitted that she cheated when she thought she could do it unobserved, but who nevertheless seemed able to produce paranormal effects when she knew the observation conditions were rigorous. They therefore still examine with interest those reports of Geller's activity or of activity of the same type which seem to have been conducted under proper conditions.

One such report was published by Cox (1974), who is both a parapsychologist and a magician. Cox stated, for example, that he laid a key on a table and saw that it was straight, then held it lightly with his forefinger while Geller gently stroked the narrower part. "The key began to bend slowly at a point just beyond my finger, stopping at above 6°. Any pressure he [Geller] might have applied would have been against the direction of bend (p. 409)." To check on watch repair, Cox had a jeweler insert aluminum foil into the balance wheel bridge and beneath the regulator arm of a watch that had two lids on the back. Geller held the closed watch and shook it slightly, then returned it to Cox. Cox found the watch was ticking and on opening it found that the regulator arm had moved to an extreme position beyond the slow setting, that the foil had been broken, and that wax on the underside of the foil was sticking to the mainspring plate, implying that it had been heated. Cox considered these changes paranormal. Many similar claims of even stronger changes under what seem proper observational conditions have also been published.

A related claim is that those who watch Geller on television often observe PK changes in objects near them, or think they have acquired the ability to make such changes themselves. Bender, Vandrey, and Wendlandt (1976) report a follow-up of a thousand such claims, where many were found to be trickery but some were not. Especially noteworthy is one boy's ability to deform spoons which the investigators put into sealed containers, something which Geller seems unwilling to attempt. Bender (1977), Hasted (1976), and others have reported similar changes under what seem to be extremely well-controlled conditions. I. M. Owen (1975) reports similar metal bending both by a former poltergeist agent, Matthew Manning, and also by the Philip group.

Since 1968, special interest has attached to a middle-aged Soviet woman, Nina Kulagina, who seems able to make small objects move by PK. Movies show her near but not touching objects on a table before her, and then show the objects moving as she sits tensely and makes small hand movements. Both Soviet and Western scientists have tested her under more or less formal conditions and have confirmed the effect. A full summary (Keil, Ullman, Herbert, and Pratt, 1976) of these reports indicates that there is good reason to accept them as authentic PK. Typical of the most striking changes is a series of observations on objects that would not be influenced by concealed magnets, such as a cigarette. The investigator brings in the objects, puts them on a table sometimes covered with a cloth, and sometimes covers the assembly, for example, with a small transparent dome. Observers tell of—and film records show—movement of one or several adjacent objects, typically in jerks, over a few centimeters. The movements are sometimes bizarre: an upright cigarette, for example, stayed upright as it moved. Although a loose screen between Kulagina and the object seems to have little effect, a well-sealed container apparently stops most or all of the movement. Physiological records of Kulagina's body changes during these exhibitions showed intense exertion, although overt movements were small.

Support for the possibility of such PK comes from accounts of others who heard of Kulagina, practiced her feats, and seem to have succeeded in doing something similar. The best authenticated report is that of Felicia Parise (Honorton, 1974), a research technician who practiced at home and was able to demonstrate movements of a bottle under which Honorton considered adequately controlled conditions in her own kitchen. She also produced compass deflections in the laboratory but could not repeat her effect on the bottle.

The contemporary subject most intensively studied with careful controls is Ted Serios, a hotel elevator operator, who is frequently able, especially when drunk, to make camera film changes which seem paranormal (Eisenbud, 1967). These changes have been recorded by polaroid and television as well as conventional cameras. Excellent controls ensure that the film and the development conditions are not suspect. Often the film comes out all white or all black, although this seems unexplainable under the conditions when it was exposed. Most striking are the times when a picture appears on the film which corresponds to something Serios had seen or was thinking about. Serios usually insists on having a rolled piece of paper, a "gismo," pointed at the camera. Investigators naturally suspect that this contains a miniaturized picture but have repeatedly examined the gismo before and after use and have seen that no such picture was there. The gismo is reminiscent of the cabinet which some séance-room mediums used and claimed was necessary to concentrate the power for their feats. The most remarkable of the published pictures are a series from a TV camera which first show Serios's face (at which the camera had been aimed), then a cloudlike formation over his face which in successive pictures grows larger and develops progressively clearer detail until finally a different picture, clear in some parts and vague in others, emerges. Strong support for Eisenbud's care as an investigator comes from similar effects that Serios produced in another laboratory (Stevenson and Pratt, 1968). It is of interest that Kulagina also has been reported able to make changes in unexposed photographic film.

7.2. Body Changes

Many individuals report that they have been able to produce psychic healing of physical disorders; sometimes the same individuals but more often different ones claim to be able to produce body injury or death through psychic means. Reports of the latter come chiefly from anthropologists, or scattered and ambiguous medical records, and will not be discussed in detail, although a psychoanalytic description of those who seem to produce psychic injury is provocative in suggesting the psychodynamics of unconscious hurting.

Among the healers, some will work only with patients who continue under medical supervision; others prefer to do so but do not insist on it; still others consider it unnecessary. Published reports of their success are impressive on reading but are usually impossible to evaluate for two reasons. One is that it is not clear how the published cases were selected out of all the cases available, and the other is that we seldom know if a medical analysis substantiated the statements of initial problem and cure (e.g., see Kruger, 1974). Work with two healers will be reported in some detail, followed by a brief statement about another, and an extremely brief survey of psychic surgery. It should also be mentioned here that Kulagina has claimed that after goldfish were dead she could make them swim again, although their swimming was clumsy. Laboratory records also show that she stopped the beating of a dissected frog heart which would otherwise have been expected to continue beating for about four hours (Keil et al., 1976).

Perhaps the best known faith healer in England is Harry Edwards. He is considered highly ethical and has such strong faith in his own powers that he gave full cooperation to a physician, L. Rose (1971), who conducted a careful, critical investigation of his work. Rose discounts cases—and there were many—in which the patient gave contradictory reports, in which medical records were lacking or inadequate, and in which the diagnosis was for a psychogenic disorder that is ordinarily curable without medical intervention. Relatively few cases remain. Some seem startling to me, such as the one in which a biopsy showed a malignant tumor in a patient who went to Edwards for healing. Medical follow-up records of the patient over a long period showed no sign of cancer thereafter. Rose, however, considers that each of these cases should also be discounted either as a fortunate accident (maybe the biopsy removed the entire cancer) or as showing only the spontaneous recovery which sometimes is reported by physicians when there has been no intervention by a psychic healer.

Olga Worrall is probably the best known of contemporary American psychic healers. She used to work in conjunction with her husband, Ambrose, but since his death has continued alone. Testimonials of her ability abound (Worrall and Worrall, 1965), and there are many remarkable case reports which seem to show healing not attributable to suggestion, such as of emphysema, or of bone deformity in an infant. The kind of critical analysis of cases which Rose undertook, with a survey of a representative sample of cases, has not been made. It is of particular interest, however, that other forms of PK are also reported for her, such as the increased growth of plant seedlings that was cited above, and in one extraordinary incident a physical change in the instruments of a distant laboratory (MacDonald et al., 1977). A recent biography (Cerutti, 1975) of Mrs. Worrall gives examples of ESP ability as well.

A clinical psychologist (LeShan, 1974) has recently described success in psychic healing but has so far reported only preliminary statements without full documentation. His work is of special interest because it is conducted systematically to develop further a theory that ESP and PK relate to an altered state of consciousness in which time, space, and energy relationships show patterns more like those described by modern physics than like those we ordinarily conceptualize in our everyday, stable, three-dimensional world.

A special subtopic within psychic healing is psychic surgery, in which claims are made of incisions which heal instantly, after being made by surgeons who have had no medical training and who use dull or dirty instruments, but which nevertheless permit removal of diseased tissue and result in instant cures with little or no bleeding. Physicians who have investigated these claims and analyzed the tissues supposedly removed from the patients tell us that laboratory analysis often shows that the tissues were not human tissue but instead were inorganic stones, chicken parts and blood, etc. The implication is that the supposed psychic surgery is frequently a combination of the psychic surgeon's ability at sleight of hand and effective suggestion (Krippner and Villoldo, 1976). Investigators also report that movie cameras can seldom take pictures at an angle which permits accurate observation. Movies and several accounts of a Brazilian psychic surgeon, Arigo, look impressive, but commercial films have shown us how effectively illusions can be produced with a movie camera, and it would be reckless to draw firm conclusions from the records that exist. We can only regret the lack of careful, controlled study while Arigo was alive. Investigations are continuing, and this indicates that some research workers think there is a possibility that some psychic surgery is not fraudulent.

8. Poltergeists

Massive and inexplicable physical effects sometimes occur so often in a household or small area that they become the talk of the neighborhood and then attract the attention of notables who come from far away to investigate them. Stones fall from nowhere, objects fly, furniture moves, bedding is disarranged, fires break out, strange noises are heard, and a variety of other rarer events are reported: bottle caps unscrew, strange lights appear, telephones ring, radios register disturbances—the list seems endless.

Because these poltergeist reports typically center around a single person (usually a young person), and because they are usually confined to a small area, investigators always examine two possibilities with special interest. One is the naughty child theory: that the strange events are attention-getting devices produced by trickery. The other is that there is some unusual physical condition in that locality, such as a change in water level due to drought or flood which shifts a building and causes the objects in it to move. Astonishingly often, teams of careful investigators can find no normal cause.

An excellent compilation of the older cases (A. R. G. Owen, 1964) reports many instances in which skeptical observers arranged conditions to prevent trickery but nevertheless all saw the strange occurrences: "One great stone that lay on a spinning wheel to keep it steady, was thrown to the other side of the room " (p. 95). Pecularities in movement are frequent, for example, "A large stone seemed to be falling perpendicularly and with great velocity right on the minister's head. But it turned aside in full career" (p. 98). Some reports describe not only changes in direction but also changes in speed, such as a rapidly moving object slowing down in midair so that it settles gently on the floor. When the person around whom the events seem to center goes somewhere else, the events sometimes stop abruptly but sometimes linger for a short while, and occasionally occur in the new place to which the person has gone.

Recent cases are of special interest because of the controls that can now be introduced. Bender (1971), in summary, has reported of investigations in which he worked closely with physicists. He describes events in the classic poltergeist tradition which occurred while they were monitored by sophisticated instruments. Most striking is his Rosenheim case. In a Bavarian law office, light bulbs exploded or turned on and off, and there were telephone disturbances, for example, calls which had not been made were registered. Because these events suggested some fault in the power supply, a line recorder fitted with a voltage magnifier was brought in to record the voltage. It showed maximal deflections, often occurring with the abnormal events. Since Bender suspected that PK was affecting the instrument, his cooperating physicists disconnected the device from the circuit and supplied it with a battery instead; the deflections continued. In addition, nonelectrical events occurred: a 400-pound shelf moved, developer fluid spilled, and paintings rotated on the walls. The events stopped when the 19-year-old girl whom Bender suspected of being the poltergeist figure was sent to another place to work. But, later, new electronic disturbances repeatedly upset the equipment at a bowling alley she visited with her fiancé (who was an enthusiastic bowler) shortly before he broke their engagement.

Bender reports several other cases, including one in a house in which a figurine was displaced while contained in a specially constructed box that was monitored by a photoelectric light curtain. The displacement occurred when Bender and all other people from the house were outdoors. The photographic equipment which would have been triggered by interruption of the light curtain did not go on.

Other careful investigations are reported by Roll (1972/1976). For example, one family which he studied had been so perturbed by objects that flew about in their house and bottle caps that unscrewed that they called the police. When no culprit could be found, other community services including the fire department, the lighting company, and the town's building department were brought in. Eventually four engineers tried in vain to find the cause. Underground water and airplane take-offs and landings as well as electrical or radio disturbances were ruled out. A fresh cap was put on the chimney, plumbing was checked, and the house was ruled structurally sound. The odd events were well-attested, and the case seemed clearly to be one of a poltergeist. The events seemed to center around the 12-year-old son of the family, and psychological tests of him indicated strong repressed aggression.

In another long-lasting case, the central figure seemed to be the 19-year-old clerk who was working, unfortunately, in a warehouse in which small, breakable novelties were stored. The events continued so long that systematic studies could be made, for example, that some types of objects were more likely to move inexplicably than were others. Roll put some mugs, which he had found to be good candidates for breakage, at the rear of a shelf, placed other less breakable candidates in front of the mugs, and observed the area closely. At a time when no one was or had been near, a mug crashed to the floor, although the cartons in front of it were undisturbed. Further observations indicated that the movements diminished exponentially with distance from the key person, in this case and in another. Personality tests of the key person here also indicated considerable aggression that was denied normal outlets. It is interesting that when the clerk was brought to Roll's laboratory and tested for PK, his formal scores were only slightly better than chance expectation—but the sturdy machine used for the tests broke twice during the session, and broke again in a later session with him.

No two poltergeist cases are alike, and although it would be tempting to describe many, I will cite only one more, of interest both because the events continued so long and because the interpretation of the identity of the central figure changed. The first reports described odors and sounds that seemed unaccountable and objects that moved, notably a thermometer that wafted into the air with no one touching it. The events were associated with the emotional difficulties of the seven-year-old daughter of the family. But when other striking events, such as a hammer's moving unexplicably, occurred ten years after the original events, it was revealed that the mother of the family had also had severe emotional disturbances at the times of the earlier occurrences (Barrington, 1976). The case suggests, as do some of Roll's, and the Philip sittings, that PK may gather strength from more than one individual.

9. Isolated Instances

Many cases of apparent spontaneous PK are reported by persons who say they have had only one or only a few such experiences. A clock stops, a picture falls, glasses shatter, a chair starts rocking when no one touches it and there is no air current or floor vibration, and the odd event coincides with a crisis that makes it meaningful. Many cases are reported to coincide with death or with a dangerous accident to some loved person at a distant place, and a substantial number of cases are associated with an emotional crisis (L. E. Rhine, 1970). Some events have been carefully investigated and confirmed by several witnesses; but as with all spontaneous cases there is no baseline by which to judge whether the apparently meaningful coincidences are more frequent than expected by chance.

Consider this account (L. E. Rhine, 1963) as an example of the difficulties in classifying the story as PK.

> My sister lives on Long Island..., I lived in Indianapolis, and my brother lived in the suburbs of the same city. One night about 2:00 A.M. in each of our homes a window shade ran to the top making a dreadful noise and waking each of us in our separate homes. The next morning we learned our mother had died. When we had all gathered together the evening after the funeral, my sister spoke of feeling something was wrong somewhere because of the strange incident of the shade. My brother and I, both speaking at the same time, said, "Why, that happened at our house, too!" Of course, we realized it was something more than coincidence. (pp. 110–111)

What is the likelihood that window shades would run to the top at night, making enough noise to wake a sleeper? It happens every so often but it is not usually reported; the likelihood seems impossible to estimate. There is the additional factor that it was reported to have occurred on the same night and in three different homes of three siblings. Was there a natural cause for it, like thunder storms or earth tremors in Long Island and the Indianapolis area that night? How tightly do members of the family roll their shades? Were they all so anxious that evening because their mother was ill that they adjusted the shades with jerkier movements than usual?

The questions are unanswerable. The case does not lend itself to statistical evaluation, nor do most of the other more frequent cases of stopped clocks and fallen or broken objects. There seem to be good reasons to brush them aside as coincidental or as faulty reporting, but there also seem to be good reasons for accepting them as PK; surely either decision should be tentative.

Suppose then that we take as a tentative working hypothesis that this case, and others like it, were paranormal. Who was the PK agent? One possibility in this case, and in others where the event happened just after someone's death, is to interpret it as a signal that the dying or dead person is making contact with the living; that the dead still live. But consider now one more case from the same collection (L. E. Rhine, 1963) which opens up another possibility:

> I was sitting in my office. . . . At 3:00 P.M., Friday, I suddenly started to cry. My employer kept asking me what was the matter, but I could not tell him. About 3:20 P.M. a huge decorative vase fell off its shelf. No one was within fifteen feet of it. Next morning I received a call telling me my father had died of a heart attack sometime on Friday. (p. 112)

Here the interesting time sequence is that the tears came first, the vase fell second. If we take it as paranormal, it suggests repressed telepathic or precognitive information of the father's fatal heart attack, accompanied by strong emotion, then followed by a PK event. Could it have been the daughter's emotion, rather than the father's, that caused the PK? On the face of it, one seems to fit the psychological dynamics as well as the other. To put it another way, the super-psi hypothesis would interpret such cases of spontaneous PK in two steps: first information comes to the living, either normally or by ESP; then unconsciously the living person responds to the shocking information by producing PK. The accounts suggest that they do not demand a spiritistic hypothesis.

The crisis associated with the description of apparent spontaneous PK is not always a matter of life or death. One of the best known incidents comes to us from Jung (1963), who tells of a confrontation with Freud in Freud's study. A letter from Freud, written just after the incident, gives some of the emotional background: Freud, to whom the Oedipal conflict was so threatening, wrote Jung that he had just "adopted you as an oldest son, anointing you my successor and crown prince." In their talk after this symbolic adoption, Jung, who was still awed by prior PK experiences in his own family, asked for Freud's views on precognition. Freud's dismissal of it seemed so shallow that Jung recalled it was all he could do to keep from retorting sharply. With this suppression of a behavioral response, Jung felt a strange bodily one, "as if my diaphragm were made of iron and were becoming red-hot," and just then there was a loud, sudden noise in the bookcase, startling them both. Jung told Freud the noise was an exteriorization of his feelings. Freud dismissed the interpretation, and Jung predicted there would be another such noise—and there was. Dare we accept this as PK? Jung did; Freud wavered.

There are still other incidents that seem not to be associated with a crisis. An example here (Myers, 1903) comes from a clergyman who wrote that he was kneeling and praying at the bedside of a dying man while the man's wife knelt at the other side of the bed. As the prayer was ending, both saw a small table "about a yard from the foot of the bed, rise two or three times from the ground and come down with a violent thump upon the floor" (vol. 2, p. 504), spilling some medicine from a glass that was on it. They naturally thought there had been some disturbance in the room below which shook the house (although nothing else had moved). But an inquiry told them that the clergyman's wife and two others who were waiting with her in the room below "had been sitting in perfect silence" and when they heard the noise, had assumed that some furniture was knocked over in the room above. The patient did not die until about a week later. Although we can speculate that strong emotions may have been roused in him or in his wife as the prayer ended, this is only speculation.

These movements of objects and strange sounds are the kind that could have been caused by some normal though awkward activity. What is remarkable is that they apparently occurred without such a cause. The only other case I will cite is of a different, stranger type (Smythies, 1951). A man in Nepal who was with his guests after dinner was told by a servant that something was wrong in the servants' quarters. The man went back to see and found his young orderly, aged 22, sitting cross-legged with his hands clasped before him, shaking and quivering, sweating, and making extraordinary noises. After about ten minutes of this, the young man rose in the air about two feet, remained there about a second, and fell to the floor, all without a change in his position; this happened twice again. No one was nearer than about eight feet to him, the light was excellent, and there were no wires or other apparatus that could lift him. He had been sitting on a bare brick floor, and the other servants witnessed the event.

Apparent cases of PK, then, are sometimes associated with death but often are not. They are usually, but not always, reported in connection with strong emotions or emotionally charged situations. Sometimes (although the few cases I have cited do not show this) there are repeated episodes associated with similar events, such as the deaths, years apart, of different members of a family. Like all isolated reports, each may be attributed to coincidence or faulty reporting. In total, they are harder to dismiss, and, theoretically, they seem all of a piece with the reports of poltergeist phenomena.

How do the spontaneous cases relate to other material on PK? The events they describe are very like those of poltergeist cases except for being isolated rather than clustered (and also perhaps because they tend to be more associated with events that will cause grief, whereas poltergeist cases tend to be associated with repressed aggression). The sounds and movements are in general like those reported in the séance room, although the range of séance effects is perhaps even wider. And the spontaneous cases that someone takes the trouble to report to us are obviously far more massive than the small effects that are so carefully recorded in controlled, repetitious, emotionally blander laboratory experiments. Whereas the cases differ in frequency from poltergeist events, they differ in magnitude from laboratory data. The analogy that immediately comes to mind is that spontaneous cases are like flashes of lightning, but the laboratory changes are more like weak and erratic current flow between two poles of a battery with dirty terminals—except when someone with strong PK ability comes into a laboratory and produces the analog to artificial lightning. Perhaps we should take the reports of spontaneous events as suggesting the possible range of PK effects; but we should take the careful laboratory work as giving us firm data which can compel us to change our ideas and to formulate new theories.

10. References

Barrington, M. R. A poltergeist revisited: The flying thermometer case again. *Journal of the Society for Psychical Research*, 1976, *48*, 293–297.

Barry, J. General and comparative study of the psychokinetic effect on a fungus culture. *Journal of Parapsychology*, 1968, *32*, 237–243.

Batcheldor, K. J. Report on a case of table levitation and associated phenomena. *Journal of the Society for Psychical Research*, 1966, *43*, 339–356.

Bayless, R. Tape-recording of paranormally generated acoustical raps. *New Horizons*, 1976, *2*(2), 12–17.

Beloff, J. Matter and manner. *International Journal of Parapsychology*, 1964, *6*(1), 93–99.

Beloff, J., and Evans, L. A radioactivity test for psychokinesis. *Journal of the Society for Psychical Research*, 1961, *41*, 41–46.

Bender, H. New developments in poltergeist research. In W. G. Roll, R. L. Morris, and J. D. Morris (Eds.), *Proceedings of the Parapsychological Association No. 6, 1969*. Durham, N.C.: Parapsychological Association, 1971, 81–102.

Bender, H. The case of "Silvio" and of some others. In J. D. Morris, W. G. Roll, and R. L. Morris (Eds.), *Research in parapsychology 1976*. Metuchen, N.J.: Scarecrow Press, 1977, in press.

Bender, H., Vandrey, R., and Wendlandt, S. The "Geller effect" in Western Germany and Switzerland: A preliminary report on a social and experimental study. In J.

D. Morris, W. G. Roll, and R. L. Morris (Eds.), *Research in parapsychology 1975*. Metuchen, N.J.: Scarecrow Press, 1976, 141–144.

Besterman, T., Goldney, K. M., Gregory, C. C. L., and Hope, C. Rudi Schneider: Recollections and comments. *Journal of the Society for Psychical Research,* 1958, *39*, 206–215.

Bierman, D. J., and v. 't Hout, N. The performance of healers in PK tests with different RNG feedback algorithms. In J. D. Morris, W. G. Roll, and R. L. Morris (Eds.), *Research in parapsychology 1976*. Metuchen, N.J.: Scarecrow Press, 1977, in press.

Braud, W. Psychokinesis in aggressive and nonaggressive fish with mirror presentation feedback for hits. *Journal of Parapsychology,* 1976, *40,* 296–307.

Braud, W. G., Smith, G., Andrew, K., and Willis, S. Psychokinetic influences on random number generators during evocation of "analytic" vs. "nonanalytic" modes of processing information. In J. D. Morris, W. G. Roll, and R. L. Morris (Eds.), *Research in parapsychology 1975*. Metuchen, N.J.: Scarecrow Press, 1976, 85–88.

Brier, R. M. PK on a bio-electrical system. *Journal of Parapsychology,* 1969, *33,* 187–205.

Broad, C. D. Cromwell Varley's electrical tests with Florence Cook. *Proceedings of the Society for Psychical Research,* 1964, *54,* 158–172.

Brookes-Smith, C. Data-tape recorded experimental PK phenomena. *Journal of the Society for Psychical Research,* 1973, *47,* 69–89.

Brookes-Smith, C. Paranormal electrical conductance phenomena. *Journal of the Society for Psychical Research,* 1975, *48,* 73–86.

Brookes-Smith, C., and Hunt, D. W. Some experiments in psychokinesis. *Journal of the Society for Psychical Research,* 1970, *45,* 265–281.

Camstra, B. PK conditioning. In W. G. Roll, R. L. Morris, and J. D. Morris (Eds.), *Research in parapsychology 1972*. Metuchen, N.J.: Scarecrow Press, 1973, 25–27.

Cerutti, E. *Olga Worrall: Mystic with the healing hands.* New York: Harper & Row, 1975.

Chauvin, R. PK and radioactive disintegration. *Journal of Parapsychology,* 1968, *32,* 56. (Abstract)

Chauvin, R., and Genthon, J. P. An investigation of the possibility of PK experiments with uranium and a Geiger counter. *Journal of Parapsychology,* 1967, *31,* 168. (Abstract)

Cox, W. E. The effect of PK on the placement of falling objects. *Journal of Parapsychology,* 1951, *15,* 40–48.

Cox, W. E. The influence of "applied psi" upon the sex of offspring. *Journal of the Society for Psychical Research,* 1957, *39,* 65–78.

Cox, W. E. A comparison of different densities of dice in a PK task. *Journal of Parapsychology,* 1971, *35,* 108–119.

Cox, W. E. Note on some experiments with Uri Geller. *Journal of Parapsychology,* 1974, *38,* 408–411.

Cox, W. E. Blind PK with automated equipment. *Journal of Parapsychology,* 1976, *40,* 48. (Abstract)

Cox, W. E. Exploring "blind PK." In J. D. Morris, W. G. Roll, and R. L. Morris (Eds.), *Research in parapsychology 1976*. Metuchen, N.J.: Scarecrow Press, 1977, in press.

Crookes, W. *Researches in the phenomena of spiritualism.* London: J. Burns, 1874.

Dale, L. A. The psychokinetic effect: The first A.S.P.R. experiment. *Journal of the American Society for Psychical Research,* 1946, *40,* 123–151.

Dale, L. A., and Woodruff, J. L. The psychokinetic effect: Further A.S.P.R. experiments. *Journal of the American Society for Psychical Research,* 1947, *41,* 65–82.

David-Neel, A. *Initiations and initiates in Tibet.* New Hyde Park, N.Y.: University Books, 1959.

Dingwall, E. J. *Some human oddities.* London: Home and Van Thal, 1947.

Dodds, E. R. Supernormal phenomena in classical antiquity. *Proceedings of the Society for Psychical Research,* 1971, *55,* 189–237.

Donald, J. A., and Martin, B. Time-symmetric thermodynamics and causality violation. Unpublished manuscript, 1976.

Eisenbud, J. Inherent difficulties. *International Journal of Parapsychology,* 1964, *6*(1), 99–101.

Eisenbud, J. *The world of Ted Serios.* New York: William Morrow, 1967.

Ellis, D. J. Listening to the "Raudive voices." *Journal of the Society for Psychical Research,* 1975, *48,* 31–42.

Evans-Wentz, W. Y. *The fairy-faith in Celtic countries.* New Hyde Park, N.Y.: University Books, 1966.

Fahler, J. Exploratory scaled PK placement tests with nine college students with and without distance. *Journal of the American Society for Psychical Research,* 1959, *53,* 106–113.

Feather, S. R., and Rhine, L. E. PK experiments with same and different targets. *Journal of Parapsychology,* 1969, *33,* 213–227.

Fisk, G. W., and West, D. J. Die-casting with a single subject. *Journal of the Society for Psychical Research,* 1958, *39,* 277–287.

Flew, A. G. N. Something very unsatisfactory. *International Journal of Parapsychology,* 1964, *6*(1), 101–105.

Forwald, H. A further study of the PK placement effect. *Journal of Parapsychology,* 1952, *16,* 59–67.

Forwald, H. Mind, matter, and gravitation. A theoretical and experimental study (*Parapsychological monographs No. 11*). New York: Parapsychology Foundation, 1969.

Girden, E. A review of psychokinesis (PK). *Psychological Bulletin,* 1962, *59,* 353–388. (a)

Girden, E. A postscript to "A review of psychokinesis (PK)." *Psychological Bulletin,* 1962, *59,* 529–531. (b)

Goodrich, J. Studies of paranormal healing. *New Horizons,* 1976, *2*(2), 21–24.

Grad, B. A telekinetic effect on plant growth. *International Journal of Parapsychology,* 1963, *5*(2), 117–133.

Grad, B. A telekinetic effect on plant growth, II. Experiments involving treatment of saline in stoppered bottles. *International Journal of Parapsychology,* 1964, *6*(4), 473–498.

Grad, B. A telekinetic effect on yeast activity. *Journal of Parapsychology,* 1965, *29,* 285–286.

Grad, B. Psychotherapy, gentling, and the placebo effect. *Journal of the American Society for Psychical Research,* 1967, *61,* 286–305.

Grad, B. The biological effects of the "laying on of hands" on animals and plants: Implications for biology. In G. R. Schmeidler (Ed.), *Parapsychology: Its relation to physics, biology, psychology, and psychiatry.* Metuchen, N.J.: Scarecrow Press, 1976.

Grad, B., Cadoret, R. J., and Paul, G. I. The influence of an unorthodox method of treatment on wound healing in mice. *International Journal of Parapsychology*, 1961, *3*(2), 5–24.

Green, E. Report to the Third Interdisciplinary Conference on the Voluntary Control of Internal States, Council Grove, Kansas, 1971.

Greene, F. M. The feeling of luck and its effect on PK. *Journal of Parapsychology*, 1960, *24*, 129–141.

Haraldsson, E. Psychokinetic effects on yeast: An exploratory experiment. In W. G. Roll, R. L. Morris, and J. D. Morris (Eds.), *Research in parapsychology 1972*. Metuchen, N. J.: Scarecrow Press, 1973, 20–21.

Hasted, J. B. An experimental study of the validity of metal bending phenomena. *Journal of the Society for Psychical Research*, 1976, *48*, 365–383.

Honorton, C. Apparent psychokinesis on static objects by a "gifted" subject. In W. G. Roll, R. L. Morris, and J. D. Morris (Eds.), *Research in parapsychology 1973*. Metuchen, N.J.: Scarecrow Press, 1974, 128–134.

Honorton, C. Effects of meditation and feedback on psychokinetic performance: A pilot study with an instructor of TM (Transcendental Meditation). In J. D. Morris, W. G. Roll, and R. L. Morris (Eds.), *Research in parapsychology 1976*, Metuchen, N.J.: Scarecrow Press, 1977, in press.

Honorton, C., and Barksdale, W. PK performance with waking suggestions for muscle tension versus relaxation. *Journal of the American Society for Psychical Research*, 1972, *66*, 208–214.

Houtkooper, J. M. Psychokinesis, clairvoyance and personality factors. In J. D. Morris, W. G. Roll, and R. L. Morris (Eds.), *Research in parapsychology 1976*. Metuchen, N.J.: Scarecrow Press, 1977, in press.

Humphrey, B. M. Help–hinder comparison in PK tests. *Journal of Parapsychology*, 1947, *11*, 4–13.

Joyce, C. R. B., and Welldon, R. M. C. The objective efficacy of prayer. *Journal of Chronic Diseases*, 1965, *18*, 367–377.

Jung, C. G. *Memories, dreams, reflections*. New York: Pantheon, 1963.

Kamiya, J., and Nowlis, D. The control of electroencephalographic alpha rhythms through auditory feedback and the associated mental activity. *Psychophysiology*, 1970, *6*, 476–484.

Keil, J. H. J., Ullman, M., Herbert, B., and Pratt, J. G. Directly observable voluntary PK effects. *Proceedings of the Society for Psychical Research*, 1976, *56*, 197–235.

Kelly, E. F., and Kanthamani, B. K. A subject's efforts toward voluntary control. *Journal of Parapsychology*, 1972, *36*, 185–197.

Kief, H. K. A method for measuring PK ability with enzymes. In W. G. Roll, R. L. Morris, and J. D. Morris (Eds.), *Research in parapsychology 1972*. Metuchen, N.J.: Scarecrow Press, 1973, 19–20.

Knowles, E. A. G. Psi dexterity in a mixing experiment. *Journal of Parapsychology*, 1967, *31*, 214–230.

Krippner, S., and Villoldo, A. *The realms of healing*. Millbrae, Cal.: Celestial Arts, 1976.

Kruger, H. *Other healers, other cures: A guide to alternative medicine*. Indianapolis: Bobbs-Merrill, 1974.

Kuyper, O. et al. The conditioning of PK responses. *Journal of Parapsychology*, 1972, *36*, 253–254. (Abstract)

LeShan, L. *The medium, the mystic, and the physicist*. New York: Viking, 1974.

MacDonald, R. G., Hickman, J. L., and Dakin, H. S. Preliminary physical measurements of psychophysical interactions with three psychic healers. In J. D. Morris, W. G. Roll, and R. L. Morris (Eds.), *Research in parapsychology 1976*. Metuchen, N.J.: Scarecrow Press, 1977, in press.

Maher, M., and Schmeidler, G. R. Quantitative investigation of a recurrent apparition. *Journal of the American Society for Psychical Research*, 1975, *69*, 341–352.

Matas, F., and Pantas, L. A PK experiment comparing meditating versus nonmeditating subjects. In W. G. Roll, R. L. Morris, and J. D. Morris (Eds.), *Proceedings of the Parapsychological Association No. 8, 1971*. Durham, N.C.: Parapsychological Association, 1972, 12–13.

McConnell, R. A. Remote night tests for PK. *Journal of the American Society for Psychical Research*, 1955, *49*, 99–108.

McConnell, R. A., Snowdon, R. J., and Powell, R. F. Wishing with dice. *Journal of Experimental Psychology*, 1955, *50*, 269–275.

Medhurst, R. G., and Goldney, K. M. William Crookes and the physical phenomena of mediumship. *Proceedings of the Society for Psychical Research*, 1964, *54*, 25–157.

Metta, L. Psychokinesis on lepidopterous larvae. *Journal of Parapsychology*, 1972, *36*, 213–221.

Millar, B. Thermistor PK. In J. D. Morris, W. G. Roll, and R. M. Morris (Eds.), *Research in parapsychology 1975*. Metuchen, N.J.: Scarecrow Press, 1976, 71–73.

Millar, B., and Broughton, R. An investigation of the psi enhancement paradigm of Schmidt. In J. D. Morris, W. G. Roll, and R. L. Morris (Eds.), *Research in parapsychology 1976*. Metuchen, N.J.: Scarecrow Press, 1977, in press.

Mischo, J. Personality structure of psychokinetic mediums. In W. G. Roll, R. L. Morris, and J. D. Morris (Eds.), *Proceedings of the Parapsychological Association No. 5, 1968*. Durham, N.C.: Parapsychological Association, 1971, 35–37.

Mischo, J., and Weis, R. A pilot study on the relations between PK scores and personality variables. In W. G. Roll, R. L. Morris, and J. D. Morris (Eds.), *Research in parapsychology 1972*, Metuchen, N.J.: Scarecrow Press, 1973, 21–23.

Mitchell, A. M. J., and Fisk, G. W. The application of differential scoring methods to PK tests. *Journal of the Society for Psychical Research*, 1953, *37*, 45–61.

Mitchell, J. L., and Perskari, B. Instrument note: A table to measure levitation and to control normal pressure. *Journal of the American Society for Psychical Research*, 1977, *71*, 51–53.

Murphy, G. Report on paper by Edward Girden on psychokinesis. *Psychological Bulletin*, 1962, *59*, 520–528.

Myers, F. W. H. *Human personality and its survival of bodily death*. London: Longmans, Green, 1903.

Nash, C. B., and Nash, C. S. Effect of paranormally conditioned solution on yeast fermentation. *Journal of Parapsychology*, 1967, *31*, 314. (Abstract)

Onetto, B., and Elguin, G. H. Psychokinesis in experimental tumorigenesis. *Journal of Parapsychology*, 1966, *30*, 220. (Abstract)

Osis, K. A test of the relationship between ESP and PK. *Journal of Parapsychology*, 1953, *17*, 298–309.

Osty, E. *Supernormal aspects of energy and matter. (Third Myers memorial lecture.)* London: Society for Psychical Research, 1933.

Owen, A. R. G. *Can we explain the poltergeist?* New York: Garrett Publications, 1964.

Owen, I. M. "Philip's" story continued. *New Horizons*, 1975, *2*(1), 14–20.

Owen, I. M., and Sparrow, M. *Conjuring up Philip*. New York: Harper & Row, 1976.

Pauli, E. N. El poder de la mente sobre objectivos vivientes. *Cuadernos de Parapsicología*, 1974, *7*, 1–14.

Podmore, F. *Modern spiritualism*. London: Methuen, 1902.

Pratt, J. G. The meaning of performance curves in ESP and PK test data. *Journal of Parapsychology*, 1949, *13*, 9–23.

Pratt, J. G. The case for psychokinesis. *Journal of Parapsychology*, 1960, *24*, 171–188.

Pratt, J. G., and Forwald, H. Confirmation of the PK placement effect. *Journal of Parapsychology*, 1958, *22*, 1–19.

Price, H. *Fifty years of psychical research*. London: Longmans, Green, 1939.

Puthoff, H., and Targ, R. Psychic research and modern physics. In E. D. Mitchell, and others. *Psychic exploration: A challenge for science*. New York: Putnam's, 1974.

Randall, J. L. An attempt to detect psi effects with protozoa. *Journal of the Society for Psychical Research*, 1970, *45*, 294–296.

Randall, J. L. Experiments to detect a psi effect with small animals. *Journal of the Society for Psychical Research*, 1971, 46, 31–39.

Randall, J. L. Two psi experiments with gerbils. *Journal of the Society for Psychical Research*, 1972, *46*, 22–30.

Rao, K. R. The bidirectionality of psi. *Journal of Parapsychology*, 1965, *29*, 130–250.

Ratte, R. J. Comparison of game and standard PK testing techniques under competitive and noncompetitive conditions. *Journal of Parapsychology*, 1960, *24*, 235–244.

Raudive, K. *Breakthrough*. New York: Taplinger, 1971.

Rhine, J. B., and Humphrey, B. M. The PK effect: Special evidence from hit patterns. I. Quarter distributions of the page. *Journal of Parapsychology*, 1944, *8*, 18–60.

Rhine, L. E. Spontaneous physical effects and the psi process. *Journal of Parapsychology*, 1963, *27*, 84–122.

Rhine, L. E. *Mind over matter*. New York: Macmillan, 1970.

Rhine, L. E., and Rhine, J. B. The psychokinetic effect. I. The first experiment. *Journal of Parapsychology*, 1943, *7*, 20–43.

Richet, C. *Thirty years of psychical research*. New York: Macmillan, 1923.

Richmond, N. Two series of PK tests on paramecia. *Journal of the Society for Psychical Research*, 1952, *36*, 577–588.

Roll, W. G. *The poltergeist*. Metuchen, N.J.: Scarecrow Press, 1976. (Originally published, 1972.)

Roll, W. G., and Gearhart, L. Geomagnetic perturbations and ESP. In W. G. Roll, R. L. Morris, and J. D. Morris (Eds.), *Research in parapsychology 1973*. Metuchen, N.J.: Scarecrow Press, 1974, 44–46.

Rose, L. *Faith healing*. Baltimore, Md.: Penguin Books, 1971.

Rubin, L., and Honorton, C. Separating the yins from the yangs: An experiment with the *I Ching*. In W. G. Roll, R. L. Morris, and J. D. Morris (Eds.), *Proceedings of the Parapsychological Association No. 8, 1971*. Durham, N.C.: Parapsychological Association, 1972, 6–7.

Rush, J. H. Effects are not illusory. *International Journal of Parapsychology*, 1964, *6*(1), 105–109.

S[alter], J. W. H. Three score years and ten: The S.P.R., 1882–1952. *Journal of the Society for Psychical Research*, 1952, *36*, 639–645.

Scarne, J. *Amazing world of John Scarne*. New York: Crown, 1956.

Schmeidler, G. Not for "uncritical" readers. *International Journal of Parapsychology*, 1964, *6*(1), 109–113.

Schmeidler, G. R. PK effects upon continuously recorded temperature. *Journal of the American Society for Psychical Research*, 1973, *67*, 325–340.

Schmeidler, G., Gambale, J., and Mitchell, J. PK effects on temperature recordings: An attempted replication and extension. In J. D. Morris, W. G. Roll, and R. L.

Morris (Eds.), *Research in parapsychology 1975.* Metuchen, N.J.: Scarecrow Press, 1976, 67–69.

Schmeidler, G., Mitchell, J., and Sondow, N. Further investigation of PK with temperature records. In J. D. Morris, W. G. Roll, and R. L. Morris (Eds.), *Research in parapsychology 1974.* Metuchen, N.J.: Scarecrow Press, 1975, 71–73.

Schmidt, H. Precognition of a quantum process. *Journal of Parapsychology,* 1969, *33,* 99–108.

Schmidt, H. A PK test with electronic equipment. *Journal of Parapsychology,* 1970, *34,* 175–181. (a)

Schmidt, H. PK experiments with animals as subjects. *Journal of Parapsychology,* 1970, *34,* 255–261. (b)

Schmidt, H. Animal PK tests with time displacement. *Journal of Parapsychology,* 1974, *38,* 244–245.

Schmidt, H. PK effect on pre-recorded targets. *Journal of the American Society for Psychical Research,* 1976, *70,* 267–291.

Schmidt, H., and Pantas, L. Psi tests with internally different machines. *Journal of Parapsychology,* 1972, *36,* 222–232.

Smith, M. J. Paranormal effects on enzyme activity. *Human Dimensions,* 1972, *1*(2), 15–19.

Smythies, E. A. A case of levitation in Nepal. *Journal of the Society for Psychical Research,* 1951, *36,* 415–426.

Stanford, R. G. "Associative activation of the unconscious" and "visualization" as methods for influencing the PK target. *Journal of the American Society for Psychical Research,* 1969, *63,* 338–351.

Stanford, R. G., Zenhausern, R., Taylor, A., and Dwyer, M. A. Psychokinesis as psi-mediated instrumental response. *Journal of the American Society for Psychical Research,* 1975, *69,* 127–133.

Stephenson, C. J. Further comments on Cromwell Varley's electrical test on Florence Cook. *Proceedings of the Society for Psychical Research,* 1966, *54,* 363–417.

Stevenson, I. Cultural patterns in cases suggestive of reincarnation among the Tlingit Indians in Southeast Alaska. *Journal of the American Society for Psychical Research,* 1966, *60,* 229–243.

Stevenson, I. *Twenty cases suggestive of reincarnation* (2nd ed.). Charlottesville, Va.: University Press of Virginia, 1974.

Stevenson, I. *Cases of the reincarnation type. Vol. I, Ten cases in India.* Charlottesville, Va.: University Press of Virginia, 1975.

Stevenson, I., and Pratt, J. G. Exploratory investigations of the psychic photography of Ted Serios. *Journal of the American Society for Psychical Research,* 1968, *62,* 103–129.

Tart, C. T., Boisen, M., Lopez, V., and Maddock, R. Some studies of psychokinesis with a spinning silver coin. *Journal of the Society for Psychical Research,* 1972, *46,* 143–153.

Thouless, R. H. Toward an "authoritative" test. *International Journal of Parapsychology,* 1964, *6*(1), 113–117.

Tversky, A., and Kahneman, D. Belief in the law of small numbers. *Psychological Bulletin,* 1971, *76.* 105–110.

Van de Castle, R. L. An exploratory study of some personality correlates associated with PK performance. *Journal of the American Society for Psychical Research,* 1958, *52,* 134–150.

Varley, C. Electrical experiments with Miss Cook when entranced. *Spiritualist,* March 20, 1874.

Vasiliev, L. L. *Experiments in mental suggestion.* Church Crookham, Hampshire, England: Institute for the Study of Mental Images, 1963.

Wadhams, P., and Farrelly, B. A. The investigation of psychokinesis using β-particles. *Journal of the Society for Psychical Research,* 1968, *44,* 281–289.

Watkins, G. K. Possible PK in the lizard *Anolis sagrei.* In W. G. Roll, R. L. Morris, and J. D. Morris (Eds.), *Proceedings of the Parapsychological Association No. 8, 1971.* Durham, N.C.: Parapsychological Association, 1972, 23–25.

Watkins, G. K., and Watkins, A. M. Possible PK influence on the resuscitation of anesthetized mice. *Journal of Parapsychology,* 1971, *35,* 257–272.

Wells, R., and Klein, J. A replication of a "psychic healing" paradigm. *Journal of Parapsychology,* 1972, *36,* 144–149.

Wells, R., and Watkins, G. K. Linger effects in several PK experiments. In J. D. Morris, W. G. Roll, and R. L. Morris (Eds.), *Research in parapsychology 1974.* Metuchen, N. J.: Scarecrow Press, 1975, 143–147.

West, D. J. *Eleven Lourdes miracles.* London: Duckworth, 1957.

Whitton, J. L. Paramorphic table rappings: Acoustic analysis. *New Horizons,* 1976, *2*(2), 7–11.

Winnett, R., and Honorton, C. Effects of meditation and feedback on psychokinetic performance: Results with practitioners of Ajapa yoga. In J. D. Morris, W. G. Roll, and R. L. Morris (Eds.), *Research in parapsychology 1976.* Metuchen, N.J.: Scarecrow Press, 1977, in press.

Worrall, A., and Worrall, O. *The gift of healing.* New York: Harper & Row, 1965.

Therapeutic Applications 3

Jan Ehrenwald

1. Psi and Psychotherapy

The proposition that psi phenomena play an important part in interpersonal relationships is now gaining increasing acceptance. But the form or type or category of psi that is involved in the origin of mental illness is an open question. Still more problematic is the part played by the psi factor in its treatment: in psychotherapy, both scientific and prescientific.

I submit that for a reasonable discussion of what amounts to the diagnostic and therapeutic implications of psi, two principal modalities have to be distinguished. One is the forced-choice, card-calling type of incidents. The other is the free-response or spontaneous type occurring in dreams or in the psychoanalytic situation. We shall see that such a distinction cuts through the usual modalities of telepathy, clairvoyance, or psychokinesis and can be applied to spontaneous and experimental incidents, as well as to both medical and nonmedical models of psychotherapy.

Elsewhere I pointed to the profound cleavage between the two prototypes (Ehrenwald, 1975a). Free-response incidents are subject to familiar psychodynamic principles; they are essentially need-determined and not readily amenable to statistical treatment. By contrast, forced-choice incidents are readily quantifiable but usually random, capricious, trivial events. Viewed in isolation, they do not seem to meet the needs of either agent or percipient. An occasional "hit" in a card-calling test may happen to bear out the subject's wish to please the experimenter; it may

---

Jan Ehrenwald · The Roosevelt Hospital, New York, New York.

be subject to what I described as "doctrinal compliance" (Ehrenwald, 1957), but this does not account for the subject's selective response, then and there, to a triangle, a cross, or wavy line. The capricious nature of such guesses, I stated, is due to random fluctuations, or flaws, in the operation of the Bergsonian filter (Ehrenwald, 1975a), a neural structure presumably located in the reticular formation of the brain stem. They can be described as random, flaw-determined neurophysiological events, subject to Rhine's position or decline effects, but they do not "make sense" in psychodynamic terms.

The proper distinction between these two principal classes of psi is a crucial point in psi research and it is a recurrent theme in the pages that follow.

1.1. Four Faces of Psi in Psychotherapy

Psychotherapy is a proving ground of unique, essentially unrepeatable interpersonal events, designed to meet the needs of therapist and patient. The uniqueness and lack of replicability of therapeutic transactions closely resembles one of the major handicaps of experiments in parapsychology. The experimental approach, with opportunities for ceaseless repetition of ESP or PK tests, seeks to make up for this deficiency and has brought psychical research into the orbit of the scientific method. The parapsychologist can rely on quantifiable data, on statistical significance, on critical ratios. But, in so doing, he is apt to neglect the study of spontaneous, free-response, real-life exchanges and interactions with his subjects.

There are no such options open to the psychotherapist. This is in effect one of the reasons why the scientific status of psychotherapy— Freudian, Adlerian, Jungian or otherwise—is still being hotly contested. All the therapist can do to hold his own is to sift, assemble, and describe the cumulative evidence of recurrent interpersonal exchanges and changing interpersonal configurations that come his way in the therapeutic situation. To this comes the added advantage of dealing with people's behavior in the flesh—and not with largely flaw-determined statistical artifacts. As is true of psi when it occurs in daily life, he is dealing with need-determined, spontaneous occurrences.

We shall see presently that in the process he may stumble—inadvertently and unawares—into a variety of psi phenomena. Like Molière's *Physician against His Will,* he may turn into a parapsychologist, *malgrè lui,* as it were. It will be recalled that precisely this happened to Freud in the wake of his first psychoanalytic encounters with the "occult" (Freud, 1933).

Spontaneous psi occurrences in therapy can be methodically studied under the following four headings:

1.1.1. Tracer Effects

The earliest observations of psi in psychotherapy were included in an anthology by Devereux (1953) and were largely concerned with reporting and verifying the occurrences and commenting on their presumed psychodynamics. Typical examples included (with the original publication dates) are articles by I. Hollos (1933), E. Servadio (1935), N. Fodor (1947), and J. Eisenbud (1948), which are included in G. Devereux's volume, *Psychoanalysis and the Occult* (1953). Other pertinent contributions along the same lines were made by J. Ehrenwald (1942), M. Ullman (1959), and other members of the Medical Section of the ASPR that flourished from 1947 to 1952. Tracer elements are such specific "bits" of information as names, dates, numerals, or a combination of a multiplicity of distinctive features in a dream whose correspondence to reality (e.g., in the therapist's personal experience) cannot reasonably be attributed to chance alone. They have no direct bearing upon interpersonal dynamics but are indicative of the occurrence of telepathy in a given case. Indeed, critics like M. Balint (1955) promptly pointed out that such incidents—whatever their nature—are undesirable by-products of the analytic situation and therefore nothing to boast—or to write papers—about. Yet, gradually, the emphasis shifted to the closer study of psi in relation to the dynamics of transference, countertransference, etc. (Ehrenwald, 1954; Servadio, 1955; Ullman, 1959; Eisenbud, 1970; and others). The prevailing concern became elucidation rather than fact-finding or proof.

1.1.2. Doctrinal Compliance

But on closer scrutiny it soon became apparent that the analytic situation was fertile soil for the emergence of a more complex group of psi incidents. Time and again, patients tended to confirm with their productions the therapist's hopes and expectations regarding the validity of the doctrines held by the school of psychotherapy to which he owed his allegiance. This is what I described as *doctrinal compliance*. It is reflected by virtually the whole history of psychotherapy (Ehrenwald, 1957, 1976). Mesmer's hysterics presented all the evidence of animal magnetism the good doctor wanted them to produce. Early-nineteenth-century patients consulting phrenologists manifested all the telltale signs which the pressing or massaging of given "bumps" on their craniums was supposed to elicit. Charcot's patients regularly acted out the four stages of hysteria he had choreographed for them. Hypnosis, in particular, turned out to be the patient's well-rehearsed psychodramatic response to the hypnotist's expectations and to the "demand characteristics" of hypnotic suggestion.

It will be noted that doctrinal compliance, conceived along these lines, comes closer to the intrinsic purpose of psychotherapy. Besides imparting cognitive information of sorts, it may also affect the patient's overall behavior in the desired way: it may help the therapeutic process. Doctrinal compliance is thus closely allied to the effects of suggestion. Yet it differs from suggestion in that usually both therapist and patient are unaware of its operation. Indeed, it appears that doctrinal compliance owes much of its telepathic potential to its hidden, unconscious quality (Ehrenwald, 1957, 1976).

However, there is one flaw in such reasoning. As a general rule, doctrinal compliance lacks the criteria of specificity or tracer effects required to clinch the case in favor of a psi factor. Its involvement can at best be inferred from the concerted evidence of tracer elements emerging in the overall context of the doctor–patient relationship and from the similarity of its psychodynamics with the experimenter–subject, or mother–child configuration.

1.1.3. Direct Impact

There is a third face of psi in psychotherapy which is still more difficult to define in terms of clear-cut clinical criteria, yet it has still greater relevance to our issue. It is the potential direct therapeutic influence upon the patient of the practitioner's or healer's motivations to help, meeting halfway, as it were, with the patient's hopes and expectations to be cured (Ehrenwald, 1977). Interlacing and dovetailing psychological configurations of this order are known to set the stage for a favorable outcome. At the same time, they are conducive to the emergence of psi phenomena (Ehrenwald, 1954). As I pointed out elsewhere (Ehrenwald, 1971), the original prototype for this phenomenon is symbiosis between the mother and her infant. To put it in a capsule, the early symbiotic phase can be described as the "cradle of ESP." It should also be recalled that the psychoanalytic situation, with its tendency to "regression in the service of treatment," may be ideally suited to recapture, at least for fleeting moments, the symbiotic stage. At the same time, it may facilitate the emergence of telepathy between analyst and patient.

1.1.4. Psi-Missing

The fourth face of psi in the therapeutic situation should be mentioned, but only in passing: the tendency to psi-missing. Psi-missing is the apparent avoidance of a target more often than can be expected by chance alone. This suggests the operation of a psi factor "in reverse," due to the subject's negative motivation (Rhine, 1952). Its occurrence is even harder to pinpoint than tracer effects, doctrinal compliance, or the therapist's direct remedial impact on the patient. Indeed, critics may rightly point out that psi-missing in the clinical setting is impossible to prove. It is vitiated by Popper's principle of falsifiability.

1.2. The Uses of Psi in Psychotherapy

Inevitably, the early approach to psi in psychotherapy was aimed at "making sense" of observations. Hollos (1933: summarized in Devereux, 1953, Chapter 19), Servadio (1935), Eisenbud (1948), Ullman (1959, 1975), Ullman and Krippner, with Vaughan (1973), and Ehrenwald (1942, 1954), to name only a few, placed their chief emphasis on bringing psi incidents into sharper focus and on arriving at a better understanding of the psychodynamics of the patient's dreams and other productions. It was hoped that introducing the telepathy hypothesis would help to fill gaps in the analyst's understanding of a given case. Eisenbud (1970), in particular, felt that judicious interpretations along these lines would provide added insight, improve the transference relationship, and enhance the therapist's self-understanding. Occasionally, it could result in a liberating, cathartic experience.

I, for my part, was less sanguine on that score and cautioned against the full sharing with the patient of the therapist's unorthodox theories concerning the part played by telepathy in paranoid reactions. Caution, I felt, was particularly needed in paranoid schizophrenics in order to avoid reinforcing their delusional trend.

1.2.1. Two-Way Street

An unexpected by-product of the therapist's open-minded attitude toward psi phenomena was the observation that telepathy in psychotherapy is not a one-way street. It occasionally worked in the reverse direction: from the patient to the therapist. Here, again, clues to that effect were provided by the appearance of a few isolated tracer elements. In my own case, they were usually concerned with my own thoughts and idiosyncratic preoccupations at the time.

The following is a typical example. Mr. H is a bachelor of forty-three, a college graduate, who was referred to me for consultation on the advice of Dr. Gardner Murphy, then President of the American Society of Psychical Research. The patient presented the picture of full-fledged paranoid schizophrenia. He complained that he was under the influence of evil spirits and that he was persecuted by German barons and dukes; he was hearing voices and had developed an elaborate system of delusions which he interpreted in terms of ESP. In the course of our first interview (the only one I had with the patient), I tried to point out to him the delusional nature of his experiences. "Your German barons and dukes, and even your Barbara Hutton," I stated, "are just split-off parts of your own personality." The patient was visibly taken aback by my remark: "How do you know that Barbara Hutton is among them? Did she tell you?" The fact is that he had not, in the preceding half hour, mentioned the heiress's name to me. Nor was she referred to in a covering letter sent to me by his previous psychiatrist. Thus, my mentioning her name was either "sheer coincidence"—or it may have been determined by the fact that Barbara happened to be my daughter's name. Or else, one may argue, that my empathy with Mr. H. went so far as to reflect—or even try to improve upon—his delusional ideas: "Yes, it is possible to pick up telepathically another person's thoughts—even *I* can do it for you."

The second incident lacks comparable criteria of specificity or uniqueness, but its psychodynamics are more meaningful and transparent. Fred L., a married man of forty-nine, was working as a furrier in his uncle's firm. In one of his sessions (June, 1968) he talked at great length about his uncle reproving him for having caused some minor damage to sable skins he had prepared for a customer. Fred did not bring to an end his guilt-laden recital of the incident that day, and I opened the next session by noting that he obviously felt unduly guilty about mistreating the skins because they actually stood for women and "women's skins"; they symbolized his sadistic—destructive impulses against them. "You feel guilty about the sable skins because deep down it is a woman's skin which you want to hurt." Thereupon the patient, visibly taken aback by my remark, reported the following dream he had had the night before: "I hit Selma [the firm's telephone operator]. She complained of headaches. She said I have damaged her scalp. Her hair was falling out at places. I got scared she'll sue me. Her scalp will look like a [damaged] genital area."

So much for the dream. Fred said that in reality he had gotten angry with Selma for "messing up" his telephone messages. "Women are messy," he added by way of an afterthought.

The deeper analytic implications of this dream need not be discussed here. Yet, an added argument in support of a telepathic reading of my response to Fred's dream is the fact that in an earlier period of treatment Fred and I had been involved in a number of similar psi incidents (Ehrenwald, 1954).

I may add that in the early stages of my preoccupation with psi phenomena a growing number of tracer effects came into my purview. At a later stage—apparently associated with a shift of my interest to other aspects of the telepathic process—evidence of doctrinal compliance came to the fore. In more recent years, I am happy to report, the apparent telepathic impact of my emotionally charged therapeutic motivations has tended to hold the center of the stage. This has been coupled with the evidence of my own growing telepathic responsiveness to my patients.

1.2.2. Existential Position

Elsewhere I have described incidents of this kind in terms of an existential shift (Ehrenwald, 1966). In the present context it would be more appropriate to describe them in terms of an existential *position*: an altered state of consciousness acquired over years of patient, wishless, and objectless waiting and seeking. It is an attitude that may have come close to crystallization in a stable personality trait over the years. That it may occasionally be punctuated with brief flurries of gentle therapeutic interventions—like the sailor going into action to catch a favorable wind—is another matter. In any case, timing, in this instance, is controlled by a telepathic feedback loop rather than by the winds and the weather.

Apparently, such experiences are not exclusively my own. They are supported by C. G. Jung (1963) who has gone on record with a number of similar observations. So have Jule Eisenbud, Joost Meerloo, Gotthard Booth, and other colleagues in private conversations with me. Nevertheless, it is slightly embarrassing to "go public" with self-revelations of this kind. For better or for worse, they are more in keeping with similar claims made by diverse unorthodox healers, practitioners of assorted esoteric mind-expanding courses, and self-styled clairvoyants. Nevertheless, they may be important ingredients of the whole—or holistic—therapeutic approach and should not be dismissed without a hearing.

What, then, are the implications of a parapsychologically informed approach to need- as well as flaw-determined psi phenomena? It suggests that the occasional selective appearance of psi can be adaptive as well as maladaptive. A few clinical vignettes will illustrate the point.

2. Psychiatric Aspects

2.1. Multiple Personalities, Possession, and Mediumistic Trance

Purported possession by demons, ancestrial spirits, or devils is the oldest prototype of alleged psi phenomena in altered states of consciousness. Yet the modern clinical concept of possession has made a clean sweep of its original paranormal aspects. Some of my own cases (Ehrenwald, 1947, 1966, 1974b) were patients suffering from paranoid schizophrenic reactions or delusional responses to acute toxic conditions. A Hungarian peasant woman of 60, raped by invading soldiers in the Second World War, felt she was possessed by the devil and attributed her own repudiated sexual responses to the Evil One. Another patient, an alcoholic woman of 52, complained she was possessed by dogs and other animals. In her trance states she barked and yelped, expressing her identification with the possessing animal spirits. On coming to, she made no paranormal claims. Nor did any patient of this group show evidence of authentic psi phenomena.

Yet, other patients did, or firmly believed that they did. A Puerto Rican girl of 24 felt she was possessed by a deceased uncle and other relatives. On a later occasion, she complained that a lesbian woman teacher was "possessing" her and tried to influence her in a telepathic way. She insisted she had also experienced genuine ESP.

Her claims were unproven. Yet the mediumistic trance, multiple personalities, and the attending states of mental dissociation often become veritable breeding grounds of telepathy, clairvoyance, and precognition. The occurrence of proven PK or other physical phenomena is still controversial. So is the survival hypothesis held by spiritualists. Thus, cases ranging from acute psychotic reactions to hysterical dissociation and diverse other altered states of consciousness add up to a merging scale of mental or physical manifestations, with no evidence of paranormality on one end, and increasing evidence of psi on the other.

Yet, it goes without saying that the cleavage between the two classes is largely arbitrary and man-made. Cases of multiple personality— usually classed under the heading of mental dissociation or hysterical defensive maneuvers—can be described as *formes frustes* of the mediumistic trance with its rich yield of authentic psi incidents. On the other hand, a psychiatrist of the old school may consider trance phenomena as nothing but examples of multiple personalities, sometimes culminating in the delusional experience of possession. In either case, the possessing or secondary personality may or may not exhibit genuine psi phenomena. These may be a dramatic impersonation by the medium of a living or deceased person, using telepathic or other cues emanating from the "sitters" (the participating observers in a mediumistic séance). It is a response which I have described as *telepathic seeding* (Ehrenwald, 1975b). Telepathic seeding is facilitated by the medium's capacity to bring about closure and to fill in gaps in incomplete gestalten or configurations that make up the "message." More impressive scenarios of this type give rise to the familiar spiritualistic theories of survival after death, the emergence of ghosts or apparitions. It should be pointed out, however, that a widely held rival hypothesis of super ESP or "this-world ESP" has been invoked as a more parsimonious explanation of such incidents (Price, 1976).

The therapeutic implications of cases of this kind depend on whether or not they are viewed within a psychiatric, parapsychological, spiritualistic, or religious frame of reference. A modern psychiatrist would describe Plato's "divine madness" or the raptures of medieval saints as acute schizophrenic states. By the same token, he would consider mediumistic trance as nothing but a case of hysterical dissociation in which the medium's repressed impulses or instinctual drives are projected into the outside world and embroidered upon with the characteristics of a colorful imaginary personage.

Whether or not therapy is indicated in cases such as these depends on the existing cultural context, and on the needs, motivations, and expectations of the subject and his social environment. In my own experience the emergence of need-determined psi phenomena may have a distinctively restitutive value. It may amount to a successful attempt at self-healing. In such cases, the medium would resolutely reject any remedial aid from outside. Only if and when she fails in her attempt at integrating the secondary personalities with the rest of her ego will she seek medical or psychiatric advice. Alternatively, she may turn to an exorciser or to a priestly or rabbinical healer. If so, her "case" is likely to go on record as one of possession by a hostile, ego alien force, a demon, a dybbuk, an incubus. On the other hand, modern psychiatric management of her case would be geared to analytic psychotherapy in which the patient's underlying unconscious conflicts are brought into focus, worked through, and, hopefully, resolved. In case of need, the analytic approach will be supplemented by one of the major tranquilizers to control the patient's fears and agitation. Such drug treatment may in addition have a tempering effect on the flaw-determined, organic component of the clinical picture.

2.2. Schizophrenia and Psi Pollution

There is an embarrassing similarity between the paranoid schizophrenic's delusions of persecution, of the possibility of thought and action at a distance, and the theories held by modern parapsychologists. Yet, as I have noted in previous writings (Ehrenwald, 1974b, 1975b), on the face of it, the patient's claims are usually wholly delusional. He cannot "read" the minds of other people, nor can his enemies pick his brain. He may claim he is capable of duplicating the biblical miracles of healing. He may identify with Christ or Napoleon, while patiently lining up with his lunchtray in the cafeteria of his hospital.

Still, as I have pointed out (Ehrenwald, 1974b), there is occasional evidence of genuine psi influences from his social environment. He seems to be selectively attuned to subliminal, repressed hostility emanating from his friends and relations, from innocent bystanders—even from his therapist. Several older observations of my own illustrate this point (Ehrenwald, 1947). Paradoxically, the cumulative experimental evidence indicates that, by and large, he is neither more nor less successful in producing extrachance scores in the statistical type of card-calling tests than nonpatients serving as controls.

Yet the paradox is only apparent. There is reason to believe that precisely because of his crumbling ego defenses he is in danger of being overwhelmed by a steady barrage of telepathic stimuli impinging on him from outside. This triggers frantic attempts on his part to ward off the insidious effects of "psi pollution." The result of this defensive posture is the withdrawn, shut-in type of personality characteristic of the schizophrenic—apparently coupled with psi-missing. He surrounds himself with an exaggerated variant of the Bergsonian filter, with Wilhelm Reich's armor-plating of character, if you like. In the extreme case, he may lapse into a catatonic stupor and become unresponsive to the whole spectrum of stimuli from the outside world.

Nevertheless, here too the occasional emergence of more-organized psi phenomena may be an auspicious development. According to Ullman (1975) telepathic patient responses often usher in a tendency to resume hitherto blocked communication with their environment. I have found that it may be greatly reassuring to the patient to realize its veridical nature. It may improve—if not vindicate—his reality testing. It may allay his irrational anxieties, his fears of "going out of his mind." Indeed, he may cease to be, if he ever has been, a "true schizophrenic." In cases such as these, it is for the therapist to strike a proper balance between the adaptive and maladaptive aspects of psi phenomena, and to refrain from fostering or sustaining delusional ideas of grandeur in the patient.

He may be well advised to realize that despite the partial vindication of their delusional trends (and contrary to R. D. Laing's, Thomas Szasz's, or John Lilly's idealized pictures of the "noble" schizophrenic), paranoia creates a distorted and frankly misleading picture of social reality. "That way madness lies."

2.3. Out-of-Body Experiences

Out-of-body experiences (OBEs) have until recently remained "outside the body" of modern clinical psychiatry. Their closest approximation are reports of autoscopic or extracampine hallucinations (Bleuler, 1930), or states of partial or global depersonalization in organic conditions, in neuroses, or in borderline conditions. My own observations (Ehrenwald, 1974a, p. 229) are representative samples of some psychopathological variants of the OBE.

Yet here, again, the boundary line between the normal, the paranormal, and the pathological is blurred. One of my patients showed very little evidence of psychopathology and was referred to me by a psychoanalytic colleague who was puzzled by the patient's bizarre, out-of-the-ordinary claims. Nor was there any unequivocal evidence of authentic paranormal incidents in his case. He had his first OBE at three or four years of age, following a surgical operation. As an adult, he was persuaded by an amateur "psychic investigator" to develop his apparent gifts, but became increasingly perturbed by them. I therefore discouraged further experimentation with his OBE travels and sought to channel his interests and his drive for self-realization and self-improvement into more realistic directions.

Here, as in some of the clinical vignettes described in the preceding sections, the quest for the paranormal appeared as a miscarriage of otherwise perfectly legitimate aspirations to develop and enhance a dormant human potential. Yet, it should also be recalled that virtually all cases—from the Siberian shaman to Bal Shem, or Robert Monroe (1971), Ingo Swann (1975), and John Lilly (1972), on the contemporary scene—the first OBEs were triggered off by severe stresses or by such life threatening situations as a surgical operation, organic illness, or an anxiety attack. Alternatively, the subject himself may bring about his OBE, as it were, by imposing harrowing physical or spiritual disciplines upon himself.

Indeed, OBEs, sought and unsought, often strike the observer as deliberate attempts at playing Russian roulette with life and death itself. They amount to daring challenges to overcome or deny the reality of death, of personal extinction, and to reach out for the ultimate goal of immortality and the survival of the soul. There can be no doubt that varying degrees of psychopathology are embedded in such ventures. But more often than not, their pathological corollaries are self-inflicted, like the self-mutilations seen in the whirling dervishes or Sufi mystics in the throes of ecstasy. This aspect of the out-of-body experience certainly conforms to the medical model congenial to the Western psychiatrist. But it is only one side of the picture. It goes without saying that the yardstick of normalcy versus abnormality cannot be applied indiscriminately to experiences of this type. Nor can traditional concepts of health and disease tip the balance for or against indication for therapeutic action in a given case. It is an existential choice to be made by the subject of the OBE: it is for him to decide whether he is willing to accept the risk, the challenge, and the beckoning spiritual rewards attending his venture into the unknown.

The accounts of articulate OBE subjects (Keen, 1973; Krishna, 1971; Lilly, 1972) tend to emphasize the blissful, ecstatic nature of the experience, though they do not gloss over its occasionally terrifying aspects. The same is true for the effects of diverse psychedelic drugs, and there is as yet no objective measure to weigh the beneficial versus the potentially harmful effects of drug-induced OBE "trips." Nor do we know enough about the respective parts played by authentic ESP or "remote viewing" involved in the out-of-body experience. It may or may not serve to bolster the same ego defenses as are brought into play in diverse sensory or motor automatisms, in the mediumistic trance, or in certain schizophrenic reactions. It may well be that here, as in human affairs in general, the very effort of trying carries with it its own reward.

2.4. Poltergeist Children and Neurosis in the Family

Reports of poltergeist children are usually written by adults and not by the children themselves. Because they invariably cause a great deal of trouble in the household, the pathological nature of poltergeist incidents has rarely been questioned in the literature.

Stripped of their paranormal aspects, they represent more or less serious behavior problems encountered in disturbed families. Child psychiatrists have described such behavior as a "loudspeaker" expressing an existing conflict in the family situation (Ehrenwald, 1963). As a general rule, the behavior amounts to the youngster's rebellion against a controlling, domineering parental figure. This is true for the family situation in the Seaford (Pratt and Roll, 1958), the Newark, and many other cases. The same pattern can be discerned in the Miami or the Rosenheim poltergeists (Bender, 1974), in which a young adult seemed to be acting out a grudge against his or her employer. In an unusual case recently seen by Montague Ullman, W. G. Roll, and myself, the disturbances centered around a woman in her forties whose symptomatology amounted to paranoia in reverse, as it were, with her social environment seemingly acting out the scenario of paranoid persecutors ganging up against her. The reality of her claims is still under investigation. In typical poltergeist cases, it appears that the emergence of PK too may have a certain restitutive value—at least for the "acting out" youngster. However, given the disturbed family situation, it calls for the treatment of all those involved in the incidents (Roll, 1972; Bender, 1974; Rogo, 1974).

The story popularly described as Jung's poltergeist in Freud's book-case is another variation on the same theme (Jung, 1963). It appears that, in this case, it was Jung's rebellion against his mentor that was responsible for a psychosomatic and psychokinetic chain of events which shook both the bookcase and their friendship to its foundations. Although it would be little short of blasphemy to describe Jung, then in his middle forties, as an overgrown poltergeist child, the conflict underlying the incident closely resembles those seen in the more pedestrian cases mentioned above.

Yet, putting one's finger on a specific psychodynamic configuration is one thing, and charging it with the responsibility for the development of a specific neurotic symptom or paranormal event is a different matter. The fact is that exactly the same psychodynamic conflict and family constellation occur in the "best of families" time and again, while verified poltergeist cases are still occurrences of utmost rarity. We do not know why this should be so. But we do know that we frequently encounter the same problems of specificity of symptom choice in psychoanalysis and psychosomatic medicine. We have to assume that, contrary to Freud's early etiological thinking, genetic or constitutional factors play a much greater role in the causation of specific neurotic, psychosomatic, or parapsychological symptomatology than we were once led to believe.

Despite these gaps in our understanding, the therapeutic implications of the typical poltergeist disturbances follow from their psychodynamics outlined here. The underlying family (or social) conflict has to be brought out in the open. Those involved in the disturbances have to be identified and confronted with their respective parts in the problem. In addition, the familiar strategies or environmental manipulations have to be brought to bear on the social or family group.

A few follow-up reports about the later development of poltergeist children provide useful hints about their therapeutic management. An instructive example is the case of Matthew Manning (1975), author of a precocious autobiography, *The Link*. Matthew was a typical poltergeist child until he reached adolescence. At 18–19, he turned his attention to automatic writing and drawing. Graphic samples of his artistic output at that time are included in the book. They are surprisingly competent pen-and-ink sketches, done in the style of Dürer, Leonardo da Vinci, or Beardsley. Manning himself attributed his art work to "spirit controls" who were guiding his hand.

The striking fact is that Matthew's change of pace to motor auto- matisms and diverse forms of artistic expression went hand in hand with the cessation of his poltergeist activities. Thus, in his case, erratic, uncontrolled, and potentially destructive PK manifestations were trans- formed, channeled, and sublimated into creative activity of a highly organized and socially desirable kind.

It is interesting to note at this point that passages in Jung's *Memories, Dreams, Reflections* (1963) point in the same direction. He describes the weeks and months of self-imposed exile and isolation in his tower at Bollingen following the break with Freud. It was a time of solitary meditation, part of it spent drawing and painting a brilliant array of mandala images, closely reminiscent of the work of anonymous Far Eastern and medieval Christian painters.

We do not know whether and how far a genuine psi factor was involved in these activities, but there is reason to believe that psi is in fact omnipresent in the workshop of genius—if not in the daily lives of ordinary men and women. The available evidence is incomplete and it would be premature to draw any far-reaching conclusions from it. Yet, the material reviewed here goes far to show that psi phenomena—both need- and flaw-determined—are themselves groping attempts at making up or compensating for a flaw or "minus function" in our mental organization. They are unconscious strategies aiming at alleviating the human situation, if not at self-healing.

3. References

Balint, M. Notes on parapsychology and parapsychological healing. *International Journal of Psychoanalysis*, 1955, *36*, 31–35.
Bender, H. Modern poltergeist research: A plea for an unprejudiced approach. In J. Beloff (Ed.), *New directions in parapsychology*. London: Elek Science, 1974.
Bleuler, E. *Textbook of psychiatry*. New York: Macmillan, 1930.

Devereux, G. (Ed.), *Psychoanalysis and the occult.* New York: International Universities Press, 1953.

Ehrenwald, J. Telepathy in dreams. *British Journal of Medical Psychology,* 1942, *19,* 313–323.

Ehrenwald, J. Exploring telepathy. *Journal of the American Society of Psychical Research,* 1947, *41,* 145–154.

Ehrenwald, J. *New dimensions of deep analysis.* New York: Grune & Stratton, 1954.

Ehrenwald, J. The telepathy hypothesis and doctrinal compliance in psychotherapy. *American Journal of Psychotherapy,* 1957, *11,* 359–379.

Ehrenwald, J. *Neurosis in the family.* New York: Harper & Row, 1963.

Ehrenwald, J. *Psychotherapy: Myth and method.* New York: Grune & Stratton, 1966.

Ehrenwald, J. Mother–child symbiosis: Cradle of ESP. *Psychoanalytic Review,* 1971, *58,* 455–466.

Ehrenwald, J. Out-of-the-body experiences and the denial of death. *Journal of Nervous and Mental Disease,* 1974, *159,* 227–233. (a)

Ehrenwald, J. The telepathy hypothesis and schizophrenia. *Journal of the American Academy of Psychoanalysis,* 1974, *2,* 159–169. (b)

Ehrenwald, J. Cerebral localization and the psi syndrome. *Journal of Nervous and Mental Disease,* 1975, *161,* 393–398. (a)

Ehrenwald, J. Possession and exorcism: Delusion shared and compounded. *Journal of the American Academy of Psychoanalysis,* 1975, *3,* 105–119. (b)

Ehrenwald, J. *History of psychotherapy: From healing magic to encounter.* New York: Jason Aronson, 1976.

Ehrenwald, J. Varieties of unorthodox healing. In B. Wolman (Ed.), *Handbook of parapsychology.* New York: Van Nostrand Reinhold, 1977.

Eisenbud, J. Analysis of a presumptively telepathic dream. *Psychiatric Quarterly,* 1948, *22,* 103–135. In G. Devereux (Ed.), *Psychoanalysis and the occult.* New York: International Universities Press, 1953.

Eisenbud, J. *Psi and psychoanalysis.* New York: Grune & Stratton, 1970.

Fodor, N. Telepathy in analysis. In G. Devereux (Ed.), *Psychoanalysis and the occult.* New York: International Universities Press, 1953. (Originally published, 1947.)

Freud, S. Dreams and the occult. In G. Devereux (Ed.), *Psychoanalysis and the occult.* New York: International Universities Press, 1953. (Originally published, 1933.)

Hollos, I. Psychopathologie alltäglicher telepathischer Erscheinungen. *Imago,* 1933, *19,* 529–546. In G. Devereux (Ed.), *Psychoanalysis and the occult.* New York: International Universities Press, 1953.

Jung, C. G. *Memories, dreams, reflections.* New York: Pantheon, 1963.

Keen, S. "We have no desire to strengthen the ego or make it happy," A conversation about ego destruction with Oscar Ichazo. *Psychology Today,* 1973, *7*(2), 64–72.

Krishna, G. *Kundalini: The evolutionary energy in man.* Berkeley, California: Shambala, 1971.

Lilly, J. C. *The center of the cyclone: An autobiography of inner space.* New York: Julian Press, 1972.

Manning, M. *The link.* New York: Holt, Rinehart, Winston, 1975.

Monroe, R. A. *Journeys out of the body*. Garden City, N.Y.: Doubleday, 1971.

Pratt, J. G., and Roll, W. G. The Seaford disturbances. *Journal of Parapsychology*, 1958, *22*, 399–410.

Price, H. H. Mediumship and human survival. In J. M. O. Wheatley and H. L. Edge (Eds.), *Philosophical dimensions of parapsychology*. Springfield, Illinois: Charles C Thomas, 1976.

Rhine, J. B. The problem of psi missing. *Journal of Parapsychology*, 1952, *16*, 90–129.

Roll, W. G. *The poltergeist*. Garden City, N.Y.: Nelson Doubleday, 1972.

Rogo, S. Psychotherapy and the poltergeist. *Journal of the Society of Psychical Research*, 1974, *47*, 433–461.

Schwarz, B. *Parent–child telepathy*. New York: Garrett Publications, 1971.

Servadio, E. Psychoanalysis and telepathy. In G. Devereux (Ed.), *Psychoanalysis and the occult*. New York: International Universities Press, 1953. (Originally published, 1935.)

Servadio, E. A Presumptively telepathic–precognitive dream during analysis. *International Journal of Psychoanalysis*, 1955, *36*, 27–30.

Swann, I. *To kiss earth good-bye*. New York: Hawthorn Books, 1975.

Ullman, M. On the occurrence of telepathic dreams. *Journal of the American Society for Psychical Research*, 1959, *53*, 50–61.

Ullman, M. Parapsychology and psychiatry. In A. M. Freedman, H. E. Kaplan and B. J. Sadock (Eds.), *Comprehensive textbook of psychiatry*. *II* (2nd ed.). Baltimore, Md.: Williams and Wilkins, 1975.

Ullman, M., and Krippner, S., with Vaughan, A. *Dream telepathy*. New York: Macmillan, 1973.

Implications for Philosophy

4

James M. O. Wheatley

1. Introduction

In their textbook on parapsychology, Rhine and Pratt (1957) distinguish two stages of scientific inquiry, the exploratory and the conclusive. The latter is marked by emphasis on reliability and on verification through rigorously designed and executed experiments. The former has as its chief characteristic that "in it the explorer is permitted to range widely, venture freely, and look into everything that might be important . . . without being burdened with too much precautionary concern. It is a more venturesome, a more extravagant phase . . . " (p. 19). I am tempted to say that this chapter is exploratory in Rhine and Pratt's sense, but there is a difficulty. The difficulty is that in philosophy there is nothing really to compare with their other, conclusive, stage of inquiry, and not merely because one does not verify philosophical hypotheses experimentally. Rhine and Pratt also speak of an emphasis on reliability. But reliability is hardly a hallmark of philosophy. Moreover, in philosophy there may not be any truths to verify at all. Whether this is so is itself a philosophical (more strictly, a metaphilosophical) question. Although some hold that there are philosophical truths (see, e.g., Lange, 1970), many take the contrary view that philosophical conclusions, doctrines, and so on are to be construed as proposals and, therefore, as neither true nor false. This is an issue that I shall not discuss. For the present chapter can be taken as exploratory regardless—if not quite in the Rhine—Pratt sense, then in an analogous one. Although it will not "look into everything that might be important," certainly it is tentative,

James M. O. Wheatley · Department of Philosophy, University of Toronto, Toronto, Ontario, Canada.

wide-ranging, and unburdened with too much precautionary concern. Many readers will doubtless find it extravagant, as well—both in the sense of "exceeding the limits of necessity or reason" and in the sense of "wandering."

If philosophical claims are really proposals, some of them are more, or less, plausible than others. To relate this illustratively to the matter at hand, the following example will do. If parapsychology were to produce convincing evidence for personal survival of death, then patently this would show that a philosophical analysis of personal identity in terms of the physical organism's continuity is highly implausible. (Just as, if philosophical claims are true or false, the verification of survival would show that it is *false.*) In fact, of course, though some of its observations appear to be consistent with some possible forms of survival, parapsychology seems to be far from marshaling convincing evidence for life after death. And that observation, as well as any, brings up a difficulty in talking at all about parapsychological implications for philosophy, a difficulty that centers on how very little is known or even highly confirmed in parapsychology today. Myriad observations have been made under excellent experimental conditions, there is a wealth of intriguing suggestions and interesting explorations, and there are possibilities and conjectures aplenty. But there are few if any *solid facts* in parapsychology, in a sense explained by Gardner Murphy (1970). In a solid evaluation of the state of the science, he refers to " 'solid' facts . . . in the sense in which the events that we find described in scientific textbooks are solid facts—that is, ordered within a conceptual system" (p. 3), and he concludes by predicting that "we shall have 'hard facts' in psychical research only when we can relate our many observations to one another in a meaningful way and fit them all into a coherent system of ideas" (p. 16).

Faced, accordingly, with a paucity of solid facts—let alone laws—in parapsychology, one who tries to discuss its philosophical implications cannot help feeling that he is standing on spongy ground. Perhaps it is most appropriate to regard those implications neither as philosophical truths or probabilities nor as philosophical proposals, but as philosophical questions. That is to say, parapsychology's present importance for philosophy lies in its ability to generate philosophical questions, rather than answers: questions about the concept of paranormal, perception, memory, knowledge, reality, science, mental events, the self, death, etc. And in this chapter I shall consider a few of these questions, in some cases very briefly, but in most, I hope, suggestively.

First, though, a prelude. There is a sort of ambivalence toward the advance of parapsychology that I suspect is fairly widespread among those who seek to promote its advance and that is tellingly illustrated by views held by the late Cambridge philosopher C. D. Broad. Among recent outstanding thinkers, he probably contributed most to the development of a philosophical perspective of parapsychology, and I shall consider his definition of the field a little later. For other philosophical discussions of parapsychology, the reader may consult, in addition to works mentioned in the following section, Ducasse (1954, 1961), Flew (1953), Hart (1965), Murphy and Ballou (1960), Price (1959, 1972), Scriven (1962), and Shewmaker and Berenda (1962).

Motivated deeply by a desire to see scientific materialism (which he evidently regarded as incompatible with the existence of paranormal phenomena) totally undermined, Broad was greatly attracted by the apparent potential of psychical research to be its undoing. Contrarily, reflection on some of the possibilities suggested by psychical research—especially in the area of life after death—led him to think that if scientific materialism were after all true, then the world as man's habitation might well be a much nicer place than it would be if scientific materialism were false. Thus parapsychology, as a science judged by many to be capable of making profound discoveries about the mind and its place in nature, thereby telling elusive truths about the mind's potentialities and susceptibilities, is a science apt to both attract and repel by what it promises to disclose. It is all very well and scientifically most interesting to discover, for example, that some dreams foretell events and that cognition sometimes assumes a telepathic cast. But, caution advises, let us not get carried away: Do we really wish to pursue the implications of these seemingly innocuous facts to the extent that more may be revealed about the mind than is in keeping with its own peace?

In an autobiographical essay, Broad (1959) speaks of his strong and enduring interest in parapsychology. He writes:

> I feel in my bones that the orthodox scientific account of man as an undesigned calculating-machine, and of non-human nature as a wider mechanism which turns out such machines among its other products, is fantastic nonsense. . . . I should be sorry if anything so absurd and . . . so dull and boring were to be true. . . . (p. 58)

And he goes on to express longing for "the irrefutable establishment of alleged [paranormal] facts, which, if genuine, would be so palpably inconsistent with this view as to leave it without a leg to stand upon" (p. 58). Elsewhere, though, he strikes a more somber note. At the conclusion of a trenchant examination of personal identity and the question of personal survival after death, Broad (1958) invites reflection:

> It is worthwhile to remember, though there is nothing that we can do
> about it, that the world as it really is may easily be a far nastier place
> than it would be if scientific materialism were the whole truth and
> nothing but the truth. (p. 32)

How, then, did Broad conceive of the area of psychical research or
parapsychology, whose findings, it is plain, caused him to believe that
scientific materialism, for better or for worse, is most probably *not* "the
whole truth and nothing but the truth"?

2. The Concept of Paranormal and Basic Principles

What has become the orthodox view of parapsychology is that it is
the study of the paranormal—paranormal events, occurrences, phenomena, etc. The first question, therefore, is what is meant by the term
"paranormal." I am aware of no answer that is entirely satisfactory, but
probably the most elaborate attempt to define it is Broad's. I shall now
discuss his definition and then comment on some more recent approaches to the problem.

Essentially, Broad's idea is that an event or occurrence is (a)
ostensibly paranormal if its existence seems *prima facie* (presumably in
the opinion of a competent investigator) to conflict with one or more
general principles or assumptions that he calls basic limiting principles;
and (b) *actually* paranormal if it does conflict with some of the principles. In *Religion, Philosophy and Psychical Research,* Broad (1953)
explains what he means by "basic limiting principles" as follows:

> There are certain limiting principles which we unhesitatingly take for
> granted as the framework within which all our practical activities and
> our scientific theories are confined. Some of these seem to be self-evi-
> dent. Others are so overwhelmingly supported by all the empirical facts
> which fall within the range of ordinary experience and the scientific
> elaborations of it . . . that it hardly enters our heads to question them.
> (p. 7)

This description tends, however, to blur the distinction that needs to be
made between the basic limiting principles and the established laws and
theories of science. Broad's reference to the principles as being overwhelmingly supported by empirical facts may be misleading.

Whereas mostly in science, data are surprising because they seem to
be in conflict with some accepted scientific law or theory, generally in
parapsychology, on the contrary, its findings are surprising just because they seem to clash with such a body of assumptions as Broad has
in mind, assumptions that we tacitly suppose are true of the world, ones

that "we unhesitatingly take for granted." Indeed, it is not easy to cite a specific scientific law or proven theory with which established results of parapsychology conflict. It is not so much that, excluding parapsychology, we have scientific reason not to expect its findings, as that, again excluding parapsychology, we have no scientific reason to expect them. To state (what is true) that there are no known scientific laws or theories that *explain* the established findings of parapsychological research by no means implies (what I am inclined to think is false) that those findings actually *contradict* any such laws and theories. It has been *said*—for example, by Wesley Salmon (1968)—that certain parapsychological hypotheses *are* logically incompatible with "well-established portions of physical science" (p. 14), and are highly implausible for that reason. Salmon cites the hypothesis that telepathy involves the instantaneous transference of thought from one person to another and the hypothesis that precognition (interpreted as a "process of direct perception of future occurrences" [p. 14]) involves the transmission of messages backward in time. However, I doubt that any parapsychologist is, or needs to be, committed to either of those hypotheses. In any case, Broad's basic limiting principles, in terms of which he defines "paranormal," are in the main not laws of nature or well-established scientific theories. And this is a point made by Broad himself in a later explanation than the one I have quoted.

In *Lectures on Psychical Research,* Broad (1962) describes the basic limiting principles as follows:

> [They are] mostly of a negative or restrictive kind, which practically everyone who has been brought up . . . under the influence of Western industrial societies assumes without question nowadays. They form the framework within which the practical life, the scientific theories, and even most of the fiction of contemporary industrial civilizations are confined. (p. 3)

It is true that he leaves the distinction between his principles and scientific laws vague, and this is a possible weakness in his account, but at least it is now acknowledged, and hence I believe that this later statement is preferable to the earlier one. Regarding the distinction, Broad (1962) asserts:

> I do not think that it is possible to draw a hard-and-fast line between certain of the most fundamental . . . negative principles of physics, e.g., the Second Law of Thermodynamics, and what I have called "basic limiting principles." But. . . . *most* of the generally accepted laws of nature would *not* count as basic limiting principles. . . . And *all* the basic limiting principles . . . are *tacitly* assumed, but not often explicitly formulated, in treatises on physics . . . and other natural sciences. (p. 4)

Examining the instances Broad gives of basic limiting principles in the two works cited, we find that he gives nine in the earlier (1953) and adds a tenth in the later (1962). The original nine comprise four divisions: (1) general principles of causation, (2) limitations on the action of mind on matter, (3) dependence of mind on brain, and (4) limitations on ways of acquiring knowledge. Both (1) and (4) contain several principles, (2) and (3) one apiece. For illustration, I shall first cite one principle from each of divisions (1) and (4), then summarily state the two principles that make up (2) and (3), and finally quote the principle added in the later work. One of the first-division principles is that "it is self-evidently impossible that an event should begin to have any effects before it has happened" (Broad, 1953, p. 9): *Does precognition conflict with this?* One of the fourth-division principles is that "it is impossible for a person to perceive a physical event or a material thing except by means of sensations which that event or thing produces in his mind" (p. 10): *Does clairvoyance conflict with this?* Principle (2) is to the effect that "it is impossible for an event in a person's mind to produce *directly* any change in the material world except changes in his own brain" (p. 9): *Does psychokinesis conflict with this?* And Principle (3) is to the effect that a necessary "condition of any mental event is an event in the brain of a living body" and that "mental events which are ... experiences of the same person are ... conditioned by brain-events which happen in the same brain" (p. 10): *Does telepathy conflict with this?* Last, the basic limiting principle that appears in 1962 might be seen as a corollary of Principle (3), and I quote it in full:

> As a final example, we take for granted that, when a person's body dies, the personal consciousness, which has been associated with it and expressed through it during his lifetime, either ceases altogether or, if not, ceases to be able to manifest itself in any way to those still living on earth. (p. 4)

(While some of these principles, with their allusions to minds and mental events, are formulated in blatantly dualistic terms, it seems likely that their basic intent could be reformulated in language acceptable to a materialist.)

I have said that the vagueness of the distinction, in Broad's account, between basic limiting principles and scientific laws is a possible weakness of that account. A reason that Broad's view *requires* a distinction between them is that, for him, an "event which seems *prima facie* to conflict only with a well-established law of nature, but *not* with any basic limiting principle, may be called an '*abnormal*' phenomenon [not a *paranormal* one]" (Broad, 1962, p. 4). (Note, incidentally, that an event that seems *prima facie* to conflict with a well-established law of nature *is* abnormal, while an event that seems *prima facie* to conflict with a basic limiting principle is only *ostensibly* paranormal. Or so Broad seems to say.) Broad's account is open to other criticisms, as well. For instance, it does not provide an exhaustive list of the principles; it leaves unclear their logical status and epistemological basis*; and though Broad stresses the point that the principles are characteristic of *Western* thought-systems, he is reticent about how plausible it might seem to persons in the East, who may not accept some of the principles at all, to define "paranormal" as he does.† So unquestionably there is something loose, something arbitrary perhaps, about Broad's definition, but it nevertheless has considerable utility, and, to my knowledge, no superior definition has been proposed.

Broad seems not to question the existence of *ostensibly* paranormal phenomena. He thinks that it is for parapsychology to investigate them, "with a view to discovering whether they are or are not genuinely paranormal" (Broad, 1962, p. 5). But, he adds, its aim "is not merely to ascertain whether there are any genuinely paranormal phenomena. If . . . there are such, then its business is to try to discover the laws governing them" (p. 19). He asserts:

> To allege that a phenomenon is paranormal is to make a purely negative statement about it; it is not . . . to offer any kind of explanation of it. . . . If you hold [certain] . . . phenomena to be paranormal, then you ought to proceed to formulate explicit hypotheses, conflicting with some of the accepted basic limiting principles; to deduce consequences from them which could be experimentally tested; and then to test them by suitably designed experiments. (p. 17)

There can be no doubt that parapsychologists do formulate explicit

---

*An observation by Hesse (1961) is pertinent. She asserts that Broad's "Principles (2)–(4). . . . reduce . . . to the unfalsifiable 'all-and-some' statement: 'For every mental event there is a corresponding physical event in a brain' " and that, consequently, "they cannot be *proved* to be violated" (pp. 298, 299). In logical symbolism (where obvious abbreviations are used—for example, "M" stands for "is a mental event"), the *negation* of the statement to which Hesse says that Principles (2)–(4) reduce is "$(Ex)[Mx \& (y) \sim (Cxy \& (Py \& By))]$." As this statement, which involves a universal negative, cannot be conclusively verified, no event whose occurrence would entail it can be *proved* to occur. This is, indeed, an interesting point, but if we are willing to settle, in science, for some degree of confirmation short of absolute proof, it need not be thought to damage Broad's position. However, if the basic limiting principles are unfalsifiable and if, as many believe, laws of nature are statements that are unfalsified *but falsifiable,* Hesse's point does underscore the distinction between Broad's principles and natural laws.

† See Edge's comment on this point (Wheatley and Edge, 1976: Chapter 1).

hypotheses and test them by suitably designed experiments. What can be doubted, though, is that they often relate their data and hypotheses to basic limiting principles in order to consider with which of the principles they possibly conflict. In fact, when parapsychologists refer to the results of some study or experiment as probably involving a paranormal factor, it is often not clear with what basic limiting principle(s)—if indeed any—the results in question are supposed to conflict. Again, when it is asked whether some phenomenon—e.g., Kirlian photography—involves a paranormal element and hence falls within the range of parapsychology, it is rarely clear whether the answer is thought to depend at all on a conflict between the phenomenon and some basic limiting principles. Thus, it may well be that many parapsychologists simply have different conceptions of the paranormal than Broad's. But if they have, it remains obscure what those conceptions are. Parapsychologists themselves still ask what is meant by "paranormal," and as yet there is no consensus with respect to the answer.

What could be regarded as giving a revised and updated version of Broad's list of basic limiting principles and what is anyhow a worthwhile presentation in its own right is Willis Harman's (1976) recent account of the reason that psychical research is "a bitterly contested battleground" (p. 231). Having set forth ten principles that "the scientific paradigm, until recently, has tended to imply" (p. 230), Harman states that the data of parapsychology—and, as well, data from research into states of consciousness—challenge them all. Yet, he thinks, it was on the basis of the principles he has listed "that the increasingly prestigious scientific world view was able, in the past, to dismiss as of secondary consequence the religious, aesthetic, and intuitive experience of man . . ." (p. 231). Do we, perhaps, have in Harman's exposition the basis for a better definition of "paranormal" than that worked out by Broad? I think not. Obviously, any definition grounded in the idea that parapsychological data are ones that challenge the premises Harman sets forth will, like Broad's definition, make it negative to describe occurrences as paranormal: An occurrence is paranormal if it is not coherent with such and such assumptions, premises, or principles. And we may well think that no definition of "paranormal" is fully satisfactory or more than merely provisional unless it is such that we can, when speaking in accordance with it, say something positive about an event in calling the event paranormal. Paradoxically, however, once the term "paranormal" does connote a positive characteristic, its employment will cease to be appropriate. When enough is known about the occurrences studied by parapsychology for them to be described in terms that, unlike "paranormal" in Broad's sense, convey something positive, it will no longer be significant to refer to them in a way that suggests contrast with the normal. For they themselves will then be normal.

3. The Paranormal, Realities, and Altered States

Meanwhile, two important approaches to the concept of paranormal are being developed by Lawrence LeShan (1969, 1974) and Charles T. Tart (1972, 1975a,b), each of whom is a psychologist and a parapsychologist. Both approaches are relativistic, in a sense, and both are decidedly innovative. Tart's pioneering work, whose matrix is transpersonal psychology, is concerned with much more than the paranormal. But among its prime objectives, on my reading, is an enhanced understanding of the concept of paranormal, coupled with wider scientific appreciation of paranormal phenomena. Here I shall first discuss the way of LeShan and then briefly describe the direction of Tart's course, suggesting finally a possible convergence of the two approaches.

LeShan's approach, in which the concept of *normal* is relativized to what he calls an individual reality (IR), exhibits unusual insight. An IR comprises just those "aspects of reality" to which an individual is perceptually or otherwise responsive and with which he interacts. An IR, LeShan sometimes suggests, is a way-of-being-in-the-world. Most of us inhabit what he calls the common-sense IR, in which, roughly, Broad's basic limiting principles appear truistic, and clairvoyance, telepathy, precognition, etc., seem impossible. But, LeShan thinks, it is possible for some people (sensitives, mystics, and others), some of the time, to live in alternative IRs, to be-in-the-world in other ways: the way of the mystic, for example. And it is LeShan's hypothesis that when one is in the mystical IR, for example, paranormal phenomena seem to him to occur naturally, "that what is *normal* in the mystical IR is *paranormal* in the common-sense IR, and vice versa" (1969, p. 41). His provocative discussion of these points is elaborate. Yet, crucially, if he is wrong in holding that science can be practiced in an IR that is radically unlike the common-sense IR but closely akin to the mystical—and I find his view on this implausible—then he has a problem. For if he is wrong about that, then despite the fact (if it is one) that in the mystical IR the paranormal becomes the normal, from a scientific point of view what we call the paranormal must remain essentially nonnormal, that is, describable only in basically negative terms. I have deprecated LeShan's argument that the pursuit of science is possible in the mystical IR. Let me explain.

LeShan sees the common-sense IR, on one hand, as set over against the clairvoyant IR, the mystical IR, and the IR of modern science, on the other. He appears to regard the latter three as virtually identical: We may call this his equivalence hypothesis. Its first part (clairvoyant IR = mystical IR) is by no means unproblematic; its second part (mystical IR = scientific IR) presents more serious difficulties. LeShan is disposed to take as paradigmatic of the (composite) IR of the mystic, the clairvoyant, and the modern scientist four assumptions that collectively seem to him inconsonant with Broad's basic limiting principles. He derives them from a discussion of mysticism by Bertrand Russell (1929). LeShan (1969) states:

> The IR of the mystic. . . . involves a set of axioms about the universe which . . . Russell has described as having four principles. . . . These are: 1) that there is a better way of knowing than the senses, which, with reason and analysis are ". . . blind guides leading to the morass of illusion"; 2) that there is a fundamental unity and oneness of all things; 3) that time is an illusion; and 4) that all evil is mere appearance. (p. 19)

A few comments. It seems to me that Murphy's suggestion (1952) that the mystical and the paranormal are very different ways of responding to certain needs is more cogent than LeShan's view that the clairvoyant IR and the mystical IR are essentially the same. I find it fairly easy to believe that nonhuman animals have ESP, but very hard to believe that they have mystical experiences. Basically, perhaps, mysticism is a matter of knowledge, but the mystic's knowledge is seemingly incommensurable with ordinary, everyday knowledge. Yet, knowledge through ESP, it seems fair to say, would be like ordinary, everyday knowledge *at least* in being knowledge *about* something. It would not involve the knower's becoming identical, in a sense, with the known. But mystical experiences, as a form of knowing, imply knowing through being one with—not being one or identical with in a strict logical sense, to be sure, but in a special mystical sense that allegedly is ungraspable by a nonmystic. "Thou art that": The religious circumstances of this equation seem to me alien to paranormal transactions *per se.*

It must be acknowledged that LeShan says quite explicitly that in his use of the term "mystic," religious connotations are not included. I wonder, though, if such a quick divorce is possible or realistic, or even quite in keeping with the spirit of LeShan's own explorations. I, in any case, find it much harder than he apparently does to divorce the term from its religious significance. In discussing the mystical, he attends recurrently to the illusoriness of time and evil in the mystical IR, the intuition of pervading oneness, and the noetic theme. Do not such adversions suggest religious connotations? And I wonder, too, if LeShan does not tend to assimilate the mystic's sense of "knowledge" to the "knowledge" of common sense. (In my view, common-sense and *scientific* knowledge, though different in degree, *are* the same in kind.) For instance, in discussing the knowledge aspect of the mystical IR, in one place LeShan (1969, p. 20) speaks of there being "a better source of information than through the senses." Now I do not think that the mystical pertains to information. It is instructive to consult the full Russellian sentence on which LeShan bases his "better source of information" passage. Russell (1929) says:

> The first and most direct outcome of the moment of illumination is belief in the possibility of a way of knowledge which may be called revelation or insight or intuition, as contrasted with sense, reason, and analysis, which are regarded as blind guides leading to the morass of illusion. (p. 9)

Mysticism, accordingly, does indeed have to do with knowledge and illumination. But with information? I strongly doubt it.

Finally, when LeShan brings in the scientific IR and hypothesizes that it is essentially the same as the mystical and the clairvoyant IRs, that is, when we come to the second part of his equivalence hypothesis, the difficulties are compounded: (1) In the clairvoyant IR, LeShan (1969) says, "to *try* is to fail" (p. 94). This, I would think, is simply false of the scientific IR. The IR to which LeShan would assimilate the scientific way-of-being-in-the-world is one in which willing, trying, and effort have no place. But surely the scientist, whatever else he is, is a professional striver, and an IR where trying to do things is impossible or doomed to frustration is scarcely one in which a person could function as a scientist. (2) We are asked to believe that in the mystical experience a sense of completion and fulfillment may be achieved. Yet for the scientist, by contrast, does not precisely this remain permanently out of reach, by nature of his occupation? (3) In the mystical IR, LeShan believes, there can be no decisions. But it seems plain that decision-making is part and parcel of the scientific enterprise.

I conclude that although it is impressive, LeShan's theory is defective. Yet though I myself would hope rather for a nonrelativistic theory, his search for an explanation of psi in terms of the IR concept is audacious, and as it continues, his own position may well be rectified. His most recent book (1976) reached me as I was completing the writing of this chapter and appears to embody notable advances. It is described by LeShan as a "work in progress." Significantly similar to LeShan's approach, I think, is Tart's, and it too seems able to advance our understanding of the paranormal. It is conducted through a study of altered states of consciousness (ASCs). Tart (1972) defines an ASC "as a qualitative alteration in the overall pattern of mental functioning, such that the experiencer feels his consciousness is radically different from the way it functions ordinarily" (p. 1203). Familiar altered states, Tart observes, are dreaming states, states between sleeping and waking, and alcohol intoxication. Other altered states, he continues, are those caused by marijuana, LSD, meditation, and autohypnosis. Thus, it seems, some ASCs are natural, some artificially induced. But Tart's central contention is that science is possible not alone in the ordinary state of consciousness, but in some altered states as well. The purpose of his well-known article in *Science,* Tart (1972) writes, "is to show that it is possible to investigate and work with the important phenomena of ASC's in a manner which is perfectly compatible with the essence of scientific method" (p. 1203). He envisions the development of sciences specific to given states of consciousness, including, we may conjecture, a state of consciousness in which the paranormal (to us) will be the normal. But, and here is an element not apparent in LeShan's theory, he further envisions that in some cases scientific communication will be possible across state lines.

One possibility we can imagine is that data that appear anomalous and paranormal from the standpoint of a scientist who, engaged in one state-specific science, directly observes them will be theoretically explicable in terms of another, but interrelating, state-specific science. Tart (1972) does not mean that work in one state-specific science will validate or invalidate work in a second: "I prefer to say," he explains, "that two different state-specific sciences, where they overlap, provide quite different points of view with respect to certain kinds of theories and data, and thus complement each other" (p. 1207). As Tart observes, there clearly are great difficulties in the way of developing state-specific sciences, yet the program he has in mind does seem to offer considerable, though at present cloudy, promise of better scientific understanding of the nature of psi.

Tart's and LeShan's approaches seem to me convergent, and perhaps if LeShan's insights can somehow be integrated with Tart's vision of state-specific sciences, the result may be more promising than either by itself.* What evidently is required is an ASC or an IR that is

---

*As a preliminary to such integration, it would be necessary to compare in depth and detail the IR approach of LeShan and the ASC approach of Tart, but that task is beyond the scope of this chapter. Also beyond it is an exploration of the relationship between LeShan's and Tart's brand(s) of relativism and both the linguistic relativism associated with the Sapir–Whorf view and the cognitive relativism asso-

altered, or is at variance with common sense, not so much that science as we know it becomes impossible, but enough to assure that, within it, the paranormal (to us) coheres with whatever standards of normalcy are specific to that state or are characteristic of that reality.

The "normalization" of the paranormal, however, most likely lies quite far in the future. For some time to come, presumably, we must make do with an essentially negative notion of the paranormal. Yet, from an intuitive standpoint, this present situation is not as dark as it might appear on a discursive approach. Although the task of stating in positive terms what psi is has proved so far insurmountable, does it not seem that we do possess an intuitive, preanalytic sense of what it is, a sense that we have not yet been able to articulate discursively? A reason for thinking that we do is the fact that Broad's set of basic limiting principles and the comparable set of premises adduced by Harman do their job as well as they do. It seems almost as though they are tailor-made to place psi in an impossible light. To be sure, there are arguments about whether this or that specific principle really belongs in a set such as Broad's,* but in the main the principles included are

---

ciated with T. S. Kuhn's (1970) *The Structure of Scientific Revolutions.* The relationship between Tart's and Kuhn's work is especially intriguing, since Tart likens his states of consciousness to Kuhn's paradigms. Regarding that alleged likeness, however, I am inclined to be skeptical. As for the relationship between LeShan and Tart on one side and linguistic relativism on the other, much more would need to be known about the relations between psi and language before any exploration of it could begin.

*Consider, for instance, the opposing positions of C. J. Ducasse (1959) and Mary Hesse (1961) concerning Broad's three general principles of causation. Ducasse, who holds that it is logically impossible for an effect to precede its cause—i.e., for "backward causation" to occur—argues that it is out of the question to abandon any of the three principles, which say, among other things, that backward causation is indeed impossible. By contrast, Hesse argues that at least two of the principles, and quite possibly all three, "are by no means necessary to physics" (p. 301). (An interesting corollary of Hesse's position is that some events that are paranormal according to Broad's definition and his list of basic limiting principles are part of the subject matter of physics.) It may be wondered how Ducasse, as knowledgeable as he was about parapsychology, could hold backward causation to be impossible. Does not precognition show that it is *not* impossible? Actually, it does not. Although philosophers who hold that it is logically possible for an effect to precede its cause may well cite precognition, if they believe that it occurs, as a case in point (Brier, 1974), those more numerous philosophers who hold that backward causation is logically *im*possible may take an entirely different view of the matter. If *they* are perplexed by the seeming existence of precognition, at least two courses are open to them, apart from revising their conception of causality. One, favored by Ducasse and Broad, is to try to show that what appears to be precognition is really

strikingly apt in their assigned role: to be such that, if they are true, then clairvoyance, telepathy, precognition, psychokinesis, etc., are impossible. Indeed, Peter French (1975) thinks that the problem of parapsychology's challenge is fitly expressed by the statement that *"psychical researchers investigate the occurrence of events which are not possible"* (p. 13). At present, asking what a psi occurrence is will elicit examples or evasion. Let the question be put to us: Being unable to characterize psi in positive terms, we tend, I believe, to fall back on something like, "well, take such and such a principle, and you'll find that psi conflicts with it." But is it not the case that we can come up with such principles only because we have already an intuitive notion of what psi occurrences are, a notion that we exploit in retrieving the principles with which they conflict? Accordingly, the fact that we now know pretty well what has to be the case if psi is impossible augurs well, I think, our eventually being able to frame a positive characterization of it.

4. *"Extrasensory Perception"*

I have been discussing the general concept of paranormal. When we turn to the more specific concepts of extrasensory perception and psychokinesis, further questions arise, which I shall examine only in relation to extrasensory perception. It is notable that telepathy and clairvoyance (ESP) have been regarded by some researchers as paranormal perception and by others as paranormal communication. Obviously, many parapsychologists must have been strongly disposed to view them as some sort of perception: Rhine since he *called* them extrasensory perception, others since the term was so widely adopted. But some, finding so little of a perceptual character about ESP,* have felt

something else (see, e.g., Broad, 1937, 1967, and Ducasse, 1959). The other is to construe precognition as an acausal phenomenon. This is a position explored by Flew (1959) in a discussion of precognition and "the possibility of empirical but non-causal connections," where he asserts that "there might be laws of the form, 'In such and such conditions subjects of such and such a sort always (or to such and such a degree above bogey) guess right:' *where the possibility of causal explanation . . . of the correlation . . . is ruled out"* (p. 426). Thus it seems that precognition, if it occurs, is not apt to change any philosophical minds about the meaning of "cause." As a source of philosophical ideas about causality, physics seems to be far more fertile than parapsychology.

*Consider, for instance, how unlike perception is the ESP apparently attested by the plethysmographic studies of D. Dean and others and by many of the traditional card-guessing experiments. In these examples, there are just no introspectable components such as would give the ESP even a quasi-perceptual character.

impelled toward an alternative way of looking at it. The alternative that seems to have been most popular is to regard it as communication. Actually, F. W. H. Myers, who suggested the term "telepathy" as early as 1882, launched it in a rather "Janus" fashion: While he *christened* it more nearly in terms of perception, he *defined* it as communication. "Telepathy," he states, "may . . . be defined as 'the communication of impressions of any kind from one mind to another, independently of the recognised channels of sense' " (Myers, 1903, p. xxii). We shall recall this definition later. At least one philosopher, it should be noted here, dismisses both these models of ESP. Antony Flew (1954) comments forcibly that " 'telepathy' is not the name of a means of communication, but of a striking correlation between two people's ideas when all means of communication have been eliminated" (p. 24), and he later (1959) decries the term "extrasensory perception" as a complete misnomer.

Admittedly, the distinction between perception and communication becomes blurred in the light of some definitions of "communication," for example, that of the psychologist S. S. Stevens. For him, *"communication is the discriminatory response of an organism to a stimulus"* (quoted by Cherry, 1966, p. 7). But such a definition seems eccentric. I think that normally people would deny that when, for instance, I perceive an ashtray on my desk, I am communicating with it, or it with me. Be that as it may, there probably is little point in arguing the relative merits of the labels "ESP" and "ESC," especially as the neutral term "psi" (which, of course, covers psychokinesis as well as telepathy and clairvoyance) is fast gaining favor in the literature. Nevertheless, investigative strategies in parapsychology are supposedly affected by whether a strategist views ESP as perception, as communication, or as both. Besides, the perception/communication distinction is related to another. The latter is perhaps more substantive and appears to deserve attention. We may ask how, in the context of ESP, we are to distinguish between *medium* and *message.* (McLuhan notwithstanding, the distinction appears worthy of pursuit.) Some experimental work has viewed this distinction (see, for example, the important paper on "ESP over distance: research on the ESP channel" [Osis, Turner, and Carlson, 1971]), but so far it remains challenging. Evidently it is related in a way—indefinite, at present—to yet a third distinction: between ESP as a *process* and ESP as a *product.** Parapsychologists, I believe, should be mindful of this third distinction, although it may differ only verbally

*See Black (1952, pp. 194–195) on the process–product shift vis-a-vis "education," "selection," and like terms.

from the second. Still, while it does not seem implausible to identify the *message* of the second distinction with the *product* of the third, one senses that the *medium* of the former and the *process* of the latter are really distinct. Intuitively, "medium" appears to denote something *out there*, "process" something *in us*. If ESP is assumed to be explicable, somehow, in terms of an organism's nervous system, then that way of looking at the medium and the process seems intelligible. The process is activity of a kind *within* the organism, the medium is whatever it is *external to* the organism that conveys the psi signals to it. If, however, we think of ESP as a phenomenon not functionally dependent on the physical organism at all, but wholly a matter of mind, then it is not obvious what we could mean by talk of a medium that exists "outside" the mind and a process that occurs "inside" it.

I am sure that there is much more to be said about how ESP as a process may relate to the medium (or channel) of ESP, but I lack the knowledge to say it. For present purposes, I shall arbitrarily conflate the second and third distinctions and provisionally relate the conflation to the first. Consider, accordingly, an experiment in which paranormal results are obtained by use of a plethysmograph, which monitors purely behavioral changes in the subject (S): notably, slight changes in the volume of a finger. These changes (of which S is unaware) are found to be correlated in a statistically significant way with times (unknown to S) at which the agent, in another room, looks at certain cards. If we describe the results of this experiment as an instance of ESP, it seems likely that we have foremost in mind the process, medium, or means whereby something paranormal has occurred. Now, by way of contrast, think of the case of a precognitive dream in which the dreamer sees herself winning at the racetrack by betting on such and such a horse. If we declare *this* to be an instance of ESP, we seem to be referring primarily to a certain result or product; if you will, not to the medium but to the message: the content of the dream, rather than the means by which it was induced. Having now conflated the second and third distinctions, we can try to relate the conflux (product—message versus process—medium) to our first distinction (perception versus communication) as follows. Simply, might we not consider the dream case (where the emphasis is on product—message) as an instance of extrasensory perception and the plethysmograph one (where it is on process—medium) as an instance of extrasensory communication? I am aware that what I have said about our three distinctions is exceedingly sketchy. But if the term ESP can, in various contexts, denote perception (or quasi-perception*), communication, a medium, a message, a product, and a process, then the somewhat indiscriminate use of it that is now common may be hindering discovery.

A final word about the perception/communication distinction. It seems probable that there are some experimental cases of ESP (perhaps some of the card-guessing experiments carried out under conditions that exclude telepathy) in which we would have to say that the paranormal events bear no resemblance to either perception or communication. In other words, I suspect that we must say of *some* instances of ESP what Flew, as we have noted, seems disposed to say of all of them—that they can plausibly be classed as neither perception nor communication.

5. Psi: Universal and Nonphysical?

In *The New York Times* not long ago (Rensberger, 1976), there was an engaging article on the reality of a primate species known as Bigfoot or Sasquatch.

> Within the vast forest wilderness of the Pacific Northwest [the *Times* relates] there may live a species of shy, furry manlike creatures, perhaps relict and declining survivors from a time before modern man evolved.
> And then again there may not. (p. 33)

Having described various pieces of evidence, reports, and alleged sightings, Rensberger (1976, p. 62) quotes an anthropologist, John Napier, as saying: "I am convinced that the Sasquatch exists, but whether it is all that it is cracked up to be is another matter altogether." Dr. Napier's attitude is probably similar to that of many scientists and philosophers regarding psi. It exists, no doubt, but is it all that it is cracked up to be?

Of course, in our case the situation is complicated by the fact that psi is cracked up to be different things by different observers. Let us consider two representative examples of disputable claims made about psi: (1) Psi is cracked up by some parapsychologists as being something that practically everyone has in some measure, whether or not he is aware of it, and (2) it is cracked up, again by some parapsychologists, as being *nonphysical.* In the first case, the outcome seems to have little

---

*I include this alternative mainly out of deference to those who hold that in dreams genuine perception does not occur, thus opposing the view that dreams constitute a form of genuine, but delusive, perception. The issue itself cannot be gone into here, however.

philosophic importance; in the second, it surely has a great deal. I shall now discuss each case in turn.

(1) It seems unreasonable to me to *believe* that everyone, or nearly everyone, possesses a measure of psychic ability. On the contrary, what little hard evidence there is suggests, to my mind, that most people simply do not have psychic experiences or capabilities at all. True, as an *assumption* or a *working hypothesis,* the universality of psi among human beings, among mammals, etc., is innocuous, but at the same time its heuristic value seems quite limited. In any case, the extent to which psychic abilities are distributed among humans (for example), though of major parapsychological interest, appears to lack direct philosophical importance. Philosophical problems of perception, for instance, are little affected by the fact that most people, rather than a few, can hear; similarly, philosophical problems in the logic of discovery are little affected by the fact that few persons are creative scientists. Why should it matter philosophically whether most humans, rather than (as seems to be the case) relatively few, can perceive extrasensorily or exercise PK? It is all too apparent, to be sure, that if clairvoyance were as easily and as widely employed as vision; if everyone could, when he wished, tell telepathically what another were feeling or thinking; if normally we precognized the future as readily as we remember the past*; and if we could psychokinetically operate machines (say) as willingly as in fact we operate them manually; then all this would so alter and disrupt human societies as to make them unimaginably different than they are.† (It

---

*Actually, the sort of super-precognition that I am envisioning would presumably be wider than memory. For a seeming difference between memory and precognition is that whereas one can remember, strictly speaking, only what is in his *own* past, a corresponding restriction is not usually thought to apply to precognition.

†Would there still be a major-league baseball season? It might be pointless for there to be one, if not impossible. If there were a season, we would know beforehand how everything would turn out, as we now know how everything turned out *last* season. If there were not, we would not, of course, be able to say who *would* have won the American League batting championship (for instance) if the season *had* taken place, any more than we can now say that if last Sunday's game had not been rained out, the Tigers would have won it. Precognition, I take it, even super-precognition, does not include knowledge of the truth-values of undecidable conditionals. So if the season does not take place, we shall not know, even with the help of our super-precognition, how things would have turned out if it had taken place; and if it does take place, then we shall know in advance just what will happen—indeed, every player will foreknow the play-by-play account of every game: in which case, there would seem to be no need, even if it would be possible, for the games to be actually played (with the help of PK?). A pretty problem for the Commissioner (especially since he, and not only he, would know what his decision would be before he made it)!

might, too, unimaginably reshape philosophy itself.) But happily, such surreal possibilities seem to be one form of shock that the future does not hold for us. [At least until we die! If postmortal survival occurs, it is possible (though there seems no reason to think) that it does so in circumstances in which some such "surreal possibilities" are indeed realized. One thinks here of Moncrieff's theory, which derives from doctrines of Bergson, that "the function of the sense-organs is to restrict or canalize the clairvoyant powers which every sentient organism has; to limit them . . . by shutting out what is biologically irrelevant" (Moncrieff, 1951, p. 7; the quotation is from H. H. Price's Foreword). At bodily death, such restrictions as the nervous system imposes would be removed, and the surviving individual might find himself in a seemingly chaotic situation, bombarded with uncontrolled psi effects in such multiplicity as to imperil his sanity. This, at least, seems to be a consequence of coupling a Bergsonian view of the function of the brain with a doctrine of survival after bodily death. (Recall Broad: "The world as it really is may easily be a far nastier place. . . .")]

If, less unrealistically now, we imagine telepathy (for example) to become appreciably, but not overwhelmingly, more common than it is, we may ask whether *that* state of affairs could be expected to have major philosophic impact. As I have implied, I take the answer to be negative. But a negative answer does not mean that an epidemic of telepathy would have *no* philosophical consequences. Although it would not result in a solution of philosophical problems, some of them might come to be viewed in a changed perspective. As a brief illustration, a few comments by A. J. Ayer on the problem of knowledge of other minds will serve. First, though, I would like to advert to the problem of knowledge in general, concerning which the philosophical implications of parapsychology seem not to be far-reaching. It is, I think, less a matter of the psi-confronted philosopher's being required to make essential changes in his conception of knowledge than of his having to allow for the possibility that some persons can acquire information paranormally, and thus to make room, within his *present* theory, for this unusual way in which true beliefs may be sufficiently justified to have the status of knowledge. As far as we know, there is (at most) very little paranormal knowledge anyway. Most of the time, experimental indications of the occurrence of psi in a certain context are entirely consistent with the nonexistence in that context of paranormal *knowledge.* Indeed, so far as *experimental* parapsychology goes, there do not seem to be *any* findings that strongly suggest genuine knowledge paranormally acquired.

I shall proceed now with the promised illustration involving the problem of our knowledge of other minds. Ayer (1954, Chapter 8; 1956, Chapter 5) has occasionally and soundly argued that the possibility of telepathy is of no help to one perplexed about how he can possibly know what is going on in someone else's mind. According to Ayer, the crux of the matter is that my telepathic awareness of your pain is indeed *my* awareness of *your* pain. If I doubt that I can ever know for sure that you are in pain, then my doubt can withstand a telepathic experience on my part at least as much as it can withstand your telling me that you are in pain. No experience of mine, even if it *is* a telepathic awareness of your pain, can guarantee itself as being such an awareness. In one work, Ayer (1940) refers to the possibility that a person, perhaps telepathically, might feel pain in another's body. In such a case, he remarks, "we should still, according to our present conventions, be obliged to say that if A did feel the pain in B's body, the pain which he felt was not numerically the same as that which was felt by B" (p. 142). Ayer (1940) then conjectures that if occurrences of this kind became common:

> We should eventually alter our way of speaking so as to allow, in a case such as that which I am now considering, of there being only a single feeling of pain which was experienced by both A and B. . . . we should admit the possibility that [the series of experiences that constituted the histories of two different people] . . . could occasionally intersect. (p. 142)

But although our way of speaking might be altered, if, as we are imagining, telepathy became a lot more common, still the essential problem of other minds would remain: How can I know that, for example, you are in pain? In the changed circumstances, this question would amount to how can I know that you are now sharing the pain that I feel? Telepathy would not have brought the answer any nearer.

It might, incidentally, be thought that a shorter way to show that telepathy cannot contribute to the other-minds *problem* is to point out that it already presupposes *other minds.* However, this would be to use "telepathy" in Myers's sense, which I referred to earlier and which R. H. Thouless (1974) has described as being no longer current. Remarking an ambiguity in the term, he says that most parapsychologists do not mean by it what Myers meant by it, and he proposes that we distinguish the two senses by using the terms "telepathy$_A$" and "telepathy$_B$." The latter signifies Myers's sense of "success in an ESP situation . . . which is due to direct mind-to-mind transmission"; the former signifies the current sense of "success in an ESP situation in which there is no external target..." (pp. 421–422). Although it is clear that telepathy$_B$ presupposes other minds, telepathy$_A$ may not: Much depends on the force of Thouless's adjective "external."

In sum, even if those who crack psi up to be something that everyone has are right, it does not seem to make much philosophical difference.

(2) In turning next to the second of our two examples of disputable claims about psi, the claim that it is nonphysical, we encounter a great potential for philosophic impact. Among current issues in philosophy few seem harder to settle than the identity theory of the mind–body relationship. Confronted with the problem of the relationship between mental and physical events, to which traditional answers are the theories of interactionism, epiphenomenalism, parallelism, etc., the identity theorists cut the Gordian knot. They maintain that mental events, such as sensations, visual images, and feelings of nausea, are precisely *identical with* states or processes in the brain. "There is nothing in the universe over and above the entities postulated by physics," one identity theorist has recently declared (Smart, 1976, p. 535). Yet, while some philosophers argue subtly and vigorously for the plausibility of the identity theory, others find it merely perverse. C. J. Ducasse (1948) writes:

> No evidence . . . can be offered to support [it] . . . , because it is in fact but a disguised proposal to make the words "thought," "feeling," "sensation," "desire," and so on, denote facts quite different from those which these words are commonly employed to denote. To say that those words are but other names for certain chemical or behavioral events is as grossly arbitrary as it would be to say that "wood" is but another name for glass. . . . Certain mental events are doubtless connected in some way with certain bodily events, but they are not those bodily events themselves. The connection is not identity. (p. 7)

If, as Ducasse says, no evidence can be offered to support the identity theory, can any be offered to refute it? The situation appears about as hopeless as the kindred one that Fichte portrayed nearly two centuries ago as he pondered the antagonism between two systems of philosophy—idealism and dogmatism, where by "dogmatism" he meant a system that entails materialism. Fichte (in Heath and Lachs, 1970) declares:

> Neither of these two systems can directly refute its opposite, for their quarrel is about the first principle, which admits of no derivation from anything beyond it; each of the two, if only its first principle is granted,

refutes that of the other; each denies everything in its opposite, and they have no point at all in common from which they could arrive at mutual understanding and unity. Even if they appear to agree about the words in a sentence, each takes them in a different sense. (p. 12)

Almost, Fichte might have been talking about the sides in the battle over the identity theory. For my part, and I doubt that I am unique, I am quite unable to accept that discomfiting theory, yet equally unable to disprove it.

Now regrettably (but understandably) it is not clear just what is meant by those parapsychologists who contend that psi is nonphysical. If, however, it could eventually be established that psi is not physical in the sense in which brain states are physical, especially if "psi" in this connection could be shown to denote certain experiences, then this would have a plain and valuable bearing on the decidability of the identity theory. Moreover, if parapsychology could show that in particular some memories can occur independently of the brain—a possibility evidently presupposed by anyone who holds the belief that personal survival after death is at least conceivable*—then that would surely tend to divest the identity view of any plausibility it now has. Philosophically, therefore, for the reasons I have mentioned and others besides, the question of psi's physicality is highly sensitive.

Among philosophically significant problems of parapsychology, the most important may be the question, obliquely referred to just now, of personal survival of bodily death. Once central to the interests of psychical researchers, this intractable question was for many years all but ignored by most workers in the field. But now, with pertinent new research strategies, including research into out-of-body experiences, being developed in parapsychology, and with today's burgeoning interest in thanatology in many quarters (see, e.g., Moody, 1975 and Toynbee, 1969), the survival problem appears to be regaining lively attention. If parapsychology were to verify the survival hypothesis, the impact on philosophy, as on almost all human activities and commerce, would be immeasurable. However, it seems to me that at least in the near future that hypothesis is unlikely to be either verified or falsified.

Since philosophers have argued, convincingly to my mind, that logical considerations preclude the possibility of a person's existing

*An exception has to be made in the case of those whose conception of survival takes the form of belief in (a) reincarnation and (b) the nonexistence of the surviving person during periods between successive incarnations (which would amount to a conception of survived personal existence across temporal gaps, as it is put).

without a body,* evidently the survival hypothesis must be put in terms of the relationship between our ordinary physical bodies and the hypothetical astral (etheric,† spiritual) bodies that we are sometimes said to possess in addition to our physical ones. If parapsychology could establish the existence of such hypothetical entities as astral bodies, then that might offer a way of so posing the survival hypothesis as to accord it the crucial property, which I believe that it has hitherto lacked, of being scientifically falsifiable. Yet, the concept of astral body, in its present state, is so crude and nebulous that its scientific inutility is plain to be seen; hence, it is by no means clear that parapsychology *could* establish the existence of astral bodies‡ even if there are such entities. Greater optimism concerning a search for them would be allowable, perhaps, if it were not so intriguingly difficult to study out-of-body experiences and behavior in nonhuman animals. But as things stand, optimism would surely be misplaced: Astral bodies, if real, may continue to elude scientific detection. All the same, if we did come to know that persons possess them, it might be possible to discover whether such bodies can exist and function independently of our ordinary physical bodies. And if such functional independence were shown experimentally to be highly improbable, I think that this would provide grounds for regarding the survival theory itself as highly improbable. On the other hand, if that independence were to gain strong experimental support, this could well afford a rationale for regarding certain observations,¶ buttressed by positive results of yet-to-be-designed experiments, as providing genuine confirmation of the hypothesis that at least some persons survive death.

6. Conclusion

Discernible in the course of this chapter is an imprecise distinction, within the general philosophical concern with parapsychology, between (a) interest in parapsychological concepts themselves and (b) scrutiny of parapsychology for its possible effects on matters of philosophical con-

---

*See, for example, Broad (1962), Flew (1972), Penelhum (1970), and Wheatley (1965); but compare Edge (1976), Lewis (1973), and Nayak (1968).

†Sometimes a distinction is made *between* the astral and the etheric body, but this is a nicety that I need not try to explore.

‡For convenience, I freely use the familiar term even though, in an obvious sense, I do not know what I am talking about.

¶For example, observations of such sorts as have sometimes in the past been prematurely taken as indicating survival.

cern outside of parapsychology. An instance of (b), evidently, is attention to such parapsychological findings and conjectures as seem to bear on philosophical views of the mind—body problem. An example of (a) is the philosopher's interest in the concept of paranormal and how to explicate it. Some will object at this point that the meaning of "paranormal" is clearly a *parapsychological* question, not a philosophical one. But their objection, I believe, invites recollection of this important point made by H. H. Price (1940), who has long been concerned with the philosophical implications of parapsychology:

> Those who say that the study of supernormal phenomena may safely be left to the experts, and is none of the philosopher's business, seem to be deceived by a false analogy. For in this field there *are* as yet no experts in the sense intended, the sense in which we speak of experts in Physics or Chemistry or Physiology. All we can say is that some people are more familiar with the facts and others less. When once a science has established itself, by devising some comprehensive hypothesis which will unify all the phenomena within its field, even though in a provisional manner; and when, consequently, it has been able to formulate with tolerable clearness the questions it wishes to ask, and has devised a reliable experimental technique which can be trusted to provide the answers—once all this has been accomplished, we *can* draw a sharp distinction between the people who are experts in that science . . . and the philosophers who are not. But Psychical Research is not yet in this happy position. (p. 366)

For notwithstanding the progressive changes that have occurred since Price wrote, regrettably—and curiously—it is still true of parapsychology that it is not in the happy position he described.

7. References

Ayer, A. J. *The foundations of empirical knowledge.* London: Macmillan, 1940.
Ayer, A. J. *Philosophical essays.* London: Macmillan, 1954.
Ayer, A. J. *The problem of knowledge.* Baltimore, Md.: Penguin Books, 1956.
Black, M. *Critical thinking* (2nd ed.). New York: Prentice-Hall, 1952.
Brier, B. *Precognition and the philosophy of science: An essay on backward causation.* New York: Humanities Press, 1974.
Broad, C. D. The philosophical implications of foreknowledge. *Proceedings of the Aristotelian Society,* 1937, *Supplementary Volume 16,* 177–209.
Broad, C. D. *Religion, philosophy and psychical research.* London: Routledge & Kegan Paul, 1953.
Broad, C. D. *Personal identity and survival. (The thirteenth Frederic W. H. Myers memorial lecture.)* London: Society for Psychical Research, 1958.

Broad, C. D. Autobiography. In P. A. Schilpp (Ed.), *The philosophy of C. D. Broad.* New York: Tudor, 1959.

Broad, C. D. *Lectures on psychical research.* New York: Humanities Press, 1962.

Broad, C. D. The notion of "precognition." In J. R. Smythies (Ed.), *Science and ESP.* New York: Humanities Press, 1967.

Cherry, C. *On human communication: A review, a survey, and a criticism* (2nd ed.). Cambridge: M.I.T. Press, 1966.

Ducasse, C. J. *Is a life after death possible? (The Agnes E. and Constantine E. A. Foerster lecture on the immortality of the soul.)* Berkeley and Los Angeles: University of California Press, 1948.

Ducasse, C. J. The philosophical importance of "psychic phenomena." *Journal of Philosophy,* 1954, *51,* 810–823.

Ducasse, C. J. Broad on the relevance of psychical research to philosophy. In P. A. Schilpp (Ed.), *The philosophy of C. D. Broad.* New York: Tudor, 1959.

Ducasse, C. J. *A critical examination of the belief in a life after death.* Springfield, Ill.: Charles C Thomas, 1961.

Edge, H. L. Do spirits matter? Naturalism and disembodied survival. *Journal of the American Society for Psychical Research,* 1976, *70,* 293–301.

Flew, A. *A new approach to psychical research.* London: Watts, 1953.

Flew, A. Telepathy and statistics. *Literary Guide,* 1954, *69*(10), 22–24.

Flew, A. Broad and supernormal precognition. In P. A. Schilpp (Ed.), *The philosophy of C. D. Broad.* New York: Tudor, 1959.

Flew, A. Is there a case for disembodied survival? *Journal of the American Society for Psychical Research,* 1972, *66,* 129–144.

French, P. A. (Ed.). *Philosophers in wonderland.* St. Paul, Minn.: Llewellyn Publications, 1975.

Harman, W. W. The societal implications and social impact of psi phenomena. In J. D. Morris, W. G. Roll, and R. L. Morris (Eds.), *Research in parapsychology 1975.* Metuchen, N.J.: Scarecrow Press, 1976, 225–242.

Hart, H. *Toward a new philosophical basis for parapsychological phenomena. (Parapsychological monographs No. 6.)* New York: Parapsychology Foundation, 1965.

Heath, P., and Lachs, J. (Eds.), *Fichte: Science of knowledge.* New York: Appleton-Century-Crofts, 1970.

Hesse, M. B. *Forces and fields: The concept of action at a distance in the history of physics.* London: Thomas Nelson, 1961.

Kuhn, T. S. *The structure of scientific revolutions* (2nd ed.). Chicago: University of Chicago Press, 1970.

Lange, J. *The cognitivity paradox: An inquiry concerning the claims of philosophy.* Princeton, N.J.: Princeton University Press, 1970.

LeShan, L. *Toward a general theory of the paranormal: A report of work in progress. (Parapsychological monographs No. 9.)* New York: Parapsychology Foundation, 1969.

LeShan, L. *The medium, the mystic, and the physicist.* New York: Viking Press, 1974.

LeShan, L. *Alternate realities.* New York: M. Evans, 1976.

Lewis, H. D. *The self and immortality.* London: Macmillan, 1973.

Moncrieff, M. M. *The clairvoyant theory of perception.* London: Faber & Faber, 1951.

Moody, R. A. *Life after life.* Covington, Ga.: Mockingbird Books, 1975.

Murphy, G. The natural, the mystical, and the paranormal. *Journal of the American Society for Psychical Research,* 1952, *46,* 125–142.

Murphy, G. Are there any solid facts in psychical research? *Journal of the American Society for Psychical Research,* 1970, *64,* 3–17.

Murphy, G., and Ballou, R. O. (Eds.). *William James on psychical research.* New York: Viking Press, 1960.

Myers, F. W. H. *Human personality and its survival of bodily death* (Vol. 1). London: Longmans, Green, 1903.

Nayak, G. C. Survival, reincarnation, and the problem of personal identity. *Journal of the (Indian) Philosophical Association,* 1968, *11,* 131–143.

Osis, K., Turner, M. E., Jr., and Carlson, M. L. ESP over distance: Research on the ESP channel. *Journal of the American Society for Psychical Research,* 1971, *65,* 245–288.

Penelhum, T. *Survival and disembodied existence.* New York: Humanities Press, 1970.

Price, H. H. Some philosophical questions about telepathy and clairvoyance. *Philosophy,* 1940, *15,* 363–385.

Price, H. H. Parapsychology and human nature. *Journal of Parapsychology,* 1959, *23,* 178–195.

Price, H. H. *Essays in the philosophy of religion.* New York: Oxford University Press, 1972.

Rensberger, B. Is it Bigfoot, or can it be just a hoax? *The New York Times,* June 30, 1976, pp. 33; 62.

Rhine, J. B., and Pratt, J. G. *Parapsychology: Frontier science of the mind.* Springfield, Ill.: Charles C Thomas, 1957.

Russell, B. *Mysticism and logic.* New York: Norton, 1929.

Salmon, W. C. Inquiries into the foundations of science. In D. L. Arm (Ed.), *Vistas in science.* Albuquerque: University of New Mexico Press, 1968.

Scriven, M. The frontiers of psychology: Psychoanalysis and parapsychology. In R. G. Colodny (Ed.), *Frontiers of science and philosophy.* Pittsburgh, Pa.: University of Pittsburgh Press, 1962.

Shewmaker, K. L., and Berenda, C. W. Science and the problem of psi. *Philosophy of Science,* 1962, *29,* 195–203.

Smart, J. J. C. The revival of materialism. *The Listener,* 1976, *95,* 535–536.

Tart, C. T. States of consciousness and state-specific sciences. *Science,* 1972, *176,* 1203–1210.

Tart, C. T. *States of consciousness.* New York: Dutton, 1975. (a)

Tart, C. T. (Ed.). *Transpersonal psychologies.* New York: Harper & Row, 1975. (b)

Thouless, R. H. Letter to the editors. *Journal of Parapsychology,* 1974, *38,* 421–422.

Toynbee, A. *Man's concern with death.* New York: McGraw-Hill, 1969.

Wheatley, J. M. O. The question of survival: Some logical reflections. *Journal of the American Society for Psychical Research,* 1965, *59,* 202–210.

Wheatley, J. M. O., and Edge, H. L. (Eds.). *Philosophical dimensions of parapsychology.* Springfield, Ill.: Charles C Thomas, 1976.

Implications for Religious Studies   5

Robert H. Thouless

1. Parapsychology, Religion, and Nonordinary Reality

A distinguishing characteristic of all religions is their assumption of the existence of some kind of nonordinary reality which may be called "the spiritual world." All religions have some practices which have the purpose of establishing relationship with this supernatural world; prayer is an obvious example. Different religions differ, however, in the accounts they give of this spiritual world and also in the details of the practices they adopt to maintain relationships with it. The fact that religions are concerned with a nonordinary reality and with ways of behaving with respect to it entails that religious thinking is related to parapsychology. This is because the existence of the postulated nonordinary reality and the effectiveness of means of establishing a relationship with it belong to the class of problems with which parapsychology is concerned.

Certainly there are religious problems which cannot reasonably be expected to be resolved by parapsychology. It is difficult to see, for example, how any parapsychological observation or experiment could bear directly on the central religious question of the existence of God. Nevertheless, parapsychological findings may bear indirectly on even such a problem as this. Belief in God or in any spiritual reality has seemed to many people to have become impossible, because these beliefs contradict the expectations raised by the scientific views which have come down to us from the last century. These views regard reality as being bounded by the physical world and necessarily exclude any spiritual world. Parapsychological investigations tend to undermine this

Robert H. Thouless · Cambridge University, Cambridge, England.

"physicalistic" view of the world and, thus, to remove one of the obstacles to religious belief. The experiments, for example, which have demonstrated the existence of extrasensory perception and of psycho-kinesis have been sufficient to make it clear that the world is much more complicated than the physicalist view supposed, and this conclusion has been strengthened by the results of later research. Parapsychological research seems to reveal a world in which it is more reasonable to suppose that God and the supernatural may play a part.

A somewhat similar line of thought is suggested by LeShan's view of "alternate realities" (LeShan, 1976). The observation of the reality of paranormal events which seem to be inconsistent with the happenings of the world of common sense leads to the possibility that what at first may seem to be different and even contradictory pictures of the world may both be true. It would seem, therefore, to be rash to reject the world of the supernatural merely because it does not seem consistent with the world of everyday experience.

2. Parapsychology and Religious Beliefs

In addition to providing some empirical basis for religious belief in general, parapsychological findings may also be said to bear on some specific aspects of religious belief.

2.1. Miracles

One area of religious belief that can be related to parapsychology is the much-discussed question of miracles. Miracles are regarded from the religious point of view as spiritual interventions in the course of events. Since Hume criticized the notion of miracles in the eighteenth century, the reports of miracles in religious narratives have seemed to many to be an obstacle to the acceptance of any religious faith. This opinion has been shared by many theologians who do not accept those parts of the Christian records which assert the occurrence of miraculous events.

Accounts of miracles seem, however, to be an integral part of such records as the Gospels and these records are much altered if the miraculous element is simply left out. A study of parapsychology sug-gests an alternative. At least some of the reported miracles may be true accounts of paranormal events which owe their religious significance to the fact that such paranormal events were believed to occur more commonly in the lives of those who were at an advanced spiritual level.

An examination of the miracles reported in the New Testament shows that many of these could have been paranormal events (of ESP, of PK, of precognition, or of paranormal healing), and they were commonly regarded by observers as evidence of the spiritual authority of the one who performed them.

2.1.1. Miracles of the ESP Type

One of the many accounts of miracles of the ESP type is that of the woman of Samaria to whom Jesus said that she had had five husbands and that she was at that time living with a man who was not her husband. This demonstration of ESP is reported to have so surprised her that she replied that the speaker must be a prophet, afterward making the stronger suggestion that he must be "the Christ." The grounds for this assertion was the ESP powers shown by Jesus, of which she gave a somewhat exaggerated account when she referred to him as "a man who told me all that I ever did" (*Holy Bible,* John 4:19,29).

Similar stories are told of other religious leaders. It is reported that a hermit who was reluctant to believe in the Buddha's holiness believed only after the Buddha had performed several miracles. The first of these was of the ESP kind when the Buddha, understanding "by the power of his mind" that the hermit did not want him to be present at a sacrifice, did not, on that day, pay his customary visit to the hermit. This was sufficient only to convince the hermit that the Buddha had great faculties; full acceptance of his holiness came only after greater experience of his powers (Müller, 1881, p. 124 ff.).

A related, more recent example within the Christian tradition is that of the Curé d'Ars, who had the reputation of being able to read men's hearts and who seems to have owed his success as a confessor in large measure to this telepathic ability (Trochu, 1927, p. 286).

2.1.2. Miracles of the PK Type

As has already been pointed out, a not uncommon form of miraculous event was one that could be regarded as a case of ESP. Some other reports of miraculous events suggest the operation of PK, although often on a scale which has not been paralleled in the parapsychological laboratory. An example is to be found in the reported multiplication of food by Jesus (*Holy Bible,* Mark 6: 35 ff. and 8:1 ff.). While acquaintance with experimental work on PK may make such stories appear less incredible than is commonly supposed, they receive no direct support from parapsychological research; experimental work on PK has not yet achieved results on this scale.

2.1.3. Miracles of the Precognition Type

Another region in which there is contact between religious studies and parapsychology is that of prophecy. There is ample experimental evidence of the capacity for precognition in, at any rate, some subjects (Rhine, 1953, p. 20 ff.). The reports of prophecies in religious writings suggest a capacity for precognition among the more successful prophets, and their credibility is obviously affected by the experimental evidence for precognition. Ancient prophecies, of course, were recorded under conditions which make them no longer verifiable, but a knowledge of the relevant parapsychological research should make students of religion realize that the truth of such reports is not incredible—although we cannot, in any particular case, say that an alleged prophecy was a genuine case of precognition.

2.1.4. Miracles of the Healing Type

The miracles of healing reported in the Gospels and elsewhere in religious literature may also appear more credible in the light of parapsychology. At the present time, it must be admitted that the reality of paranormal healing (as distinct from healing by suggestion) has been less clearly demonstrated than that of ESP, PK, and precognition. A study of the Lourdes healings has been made by Donald J. West (1957) and a more general study of "faith healing" by Louis Rose (1968). Both of these investigators found the evidence they examined to be unconvincing, although they remained open to the possibility that further evidence could be more conclusive. It is to be hoped that future research will clarify this area of parapsychology.

Many of the inquiries into the reality of paranormal healing have taken the somewhat unsatisfactory form of asking whether particular cases of apparent paranormal (or spiritual) healing go beyond the possibility of explanation in terms of scientific medicine. This is a question to which a definite answer cannot be expected, as we cannot have certain knowledge of the limits of natural healing. The only satisfactory evidence of spiritual healing would be an experiment in which a group of sick persons was treated (without their knowledge) by a spiritual healer and the amount of their healing was compared with a control group of sick persons similar to the experimental group in all respects except the fact that they had not received the ministrations of a spiritual healer. The judge making the comparison would, of course, be ignorant as to which individuals belonged to the experimental group and which to the control group. This is a standard form of parapsychological experiment which has not yet, so far as I know, been applied to this problem. It would seem to be, in principle, a possible experiment although there are obvious difficulties (some ethical) in carrying it out.

Expressions of opinion as to whether cases of ostensible paranormal healing do or do not go beyond the possibilities of natural healing can only take us a first step toward proving the existence of paranormal healing or understanding its nature. More direct evidence on this subject is provided by experiments such as those which show that the healing of wounds in mice may be accelerated by psychic treatment (Grad, Cadoret, and Paul, 1961). There are also clearly relevant experiments which show that a gifted healer may be successful in accelerating the recovery of mice from an ether-induced state of anesthesia (Watkins and Watkins, 1971). While these experimental studies are not replications of miracles of healing, they suggest that miracles of healing may not be impossible events, and may, in fact, involve a principle which goes beyond the operation of suggestion.

2.2. Holiness and Paranormal Powers

Reports of extrasensory capacities among religious figures can best be understood in the light of the strong experimental and observational evidence for ESP found in parapsychological literature. From this point of view, they need not be regarded necessarily as misreports of normal events. They owed their religious importance to the fact that such extrasensory powers were regarded (along with other criteria) as indications of the holiness of the person producing them. However, they were not considered unambiguous indications, since it was believed that such events could be produced not only by a holy man but also by a sorcerer. One could express this by saying that the capacity to produce such paranormal events was supposed to be correlated with variations in either direction of the dimension of holiness. This idea has not yet had any support from parapsychology; such successful subjects as have appeared do not seem to belong either to the class of saint or sorcerer. There is no experimental evidence on the question, because holiness is not a personality dimension that parapsychologists have investigated. A preliminary study of a closely related problem is, however, to be found in an experimental investigation by Carroll B. Nash (1958) in which there was some indication of a correlation between positive ESP scores and high scores in a test of religious values. Perhaps future parapsychological studies will investigate the extent of these kinds of correlations.

Belief in the correlation of paranormal powers with holiness has been strong enough for such powers to have been accepted by religious groups as evidence of superior holiness when the person displaying them has shown other grounds (in speech or behavior) for considering him to be holy. This is, for example, implied by the traditional requirement of the Roman Catholic Church that, while at least four well-attested miracles should have been performed after the death of any person who is to be recognized as a saint, paranormal powers alone are not regarded as sufficient evidence of sanctity. It must first be proved that the candidate for sainthood had displayed heroic virtue in life (Haynes, 1970).

2.3. Survival Research and Belief in Immortality

Another important problem common to religious studies and to parapsychology is that of the survival of bodily death. This problem was one of the principal interests of such early parapsychologists, as, for example, F. W. H. Myers (1902/1975). This interest has now waned considerably, largely because of the conviction that there are other parapsychological problems that must be solved before we can hope to have a definite answer to the question of whether human consciousness survives death.

All religions teach that there is some sense in which the stream of consciousness continues after the death of the body, although they differ as to the nature of this survival. Not all would express this expectation by saying that there is an immortal soul which continues to exist after the death of the body. It is relevant to religious studies to consider the position of parapsychological research on this question. There are several points of interest: what is the evidence as to survival and how strong is it; what are the alternatives to survival as explanations of such evidence; and to what extent do the indications from parapsychological research on survival tend to confirm religious teachings on the subject?

2.3.1. Types of Survival Evidence

It must be admitted that the numerous investigations on the problem of survival have not yet led to any final answers even to the basic question of whether anything survives the death of the human organism. This is not due to lack of evidence but rather to uncertainty as to how the evidence should be interpreted. The student of religion should know something of the parapsychological evidence to be in a position to make his own interpretation.

2.3.1a. Mediumistic Communications. The primary evidence for survival is, no doubt, the occurrence of communications ostensibly from departed persons which come through mediums. These seem to point to survival as their explanation; in the best cases they point to it strongly. Recent published examples of such strong cases are to be found in the communications ostensibly from Mrs. Coombe Tennant (Cummins, 1970); from Edgar Vandy, who was accidentally drowned in a swimming pool (Gay, 1957); and from Mary Lyttleton, who was loved by A. J. Balfour (Balfour, 1960). In all three there seem to be strong indications of the communication of information which cannot easily be explained by the ESP of the medium or of the sitters and which therefore suggest communication from beyond the grave. These three cases are a small sample drawn from numerous communications which seem to point to the survival of death. Some of these, at least, should be considered by any religious writer concerned with evidence for continued existence after death.

That the communicators are the spirits of people whose bodies have died is the simplest explanation of the communications received, and many people are convinced by the evidence for the truth of this explanation. Students of religion who study such cases should, however, also consider the reasons for many parapsychologists' finding the evidence inconclusive. The general grounds for this opinion are to be found in many places in parapsychological literature. It is, for example, clearly stated in Rhine's *New World of the Mind* (1953, pp. 304–307). Although it is generally agreed that the communications received through a good medium may show a knowledge of the ostensible communicator's affairs far exceeding the normal knowledge of the medium, many parapsychologists do not feel certain that such enhanced knowledge may not be explained by the psi capacities of the medium. Survival is a problem still under research investigation and the future of this research may remove the doubts that still remain. The course of this research should be of interest to all those engaged in religious studies.

2.3.1b. Cross Correspondences. One way of trying to remove doubt from the conclusions that may be drawn from mediumistic communications is to convert such observations into the form of experiments. In a variant of this usual procedure, the "cross correspondences" of the early part of the present century had the appearance of being an experimental demonstration of survival arranged from the *other* side of the grave (Saltmarsh, 1938/1975). In these, the evidence for survival consisted of messages which were intelligible only when communications received independently through different mediums were combined. It was postulated that these messages could only result from the activity of a single surviving communicator and that they could not reasonably be attributed to ESP among the mediums. If the cross correspondences were an experiment arranged from beyond the grave, this was not a very good experiment since its results were very difficult to assess.

　　2.3.1c. "Sealed-Package" Tests. A more promising line of experimentation on survival was that of the "sealed package." This was carried out by F. W. H. Myers (Salter, 1958) and by Oliver Lodge (Jolly, 1974, pp. 233–236). Both of these left sealed packages with the Society for Psychical Research (S.P.R.) in London, intending to communicate the contents of these through a medium after their death. Neither attempt was successful; the contents of the packages were only discovered by being opened.

　　If these experiments had succeeded, they would not have offered very strong evidence for the survival of Myers and Lodge. Their design excluded the possibility of success being due to telepathy from the living but not the possibility of it being due to clairvoyance on the part of the medium. The possibility of clairvoyance was not taken very seriously in Great Britain at that time, but since Rhine's demonstration of the reality of clairvoyance (Rhine, 1934, pp. 50 ff.), the possibility of a medium's discovering the contents of a package by clairvoyance can no longer be ignored.

　　It follows that the purpose of the sealed-package test would be better achieved by a task in which there is no object to serve as a target for the medium's clairvoyance and which also can be tried out in the communicator's lifetime to see whether the answer can be obtained by the ESP of a medium. For this purpose, I have suggested a test in which what is to be communicated is the key which will enable a passage in cipher to be read (Thouless, 1972, pp. 162–163). Ian Stevenson (1968, 1976) has also made an experiment along similar lines which uses simpler material. Here the object deposited is a combination lock which has been set by the experimental subject to a number known only to himself. It is this number which he means to communicate through a medium after his bodily death.

　　Neither of these tests has yet yielded a positive result. If either does so in the future, this success will provide strong evidence for the survival of the chain of memories of a deceased person and a strong presumption of the survival of the consciousness of that person.

2.3.1d. Reincarnation and Other Beliefs. These experiments may be considered to be of particular importance to religious studies, as the traditional belief in immortality seems to be becoming weaker in many modern religious thinkers. Continued failure of such crucial experiments on survival will tend to reinforce such skepticism. If they succeed, however, they will tend to counteract this tendency and to reinforce the traditional beliefs on the subject. It is not, of course, the concern of parapsychology to provide either refutation or confirmation of religious beliefs. As a branch of scientific inquiry, parapsychology is concerned only with finding truth. In the course of this inquiry, data may be obtained which have important theological implications. Such studies have not necessarily confirmed traditional Christian religious beliefs; Stevenson (1974, 1975) has, for example, raised the question of evidence from childhood memories of previous incarnations. This research is still at an early stage, but already it has provided preliminary indications that, for some individuals at any rate, there are ostensible memories referring to previous lives on earth. If further studies along these lines strengthen the case for reincarnation, this will be a finding of parapsychology more in line with the traditions of Buddhism and Hinduism than with those of Christianity and Judaism.

2.3.1e. Out-of-Body Experiences. Another interesting aspect of the survival problem is the experimental investigation of "out-of-body" experiences (OBEs). In such cases, the person experiencing them reports that he has seemed to be outside his body, and sometimes he has perceived his body from a point of view outside it (Green, 1968). Such reported experiences might be purely hallucinatory; but if good evidence can be found for the reality of this apparent detachment of the self from the physical organism, this will have theoretical consequences of considerable interest to religious thought. It bears on the question of whether there is any nonbodily part of the self (as is assumed in the traditional concept of the soul), and so indirectly on the question of whether immortality is a reasonable expectation. Although research is still at an early stage, various ingenious experiments on the nature of the OBE have been done by parapsychologists (e.g., Morris, 1974).

2.3.1f. Experiences of Dying. A somewhat related field of inquiry is that into the experience of dying as reported by those who have been in attendance on the dying (Osis, 1961). Sometimes those who are on the point of death have experiences which seem to them to be of passing into another world or of making contact with those who are already there. These instances, obviously, cannot be treated as hard evidence of the reality of survival or of the nature of any future life, but are, however, suggestive and should be known to those concerned with the theory of a future life or with pastoral care for the dying.

2.4. Altered States of Consciousness and Mystical States

2.4.1. Nature of the dASC

The OBE is one example of an altered state of consciousness (ASC). These have been studied considerably by parapsychologists in recent years (Parker, 1975). For another type of ASC, Tart (1975, p. 5) has introduced the term "discrete altered state of consciousness" (dASC) for a changed pattern of consciousness which shows marked discontinuity from the basic state of consciousness of everyday life. Examples are to be found in the state of dreaming and the conditions of intoxication induced by alcohol and certain other drugs. The interest of this work for religious studies lies in the large part played in the development of religions by such dASCs as the mystical states of prayer described by St. Teresa of Avila (Teresa, 1588/1912, p. 58 ff.), or the "samadhi" of the Hindu tradition (M., 1944, p. 54). A more recent description of a similar state of consciousness is to be found in the work of J. H. M. Whiteman (1961, p. 47 ff.).

A characteristic of a mystical state of consciousness is that it seems to the person experiencing it that he is having direct experience of spiritual reality. If this is a purely illusory impression, such experiences are of no particular religious importance. Parapsychological investigation does, however, suggest the possibility that what are commonly regarded as illusory perceptual experiences in dASCs may be real perceptions of a nonordinary reality (Castaneda, 1968). If this is confirmed, it obviously opens the way to considering the perceptual experiences in mystical states as a genuine experience of the nonordinary reality of a spiritual world. These parapsychological studies also open the way to the exploration of another religious idea, found in Buddhism and among some Christian mystics, that of the inferior reality status of the ordinary perceived world of everyday life—the *samsara* (or illusory world) of the Buddhists (Tart, 1975, pp. 258 ff.).

2.4.2. Prayer and Meditation

There are two activities of the religious life, prayer and meditation, which are somewhat related to altered states of consciousness, although the degree to which the basic state of consciousness is changed is less than that of a true ASC. They seem to belong to the same class of mental attitudes as do concentration and relaxation. These may conveniently be called "changed states of consciousness." Either of these changed states of consciousness may pass spontaneously into the dASC of the mystical state.

Prayer and meditation are mental activities that cannot be sharply distinguished from one another. A rough distinction may be made by saying that prayer is intended as communication with the spiritual world, generally as communication with God. This communication may take the form of petition, but does not necessarily do so. Meditation, on the other hand, has the main purpose of altering the attitudes and mental habits of the meditator. An example of a course of meditation in the Christian tradition is *The Spiritual Exercises of St. Ignatius Loyola* (Longridge, 1919). There are also numerous descriptions of the various meditational techniques used in different forms of Buddhism (Goleman, 1975). There is obviously no sharp dividing line between these two activities of meditation and prayer; activity aimed at communication with the spiritual world may also have an effect on the communicator's own mind. Typical forms of the two activities are, however, sufficiently different to make it convenient to give them different names.

Prayer has not attracted much attention from parapsychologists except for the suggestion (Hardy, 1975; Heron, 1974) that, if there is communication with the spiritual world, its means must be some form of ESP. The central problem raised by the concept of prayer is that of the existence of any communication with the spiritual world. Although it is difficult to see how parapsychology could solve this problem, there seems to be no reason, in principle, why parapsychological experiments should not clarify it somewhat. An easier contact between parapsychology and the problems of prayer would seem to be in the less fundamental religious problem of the causal efficacy of petitionary prayer. The scientific study of this question was suggested by one of the pioneers of parapsychology, Sir Francis Galton (Galton, 1883, p. 277 ff.). A controlled experiment of rather primitive type is also reported to have been carried out a long time ago by the Jewish leader, Gideon, who is said to have prayed successfully that a fleece of wool should become wet with dew while the ground around it remained dry and, on the next night, that the ground should be wet with dew while the fleece remained dry (*Holy Bible,* Judges 6: 36–40). The question does not, however, seem to have been investigated by any modern parapsychologist, although there are recent experiments which, with a slight modification of design, could be made into tests of the efficacy of petitionary prayer. Examples are to be found in two experiments already mentioned: that on psi influence on healing (Grad, 1965) and on recovery from anesthesia (Watkins and Watkins, 1971).

Meditation has attracted more attention from experimenters than has prayer. These experiments should be mentioned, although they are related more closely to psychology and to psychiatry than to parapsychology. The central problem is the effect on the meditator of the activity of meditation and its contribution to mental health. Experimentation has generally been on the forms of meditation practiced in the Eastern religions, although similar problems arise in connection with the Christian tradition of meditation. Deikman (1969), for example, has studied experimentally the induction of a meditative condition of the Buddhist type. His work points strongly to the fact that changes of consciousness reportedly take place in meditation.

A variety of meditative techniques have been used for the purpose of mental healing with, on the whole, promising results (Kretschmer, 1969). This work is in a preliminary stage and more definite findings may be expected in future years. One implication of this work for religious studies may be to suggest that those religious bodies which have abandoned the practice of meditation may have sacrificed a practice of some spiritual value.

2.5. Possession and Exorcism

Another contact between religion and parapsychology is in the region of the phenomena which have been regarded as cases of invasion by hostile spirits of either places or persons. These have traditionally been dealt with by the rite of exorcism. Cases of ostensible spirit invasion of places may well all be cases of poltergeist phenomena (Owen, 1964). The parapsychologist is inclined to explain these as due not to discarnate spirits, but to a PK activity of one or more of the persons involved (Roll, 1972/1976). The case is somewhat more difficult for ostensible spirit possession of persons. It is generally agreed that most of these cases are examples of schizophrenia or of hysterical dissociation of personality. It has been argued, however, that some cases are not so easily explained and that there are occasionally sufficient indications that there is real possession of the organism by alien spirits. For such cases, exorcism or some religious activity akin to exorcism may be an appropriate treatment (Petitpierre, 1972).

3. Lack of Recognition of Parapsychology's Contribution to Religion

Although there are many ways in which parapsychological research would appear to be able to contribute to religious thought, this contribution is not yet very generally recognized from the religious viewpoint. If, at the present time, a theologian writes a book on miracles or on prophecy or even on the future life, it is not likely that he will concern himself with what parapsychology has found out about the matter. There are certainly exceptions as, for example, a book on the Resurrection by Michael Perry (1959) in which he suggests that the understanding of the nature of apparitions given by parapsychological study removes an unnecessary barrier to belief in the resurrection of Jesus Christ. In a preface to the same book, the theologian Austin Farrer expresses the opinion that it is "inexcusable at the present day, for the philosophically minded inquirer into Christian truth to leave psychical research out of his reckoning." If the neglect of the findings of parapsychology by religious inquirers is inexcusable, it still frequently happens. There are, however, indications that the isolation between these two fields of study is breaking down.

There are, for example, books written with the express purpose of informing students of religion about the findings of parapsychology (e.g., Higgins, 1976; Pearce-Higgins and Whitby, 1973). There are also societies whose members have primarily religious interests which are concerned with the implications of parapsychology for religious thinking and practice. There is, for example, in Great Britain, The Churches' Fellowship for Psychical and Spiritual Studies. A similar group in America is the Spiritual Frontiers Fellowship. *Quarterly Review* is published by the former while the latter publishes the quarterly, *Spiritual Frontiers.* Since 1975, there has also been published in London a quarterly newsletter, *The Christian Parapsychologist.*

Another bridge between parapsychology and religious studies is provided by the Religious Experience Research Unit founded at Oxford in 1969 by Sir Alister Hardy. This unit studies both religion and parapsychology from a biological point of view. In Hardy's own book on the subject, *The Biology of God* (1975), he argues that, if it can be shown without doubt that one mind can communicate with another mind by other than physical means, this fact would lend plausibility to the idea that our minds might be in touch with some larger mental field.

However, although there are these signs of awakening interest in parapsychology among religious thinkers, it remains only a minority interest; the main current of religious thought is still little affected by the progress of parapsychological research. It may well be that this will not be the case much longer.

If it is agreed that parapsychological studies are relevant to various aspects of religious studies, there remains the question of the nature of their interaction. It would be a mistake, I think, to suppose that this interaction must be the replacement of a traditional system of religious dogma by a system of new dogmas based on the assured results of parapsychological research. Such an expectation would seem to be based on a misunderstanding of the nature of scientific research. Research in parapsychology is not likely to produce the kind of assured results that lead to the positive assertions that form the basis of a belief system. Rather, it is to be expected of any research process that it will lead to a continuing system of widening insights into the nature of reality. The contribution of parapsychological research to religious studies may be expected to be not the contribution of a new dogmatic foundation of religion but a change of attitude toward dogma. It invites the religious believer to accept the necessity for a process of finding out in connection with many of the questions that the religions have traditionally regarded as closed.

4. References

Balfour, J. The "Palm Sunday" case: New light on an old love story. *Proceedings of the Society for Psychical Research,* 1960, *52,* 2–64.

Castaneda, C. *The teachings of Don Juan: A Yaqui way of knowledge.* Berkeley: University of California Press, 1968.

Cummins, G. *Swan on a black sea* (2nd ed.). London: Routledge & Kegan Paul, 1970.

Deikman, A. J. Experimental meditation. In C. T. Tart (Ed.), *Altered states of consciousness.* New York: John Wiley & Sons, 1969.

Galton, F. *Inquiries into human faculty and its development.* London: Macmillan, 1883.

Gay, K. The case of Edgar Vandy. *Journal of the Society for Psychical Research,* 1957, *39,* 2–64.

Goleman, D. The Buddha on meditation and states of consciousness. In C. T. Tart (Ed.), *Transpersonal psychologies.* New York: Harper & Row, 1975.

Grad, B. Some biological effects of the "laying-on of hands": A review of experiments with animals and plants. *Journal of the American Society for Psychical Research,* 1965, *59,* 95–129.

Grad, B., Cadoret, R. J., and Paul, G. I. The influence of an unorthodox method of treatment on wound healing in mice. *International Journal of Parapsychology,* 1961, *3*(2), 5–24.

Green, E. *Out-of-the-body experiences.* Oxford: Institute of Psychophysical Research, 1968.

Hardy, A. *The biology of God.* London: Jonathan Cape, 1975.

Haynes, R. *Philosopher king: The humanist Pope Benedict XIV.* London: Weidenfeld & Nicolson, 1970.

Heron, L. T. *ESP in the Bible.* Garden City, N.Y.: Doubleday, 1974.

Higgins, P. L. C. *Frontiers of the spirit.* Minneapolis, Minn.: Denison, 1976.

The Holy Bible. Revised standard version. New York: Thomas R. Nelson, 1952.

Jolly, W. P. *Sir Oliver Lodge.* London: Constable, 1974.

Kretschmer, W. Meditative techniques in psychotherapy. In C. Tart (Ed.), *Altered states of consciousness.* New York: John Wiley & Sons, 1969.

LeShan, L. *Alternate realities.* New York: M. Evans, 1976.

Longridge, W. H. *The spiritual exercises of Saint Ignatius Loyola.* London: Robert Scott, 1919.

M., *The gospel of Sri Ramakrishna.* Madras: Sri Ramakrishna Math, 1944.

Morris, R. L. The use of detectors for out-of-body experiences. In W. G. Roll, R. L. Morris, and J. D. Morris (Eds.), *Research in parapsychology 1973.* Metuchen, N.J.: Scarecrow Press, 1974, 114–116.

Müller, F. M. (Ed.). *Sacred books of the East XIII.* Oxford: Clarendon Press, 1881.

Myers, F. W. H. *Human personality and its survival of bodily death.* New York: Arno Press, 1975. (Originally published, 1902.)

Nash, C. B. Correlation between ESP and religious value. *Journal of Parapsychology,* 1958, *22,* 204–209.

Osis, K. *Deathbed observations by physicians and nurses. (Parapsychological monographs No. 3.)* New York: Parapsychology Foundation, 1961.

Owen, A. R. G. *Can we explain the poltergeist?* New York: Garrett/Helix, 1964.

Parker, A. *States of mind: ESP and altered states of consciousness.* New York: Taplinger, 1975.

Pearce-Higgins, J. D., and Whitby, G. S. (Eds.). *Life, death and psychical research.* London: Rider, 1973.

Perry, M. *The Easter enigma.* London: Faber & Faber, 1959.

Petitpierre, R. (Ed.). *Exorcism: The report of a commission convened by the Bishop of Exeter.* London: S.P.C.K., 1972.

Rhine, J. B. *Extrasensory perception.* Boston: Boston Society for Psychic Research, 1934.

Rhine, J. B. *New world of the mind.* New York: William Sloane Associates, 1953.

Roll, W. G. *The poltergeist.* Metuchen, N.J.: Scarecrow Press, 1976. (Originally published, 1972.)

Rose, L. *Faith healing.* London: Victor Gollancz, 1968.

Salter, W. H. F. W. H. Myers' posthumous message. *Proceedings of the Society for Psychical Research,* 1958, *52,* 1–12.

Saltmarsh, H. F. *Evidence of personal survival from cross-correspondences.* New York: Arno Press, 1975. (Originally published, 1938.)

Stevenson, I. The combination lock test for survival. *Journal of the American Society for Psychical Research,* 1968, *62,* 245–254.

Stevenson, I. *Twenty cases suggestive of reincarnation* (2nd ed.). Charlottesville, Va.: University Press of Virginia, 1974.

Stevenson, I. *Cases of the reincarnation type, Vol. 1. Ten cases in India.* Charlottesville, Va.: University Press of Virginia, 1975.

Stevenson, I. Further observations on the combination lock test for survival. *Journal of the American Society for Psychical Research,* 1976, *70,* 219–229.

Tart, C. T. *States of consciousness.* New York: Dutton, 1975.

Teresa, St. [*The interior castle*] (English translation). London: Thomas Baker, 1912. (Originally published, 1588.)

Thouless, R. H. *From anecdote to experiment in psychical research.* London: Routledge & Kegan Paul, 1972.

Trochu, F. *The Curé d'Ars* (Engl. trans.). London: Burns Oates & Washbourne, 1927.

Watkins, G. K., and Watkins, A. M. Possible PK influence on the resuscitation of anesthetised mice. *Journal of Parapsychology,* 1971, *35,* 257–272.

West, D. J. *Eleven Lourdes miracles.* London: Gerald Duckworth, 1957.

Whiteman, J. H. M. *The mystical life.* London: Faber & Faber, 1961.

A Select Bibliography of Books on Parapsychology, 1974-1976

6

Rhea A. White

1. Introduction

It is likely that the apogee of the publication of books on parapsychology was reached in the years 1974–1976, the years covered in this bibliography. During those three years nearly everyone who had anything to say on the subject, as well as those who did not, came out with books or monographs or new editions or were reprinted. It is difficult to see how much more can be published—unless and until major breakthroughs occur so that there will be something new to write about! The types of books still needed are those that most publishers do not like to underwrite: in-depth studies of a single aspect of parapsychology, serious (and to most, boring) works of reference, and methodological reviews. However, as the subject takes hold in colleges and universities—particularly as the need for graduate training grows—hopefully some reputable publishers will be perspicacious enough to fill the gaps in the literature. And then, at least in the best of all possible worlds, the bright and eager students, thus fully apprised of what has been done in parapsychology as well as equipped with a knowledge of how and why—will in their turn reciprocate by producing fresh and fruitful research and insightful and interconnected theory-building. We can only wait and hope.

The books in this annotated bibliography were selected from those I was able to inspect and read at first hand. They were chosen because, in my opinion, they are basically reliable and because they have new

Rhea A. White · Reference Department, East Meadow Public Library, East Meadow, New York.

information or offer fresh viewpoints. Popular as well as scholarly books are included, the former generally because they cover subject areas that have been neglected in the more scholarly volumes.

As indicated in the chapter title, this bibliography includes books published from 1974 through 1976 (plus two 1977 titles). Anyone wanting to learn about books on parapsychology published prior to 1974 may consult *Parapsychology: Sources of information,* complied by myself and Laura A. Dale (Scarecrow Press, 1973), which describes 282 books arranged under 24 broad subject categories.

There are 93 books in the bibliography, arranged alphabetically by the author's last name under 14 subject headings, which themselves are in alphabetical order. These headings are: Altered States and Psi; Autobiographies and Biographies; Criticisms; Education for Parapsychology; Experimental Parapsychology; Medicine, Psychiatry, and Parapsychology; Parapsychology and Other Sciences; Philosophy and Parapsychology; Practical Applications of Psi; Psychokinesis; Reference Works; Religion and Parapsychology; Spontaneous Psi Experiences; and Survival. Each book is numbered consecutively starting with the first book listed through the last one.

There is an introduction to each of the 14 subject groupings in which all books in that category are considered as a group. The introduction describes which titles stand out from the others in certain ways and sometimes compares or contrasts two or more titles in the group. It is conceivable a book could have been placed in two or more subject categories. If a book in one subject category has considerable relevance to other categories, this is pointed out in the introductions to the other sections. When books are referred to in this way only the author's last name or the title is given, followed by the number of the book in parentheses which indicates where it may be located in the bibliography.

The main or numbered listing for each book provides the following information: author, title, place of publication, publisher, date of publication, number of pages, price, and whether it has a bibliography (bibl.), index (ind.), illustrations (illus.), or other special features, such as a glossary. If these items are not specified, it can be assumed that a book does not have them.

The annotation of each book provides a brief description of its contents. Often the author's own words have been used. I have tried to point out any very strong or especially weak areas of the books and to describe special features. No attempt has been made to limit the annotations to a uniform length. The aim was to use as few words as possible to describe the book adequately.

Finally, any treatment of books published between the years 1974 and 1976 would have to give some recognition to a major publishing event concerning parapsychology which took place in that period: the publication by Arno Press of two series of reprints of books relevant to parapsychology. One series, entitled *Perspectives in Psychical Research,* consists of 33 titles selected by psychology-trained parapsychologist Robert L. Morris who heads the tutorial in parapsychology at the University of California, Santa Barbara. The other series is entitled *The Occult,* and consists of 33 titles selected by British historian of the occult, James Webb. Although almost all of the books in the two series are reprints of out-of-print classics, some titles included were published for the first time in book form: anthologies of periodical articles and in one instance, a thesis. Two of these have been treated as new titles and are included in the annotated bibliography: Roll's *Theory and Experiment in Psychical Research* and *The Subliminal Consciousness* by F. W. H. Myers. In order to take cognizance of some of the other titles in the two series, a list of reprints and new editions is given at the end of the relevant subject categories. Due to lack of space these titles have not been annotated. In addition to the Arno books, reprints of other publishers and revised editions of important books in parapsychology published during 1974–1976 are also included in these supplementary listings.

2. *Altered States and Psi*

Currently, one of the most active areas of parapsychological research is the study of psi in the context of various altered states of consciousness, or ways of experiencing other than our "normal" one. Concomitantly, in the wider world of psychology, there is also a greatly increased interest in altered states. The number of books in this section reflects the magnitude of this interest. Although nearly all these titles deal to some extent with psi and altered states, with the exception of Parker and Panati, the emphasis is on altered states. In fact, the book by Pelletier and Garfield does not deal with psi at all, but it is such an excellent basic guide to the literature of altered states that I could not possibly exclude it. The newly published Myers volume could be viewed as a collection of some of the first papers on psi and altered states. Ornstein's book is an anthology of basic articles on ASCs, three of which deal with parapsychology. In a sense, Barber's book can be looked at as its twin, except that it includes more recent material, and the number of papers on parapsychology has been increased to seven. Tart's work presents a map of the terrain for anyone interested in exploring states of consciousness, and Adam Smith's book is the diary of a man who set out to be a guinea pig for various methods of inducing ASCs. Grof's book is a report of some aspects of his longitudinal studies of LSD and psychiatry and is included here both because LSD is a major means of altering consciousness and because some of the findings Grof reports implicate various types of psi phenomena. LeShan's *Alternate Realities,* although a philosophical discussion in one sense, is actually about the practicality of altered states and how what happens "inside" can influence what is experienced as "outside." Panati's *Supersenses* is a general survey of parapsychology, but it has been placed in this section because the emphasis is on altered states and psi. Last, but of prime importance, the subject of Parker's *States of Mind* is depicted better by its subtitle: *ESP and Altered States of Consciousness.* It is the first general survey in book form of studies bearing on both psi and ASCs.

Books listed under other subject categories which have a significant amount of information on psi and altered states are Beloff (27), Dean (45), Greeley (52, 76), Higgins (79), Hintze and Pratt (30), Jacobson (89), Krippner (16), LeShan (48), Moody (90), Ornstein (26), Rogo (34), Tart (80), White (36), and Wolman (75). *Research in Parapsychology (RIP)* (38, 39, 41) is the best source for keeping up with research in altered states and psi. *RIP 1974* (38) contains Tart's long address, "On the nature of altered states of consciousness, with special reference to parapsychological phenomena."

1. Barber, Theodore X. (Ed.). *Advances in altered states of consciousness and human potentialities.* Vol. 1. New York: Psychological Dimensions, 1976. 698p. Illus. Ind. $20.00.

    This is an anthology of the most important papers and selections from books dealing with human potentialities and altered states of awareness published in recent years. Contains 43 selections, seven of which are on parapsychology: by Schmeidler, the Brauds, Palmer, Tart (2), R. V. Johnson, II, and E. L. Smith.

2. Grof, Stanislav. *Realms of the human unconscious: Observations from LSD research.* New York: Viking, 1975. 257p. Bibl. Illus. Ind. $15.00.

    Summary of basic information on LSD as a result of 18 years of research. Emphasizes a phenomenological description of experiences under LSD, including several that are possibly psi-determined: precognition, clairvoyance, retrocognition, out-of-body experiences, telepathy, and mediumistic or spiritistic experiences.

3. LeShan, Lawrence. *Alternate realities: The search for the full human being.* New York: M. Evans, 1976. (Distributed by Lippincott.) 232p. $7.95.

A continuation of the author's *Toward a general theory of the paranormal* (Parapsychology Foundation, 1969) and *The medium, the mystic and the physicist* (48). In addition to the modes of being described in these earlier books, he develops the concepts of the transpsychic and mythic modes of being. He applies his hypotheses to ESP and survival.

4. Myers, Frederic W. H. *The subliminal consciousness.* New York: Arno Press, 1976. 593p. $40.00.

An original Arno Press anthology of articles published in the *Proceedings of the Society for Psychical Research, 1885–1895.* In these papers, Myers shows how he arrived at the concept of the "subliminal self." Some of the topics covered here were not included in Myers's classic, *Human personality,* or, if included, were not treated as fully there as here.

5. Ornstein, Robert E. (Ed.). *The nature of human consciousness: A book of readings.* New York: Viking, 1974. Bibl. Ind. $15.00.

An anthology intended "to assist in a small way in regaining a lost perspective in psychology," one which views psychology as the science of consciousness, with emphasis on the intuitive mode of consciousness. There are 41 selections, three on parapsychology, and a 17-page bibliography.

6. Panati, Charles. *Supersenses: Our potential for parasensory experience.* New York Quadrangle/New York Times Book Co., 1974. 274p. Bibl. Illus. Ind. $8.95.

A popular review of current research in parapsychology with emphasis on altered states and psi. Subjects covered are the dream studies at Maimonides, hypnosis and psi, psychic healing, telepathy, the twilight mind (including automatic writing, creativity, and out-of-body experiences), clairvoyance, the mystic and psi, and PK and life fields.

7. Parker, Adrian. *States of mind: ESP and altered states of consciousness.* New York: Taplinger, 1975. 198p. Bibl. Ind. Glossary. $9.95.

The first general survey of altered states of consciousness and ESP in book form. The types of ASCs related to ESP are hypnosis, trance, OBES and lucid dreams, pathological states, psychedelic states, meditative and mystical states, and alpha states. A chapter is devoted to the question: "Is there a post-mortem ASC?" 15-page bibliography.

8. Pelletier, Kenneth R., and Garfield, Charles. *Consciousness: East
   and West.* New York: Harper & Row, 1976. 308p. Bibl. $4.95
   (pap.).

   This is a "reader's guide" to views of consciousness. The
   authors state that their aim "is to convey the sense of human
   consciousness as that aspect of being wherein the temporal and
   eternal, the complex and singular, the ancient and contemporary,
   the material and spiritual, the microcosm and macrocosm, are resolved in a moment of comprehension and insight" (p. x). 31-page
   bibliography.
9. Smith, Adam (pseudonym for Jerry Goodman). *Powers of mind.*
   New York: Dutton, 1975. 418p. Bibl. $10.00. New York: Ballan-
   tine Books, 1976. $1.95 (pap.).

   A lucid firsthand report of one man's tour through the human
   potential movement. Smith visited and participated in research at
   various key centers engaged in studying altered states, mysticism,
   and parapsychology. He interviewed Edgar Mitchell and Montague
   Ullman and researchers at Maimonides Medical Center and Stanford
   Research Institute as well as Uri Geller, James Randi, and Ingo
   Swann. 18-page bibliography.
10. Tart, Charles T. *States of consciousness.* New York: Dutton, 1975.
    305p. Bibl. Ind. $4.95 (pap.).

    In this book the author presents a "systems approach" to
    viewing consciousness. The first part, "States," describes the sys-
    tems approach, its implications, and reviews what we now know
    about states of consciousness. The second part, "Speculations,"
    "presents ideas that, while consistent with the systems approach,
    are not a necessary part of it and are more unorthodox" (p. xi).

3. Autobiographies and Biographies

Several recent books on parapsychology have been on the lives of
persons associated with the field. These books can be classified in four
ways: as biographies or autobiographies, and as being about parapsychologists (researchers or investigators of psi phenomena) or about
mediums, sensitives, high-scoring subjects, healers, etc. (those who are
investigated by parapsychologists). The books in this section fall mainly
in this last grouping and are primarily autobiographies. However, there
are two autobiographies of current parapsychologists, Stanley Krippner
and Scott Rogo, and a biography of Sir Oliver Lodge, one of the first
scientists to be associated with parapsychology. There also are biogra-

phies of Bishop Pike, who in his last years was associated with parapsychology, and of Eileen Garrett and Olga Worrall. The remaining books
are all autobiographies by sensitives who are dominating the current
parapsychological scene: Uri Geller, Sean Harribance, Matthew Manning,
Ingo Swann, and Alex Tanous. Their stories may one day be useful as
psychological documents.

Books in other subject categories that have an autobiographical
slant are those by LeShan (48) and Smith (9). Three books listed under
"Psychokinesis" are full-length studies of Geller: those by Ebon (64),
Panati (67), and Randi (68). However, their emphasis is on Geller's
phenomena rather than his life. Several books have chapters on individual psychics: Christopher (22), Krippner and Villoldo (47), Nolen
(49), and Wilhelm (44). Some biographical information on Jeane Dixon
may be found in the book by Brian (82).

11. Angoff, Allan. *Eileen Garrett and the world beyond the senses.* New
York: William Morrow, 1974. 241p. Bibl. Ind. $6.95.

Biography of a gifted medium, administrator, publisher, and
writer. The first four chapters are about Mrs. Garrett as a medium
and her work in parapsychology. The remaining 12 present a
chronological review of her life and accomplishments.

12. Cerutti, Edwina. *Olga Worrall: Mystic with the healing hands.* New
York: Harper & Row, 1975. 169p. $7.95.

Contains firsthand observations of the healing and psi ability
of Olga Worrall and an account of her convictions regarding survival
and of the "spirit" teachings and guidance both Olga and Ambrose
Worrall received, and which he began to communicate to Olga after
his death. Some investigations of Olga Worrall made by scientists
are described.

13. Geller, Uri. *My story.* New York: Praeger, 1975. 282p. Illus. $8.95.

In this autobiography, Geller describes his life, how he became
aware of his psi ability, what he has done with his powers thus far,
and where he thinks they are leading.

14. Harribance, Sean, as told to N. Richard Neff. *This man knows you.*
San Antonio, Texas: Naylor Co., 1976. 138p. Bibl. Partial list of
public appearances. $8.95.

Harribance, a high scoring ESP subject who has succeeded in
several parapsychological laboratories, here provides some autobiographical information and an account of his work as a psychic.

15. Jolly, W. P. *Sir Oliver Lodge.* Rutherford, N.J.: Fairleigh Dickinson
University Press, 1975 (©1974). 256p. Illus. Ind. $10.00.

Biography of a man who was a pioneer in parapsychology as

well as physics. Half of the book is devoted to Lodge's work in psychical research, including early ESP experiments, research with mediums, and cross correspondences.

16. Krippner, Stanley. *Song of the siren: A parapsychological odyssey.* New York: Harper & Row, 1975. 311p. Bibl. Ind. $12.50.

An account of the ten years in which Krippner devoted most of his time to parapsychology. He describes the research he has engaged in, his visits to parapsychological centers throughout the world, and his views concerning the nature of psi and the conduct of parapsychological research.

17. Manning, Matthew. *The link.* New York: Holt, Rinehart and Winston, 1974. 200p. Illus. $7.95; New York: Ballantine, 1976. $1.95 (pap.).

Autobiography of the young British psychic who is also a metal bender and healer. Peter Bander provides a survey of the scientific investigations of Manning in a 26-page introduction, and A.R.G. Owen provides an overview of research with Manning in Canada.

18. Rogo, D. Scott. *In search of the unknown: The odyssey of a psychical researcher.* New York: Taplinger, 1976. 190p. $9.95.

Autobiographical account of Rogo's work in parapsychology as a field investigator. Its value is not so much in the genuine phenomena he observed as in his descriptions of the many normal means that can account for what naive persons might assume to be genuine psi phenomena.

19. Stringfellow, William, and Towne, Anthony. *The death and life of Bishop Pike.* Garden City, N.Y.: Doubleday, 1976. 446p. Bibl. Illus. $10.00.

This detailed and honest biography covers the entire life of Bishop Pike, but roughly half is devoted to Pike's parapsychological concerns. Commissioned by Pike before his death, it provides many details missing from Pike's book, *The other side* (Doubleday, 1968).

20. Swann, Ingo. *To kiss earth good-bye.* New York: Hawthorn Books, 1975. 217p. Bibl. Illus. Ind. $10.00.

An autobiographical account of Swann's psi abilities, which include PK, precognition, and out-of-body experiences. He describes research with him as subject conducted by Targ and Puthoff at Stanford Research Institute, by Osis at the American Society for Psychical Research, and by Schmeidler at City College. Swann not only describes his experiences but reviews the literature and attempts to explain what is happening.

21. Tanous, Alex, with Harvey Ardman. *Beyond coincidence: One man's experiences with psychic phenomena.* Garden City, N.Y.: Doubleday, 1976. 195p. $7.95.

   This autobiography of a psychic gives examples of how his psi has been expressed: precognition, psychic diagnosis and healing, psychic photography, OBEs, and communication with the "dead." He also describes scientific investigation of him, comments on how it feels to experience psi impressions, and offers suggestions for developing psi.

3.1. Reprints and New Editions

Garrett, Eileen J. *My life as a search for the meaning of mediumship.* New York: Arno Press, 1975 (c 1939). $13.00.

Home, Mrs. D. D. *D.D. Home: His life and mission.* New York: Arno Press, 1976 (©1888). $24.00.

4. Criticisms

   The newest crop of books presenting critical views of parapsychology or aspects of it is somewhat different from earlier ones. Christopher's book, like his earlier *ESP, seers, and psychics* (Crowell, 1970), is more or less standard criticism, but the books by Ebon and Gruss in a sense are predicated on the fact that psi phenomena exist. They are not out to criticize the evidence in parapsychology, but to educate—to warn, even—the gullible and unwary concerning the dangers involved in dabbling with psychic abilities and the occult. Their books are directed (as is Ornstein's, to be described next) more at the "occult fringe" than at parapsychologists, and yet—just as the smoke in any occult fire is most likely due to the presence of a psi factor beneath the trappings of ritual and symbolism, so anyone who sets out to harness or train psi abilities, as of course parapsychologists would like very much to do—would be wise to read *The ouija board* and *The Satan trap.* Ornstein's book has a chapter on parapsychology, but it is mainly concerned with current Western interest in consciousness, mysticism, altered states of consciousness, and occultism. It is critical on two fronts: he exposes the excessive promises made by self-improvement hucksters on the one hand, and on the other he takes to task the overly rational "scientists" who are unable to see the value of studies of the "other" side of the mind. Keene's book is an exposé of fraudulent mediumship.

Criticisms in other books listed in the bibliography may be found in Brier (56), which provides a pro and con survey of philosophic views of the possibility of backward causation: Ebon (64), which contains several anti-Geller articles; French (57), which has a number of critical philosophical articles on aspects of parapsychology or subjects tangentially relevant to it; Nolen (49), which is an exposé of faith healers and psychic surgeons; Randi (68), which is anti-Geller; Rogo (18), who spells out various forms of trickery and is also critical of the over-conservatism of many parapsychologists; Stringfellow and Towne (19), who take a careful, critical look at the psychic experiences of Bishop Pike; and White (36), which has a section of three critical articles, together with a bibliography of further criticisms.

22. Christopher, Milbourne. *Mediums, mystics, & the occult.* New York: Thomas Y. Crowell, 1975. 275p. Bibl. Ind. Illus. $6.95.

The subjects covered in this book are Uri Geller, psychic surgery, Peter Hurkos, eyeless vision, Mitchell's outer space experiment, Ted Serios, Arthur Ford, some "mystics from the East," research on survival financed by the Kidd legacy, Margery Crandon, the *Scientific American* investigations, and Annie Eva Fay. In each case Christopher tries to show how the investigators were hoodwinked by the psychics being studied.

23. Ebon, Martin (Ed.). *The Satan trap: Dangers of the occult.* Garden City, N.Y.: Doubleday, 1976. 276p. $7.95.

Presents the dark side of psychic and occult phenomena. Ebon warns: ". . . we are . . . experiencing a virtual epidemic of irresponsible toying with psychic powers" (p. vii). There are 25 selections by parapsychologists, psychiatrists, psychologists, and writers who describe the potential dangers involved in the overzealous pursuit of personal psychic experience.

24. Gruss, Edmond C., with John G. Hotchkiss. *The Ouija board: Doorway to the occult.* Chicago: Moody Press, 1975. 191p. Bibl. $1.50 (pap.).

In spite of the current popularity of the Ouija board, it is difficult to find any literature on it. This gap is filled by this book which is on automatisms in general and the Ouija board in particular. It contains a history of the board, a chapter on what makes it work, and one on its use in psychic development and the dangers involved in so doing. There are also three chapters on possession and demonology.

25. Keene, M. Lamar, as told to Allen Spraggett. *The psychic mafia.* New York: St. Martin's Press, 1976. 177p. Bibl. Illus. $7.95.

This book is written by a former fraudulent medium, now reformed. He tells how he became a fake medium and describes the tricks mediums use to make a living by duping people into believing they are actually communicating with deceased loved ones. 13-page bibliography.

26. Ornstein, Robert E. *The mind field; a personal essay.* New York: Grossman, 1976. 142p. $7.95.

There are seven chapters in this book, one of which is on parapsychology. Each chapter is a commentary on various approaches to consciousness and the pitfalls involved both in trying to develop consciousness as well as to study it. Ornstein cautions that we should neither summarily reject these "mind fields" nor accept them uncritically as the answer to all our problems.

4.1. Reprints and New Editions

Cumberland, Stuart. *A thought-reader's thoughts: Being the impressions and confessions of Stuart Cumberland.* New York: Arno Press, 1975 (© 1888). $19.00.

Mulholland, John. *Beware familiar spirits.* New York: Arno Press, 1975 (© 1938). $20.00.

Murchison, Carl (Ed.). *The case for and against psychical belief.* New York: Arno Press, 1975 (© 1927). $22.00.

Price, Harry, and Dingwall, E. J. *Revelations of a spirit medium.* New York: Arno Press, 1975 (© 1922). $22.00.

5. Education for Parapsychology

Although the 1970s have witnessed a great increase in the number of courses on parapsychology, not only at the college level but also in high school and adult education classes, there is a dearth of qualified instructors to teach such courses. Moreover, even the handful of qualified teachers, to say nothing of those who have little background in the subject, are very much handicapped by the lack of textbooks, books of readings, and other handbooks which form a regular part of the teaching arsenal in most fields. As the books listed below indicate, this situation is finally being rectified to some extent. The books described in this section are either about education for parapsychology (for example, the Parapsychology Foundation proceedings) or are books aimed, at least in part, at teachers of parapsychology and their students, as well as the independent learner. Since the only book on parapsychology specifically written as a textbook was published in 1957 (Rhine and Pratt's *Parapsychology*, Charles C Thomas), general surveys and collections of articles have had to serve as textbooks in more recent years. Fortunately, R. L. Morris and J. H. Rush are writing a textbook, as is C. B. Nash. And K. R. Rao is preparing a completely revised edition of his review of the experimental literature, *Experimental parapsychology* (Charles C Thomas, 1964). In the meantime, instructors and students will find considerable assistance in the materials listed below. Several of the books are aimed at high school students and readers with little or no background in parapsychology: Ebon, Hintze and Pratt, Owen, and L. E. Rhine; others are directed at the more advanced student: Beloff, Mitchell, Rogo, and White.

Elsewhere in the bibliography all the books listed under "Reference" would be useful at one step or another of the educational ladder, but especially Cavendish (72) and Wolman (75). The review articles in Schmeidler (55) provide excellent state-of-the-art summaries of parapsychology as well as surveys of parapsychology in relation to several of the major sciences which should be helpful to students in choosing subjects for research and also for deciding on subjects in which to specialize. Wheatley and Edge (59) also have several review articles which should be helpful to students, especially regarding the scientific status of parapsychology. The books by Feola (65) and Sibley (91) are specifically aimed at high school students. Finally, *Research in Parapsychology* (38, 39, 41) is a must for serious students of parapsychology in order to keep abreast of both research findings and methodology.

27. Beloff, John. *New directions in parapsychology.* With a postscript by Arthur Koestler. Metuchen, N.J.: Scarecrow Press, 1975. 174p. Illus. Ind. Glossary. $8.50.

    This anthology of original papers stresses current parapsychological research strategies. Methodologies, findings, and theoretical implications are described by experts in key areas: instrumentation (H. Schmidt), altered states and ESP (C. Honorton), personality and psi (K. R. Rao), biology and psi (J. Randall), poltergeists (H. Bender), and survival (W. G. Roll).

28. Ebon, Martin. *What's new in ESP.* New York: Pyramid Books, 1976. 192p. Bibl. Ind. $1.50 (pap.).

    This is a popular survey of current happenings in parapsychology. After an opening chapter on self-testing, there are three sections: "leading contemporary psychics" (Geller, Manning, Swann, Ganzfeld experiments); "ESP enters other areas" (anpsi, psychic archaeology, and psi and religion); and "Cases for survival after death" (exorcism, OBE research, xenoglossy, and reincarnation). A final chapter relates parapsychology to other scientific disciplines.

29. Education Dept., American Society for Psychical Research. *Courses and other study opportunities in parapsychology.* Revised edition. New York: American Society for Psychical Research, 1976. 16p. $2.00.

This pamphlet is an annual and lists courses and other study opportunities in parapsychology throughout the world. The school, name of course and instructor, type of course and level, and name and address of person to contact for further information is provided.

30. Hintze, Naomi, and Pratt, J. G. *The psychic realm: What can you believe?* New York: Random House, 1975. 269p. Bibl. Ind. $8.95.

The aim of this book is to provide an accurate and comprehensive introduction to all aspects of parapsychology in language that the average reader can easily understand. Hintze vividly describes the subject matter in the first half of each chapter followed by Pratt's scientific evaluation of the subject matter.

31. Mitchell, Edgar D., and others. *Psychic exploration; a challenge for science.* John White (Ed.). New York: Putnam's, 1974. 708p. Illus. Ind. Glossary. $17.50· $4.95 (pap.).

An anthology of 29 original papers written specifically for this volume and covering the major areas of parapsychology and its relation to other disciplines. The chapters are not equally authoritative and the treatment in some is much more superficial and speculative than others, but on the whole the contributors, who are primarily parapsychologists, physicists, and transpersonal psychologists, have provided good overviews of current parapsychology.

32. Owen, A. R. G. *Psychic mysteries of the North: Discoveries from the Maritime Provinces and beyond.* New York: Harper & Row, 1975. 243p. Bibl. Ind. $8.95.

A good introduction to parapsychology for beginners because throughout Owen distinguishes between the scientific and the pseudo-scientific approaches to psi. It is primarily both a history and a survey of current parapsychology in Canada.

33. Rhine, Louisa E. *Psi, what is it? The story of ESP and PK.* New York: Harper & Row, 1975. 247p. Bibl. Ind. $10.00; $1.95 (pap.).

A nontechnical "account of parapsychology today, written for inquiring minds of any age" (p. 9). It is primarily the story of parapsychology as it developed at the Duke University Parapsychology Laboratory. In addition to reviewing major research methods and findings, it contains a section on the occult in school, how to get into parapsychology, and how to conduct psi tests.

34. Rogo, D. Scott. *Parapsychology: A century of inquiry.* New York: Taplinger, 1975. 319p. Bibl. Ind. $12.50.

    An attempt to present the major findings of all aspects of parapsychology. It weaves together historical investigations, mediumship and survival, laboratory research, and studies of spontaneous psi in a single tapestry. It is not error-free and bibliographic citations are difficult to find, but it has a good index and on the whole is a compact, useful, and up-to-date introduction to the entire field.

35. Shapin, Betty, and Coly, Lisette (Eds.). *Education in parapsychology.* New York: Parapsychology Foundation, 1976. 313p. $12.50.

    This volume consists of the 16 papers and the discussions that followed them given at the Parapsychology Foundation's 1975 conference. It is a useful volume for teachers of parapsychology and for students or anyone aspiring to enter the field.

36. White, Rhea A., compiler. *Surveys in parapsychology: Reviews of the literature with updated bibliographies.* Metuchen, N.J.: Scarecrow Press, 1976. 484p. Bibl. Ind. $17.50.

    An anthology of 19 state-of-the-art reviews originally published in parapsychology journals and aimed at providing in-depth coverage of key aspects of parapsychology. There are five sections: basic areas of study, special subject populations, insights into how psi operates, theories of psi, and criticisms. The already-lengthy bibliographies have been updated by the compiler thus making the book a bibliographic guide to further information as well as a basic source book.

5.1. Reprints and New Editions

Gudas, Fabian (Ed.). *Extrasensory perception.* New York: Arno Press, 1975 (© 1961). $10.00.

Price, Harry. *Fifty years of psychical research; a critical survey.* New York: Arno Press, 1975 (© 1939). $23.00.

Tyrrell, G. N. M. *Science and psychical phenomena.* New York: Arno Press, 1975 (© 1938). $22.00.

6. Experimental Parapsychology

Most parapsychological research, as in any other science, is published initially in the professional journals, the chief ones being the *Journal of the American Society for Psychical Research* and the *Journal of Parapsychology*. However, the majority of the research is reported for the first time at the yearly convention of the Parapsychological Association and is published in abbreviated form in its annual proceedings, *Research in parapsychology (RIP)*. Much of the research reported in *RIP* will later be published in more detail in the form of journal articles, but the best overview of research in parapsychology for any given year is *RIP*, the three latest of which are listed below in order to provide a cross-section of its contents. The Hardy book and the one by Tart are actually extended research reports. *Experiments in distant influence* offers the most complete account in book form of the research of the pioneer Russian parapsychologist, L. L. Vasiliev. Roll's book, although published for the first time in 1975, was first written in 1959 and was later updated. It contains reports of original research, surveys of research, and is a good source of research hypotheses. Wilhelm's book is about the parapsychological research being undertaken at one of the major research centers in the United States—Stanford Research Institute (SRI).

Elsewhere in the bibliography books which give major emphasis to empirical research are Beloff (27), Hintze and Pratt (30), Jacobson (89), Parker (7), Randall (54), L. E. Rhine (33), Rogo (34), Schmeidler (55), White (36), and Wolman (75). Targ and Puthoff have a paper describing their "remote viewing" experiments in Oteri (53).

37. Hardy, Alister, Harvie, Robert, and Koestler, Arthur. *The challenge of chance; a mass experiment in telepathy and its unexpected outcome.* New York: Random House, 1974. 280p. Illus. Ind. $8.95; $2.95 (pap.).

    This book describes Hardy's Caxton Hall GESP experiment in which 200 agents concentrated on pictures while 20 subjects tried to draw the targets. Some unusual coincidences in the results are examined by Harvie, and Koestler presents many instances involving unusual coincidences in daily life and offers a theory to explain them.

38. Morris, Joanna D., Roll, William G., and Morris, Robert L. (Eds.). *Research in parapsychology 1974.* Metuchen, N.J.: Scarecrow Press, 1975. 265p. Ind. Glossary. $9.00.

The proceedings of the seventeenth convention of the Parapsychological Association contain comments on the Levy affair (the case of a fraudulent experimenter) by James Davis, and 31 research briefs and 17 papers under the following session headings: altered states of consciousness, animal studies, theory and methods, psychokinesis with human subjects, out-of-body experiences, spontaneous case trends, and ESP and "normal" cognition. There were two symposia: "Energy focusing and lingering effects in poltergeist cases and experimental studies" and "Ethical issues confronting parapsychologists." The full text is given of the presidential address, "Tacit communication and experimental theology," by R. L. Morris, and the invited address, "Biofeedback and pattern self-regulation in biological perspective: A critical analysis of extrasensitive perception," by Gary E. Schwarz.

39.   Morris, Joanna D., Roll, William G., and Morris, Robert L. (Eds.). *Research in parapsychology 1975*. Metuchen, N.J.: Scarecrow Press, 1976. 277p. Ind. Glossary. $8.00.

The eighteenth convention of the Parapsychological Association as presented in this volume consisted of 41 research briefs under the following categories: Levy replications, instrumentation, psychophysiological studies, attitudinal variables, variations on forced-choice testing procedures, utilization of natural targets, psychokinesis on stable systems, commercial claims, application of conventional learning theory, psychokinesis on dynamic systems, mental retardation, subliminal stimulation, field studies, cognitive variables, internally-deployed attention states: relaxation, and internally-deployed attention states: perceptual isolation. There were 15 papers given in five sessions devoted to the following topics: unconscious psi processing, internal states and ESP, psychokinesis: experiments and field investigations, memory and ESP, and imagery and ESP. The texts are included of Charles Honorton's presidential address, "Has science developed the competence to deal with the paranormal?" and Willis W. Harman's invited address, "The societal implications and social impact of psi phenomena."

40.   Roll, William G. *Theory and experiment in psychical research*. New York: Arno Press, 1975. 510p. Bibl. Illus. Ind. $29.00.

This was originally submitted in 1959 as a thesis at Oxford University and was later revised and expanded. Roll describes his research on hypnosis and ESP, personality variables and ESP, and habit-patterns in ESP testing. He also provides a review of psychometry. Several models of psi are described and discussed, and hypotheses capable of being tested empirically are presented. The book reflects on extensive acquaintance with the literature, and there is a 30-page bibliography.

41. Roll, William G., Morris, Robert L., and Morris, Joanna D. (Eds.). *Research in parapsychology 1973.* Metuchen, N.J.: Scarecrow Press, 1974. 249p. Ind. Glossary. $9.00.

    This is the proceedings of the sixteenth annual Parapsychological Association convention. There were 20 research briefs and 14 papers presented under the following subject categories: work with special subjects, PK, animal psi, ASCs, methodology, and nonintentional psi events: experimental approaches. There were two symposia entitled "Research on out-of-body experiences: where do we go from here?" and "Psychokinesis on stable systems: work in progress." The complete texts of the presidential address by Rex Stanford, "Concept and psi," and of the invited address by Charles Tart, "On the nature of altered states of consciousness, with special reference to parapsychological phenomena," are given.

42. Tart, Charles T. *Learning to use extrasensory perception.* Chicago: University of Chicago Press, 1976. 170 p. Bibl. Illus. Ind. $12.50; $3.95 (pap.).

    This book revises and expands the author's earlier Parapsychology Foundation monograph. He presents a survey of the literature on ESP and learning theory, and reports on a series of experiments he conducted to show that by providing immediate feedback to ESP test subjects when a response is correct, customary scoring declines may be eliminated and some subjects may even increase their performance.

43. Vasiliev, Leonid L. *Experiments in distant influence.* Translation and introduction by Anita Gregory. New York: Dutton, 1976. 204p. Illus. $4.95 (pap.).

    This is the first American edition of a book that was published in English in 1963 by the Institute for the Study of Mental Images, Church Crookham. This edition is enhanced by a long introduction by Anita Gregory which surveys not only Vasiliev's work in parapsychology but Soviet parapsychology in general. Vasiliev describes his experiments with mental suggestion with and without hypnosis and offers an electromagnetic theory to account for the results.

44. Wilhelm, John L. *The search for superman.* New York: Pocket Books, 1976. 286p. Bibl. Illus. $1.95 (pap.).

    This is a journalist's account of the parapsychological research conducted at the Stanford Research Institute. The bulk of the book is devoted to Geller, but research with Ingo Swann and Pat Price is also covered. There is a chapter on government-sponsored psi research.

6.1. Reprints and New Editions

Carrington, Hereward. *Laboratory investigations into psychic phenomena.* New York: Arno Press, 1975 (© 1939). $14.00.

Coover, John E. *Experiments in psychical research at Leland Stanford Junior University.* New York: Arno Press, 1975 (© 1917). $37.00.

Warcollier, Rene. *Experimental telepathy.* Edited and abridged by Gardner Murphy. New York: Arno Press, 1975 (© 1938). $17.00.

7. Medicine, Psychiatry, and Parapsychology

Psi may be involved in healing, not only in the case of physical lesions and disorders, but also in the successful practice of psychotherapy. In a new comprehensive survey, Ehrenwald provides an historical overview of mental healing, including psi applications. The book edited by Dean contains papers on diverse subjects, but the majority have to do with the relation of psychiatry to mysticism and/or parapsychology. LeShan's book is an account of the steps he followed in becoming a healer and how he teaches others to heal. The Krippner and Villoldo work is a survey of many of the major types of psychic healing, as well as a review of the laboratory evidence. The foregoing presentations, all of which may be characterized as primarily "pro-healing," are balanced by Nolen's firsthand, critical survey of unorthodox healing.

Other books in the bibliography of relevance to healing are Angoff (50), which includes three papers on psychiatry and parapsychology; Angoff and Barth (51), which has a chapter on peasant healers; Cerutti (12), which is a biography of healer Olga Worrall; Harribance (14), who describes his healing abilities; Hintze and Pratt (30), Mitchell (31), which contains an excellent review of psi and psychiatry by Ullman; Panati (6), who has a section on psychic healing; Rogo (18), who is critical of healing and psychic surgery; White (36), which contains a review of the medical applications of psi by C. B. Nash; and Wolman (75), which has three chapters on parapsychology and healing. In addition, Grof (2) discusses the relation of transpersonal experiences engendered by LSD to psychotherapy and Pelletier and Garfield (8) have chapters on altered states and psychotherapy and on transpersonal psychotherapy.

45. Dean, Stanley R. (Ed.). *Psychiatry and mysticism.* Chicago: Nelson-Hall, 1975. 424p. Illus. Ind. $15.00.

   A collection of 26 papers read at three symposia on psychic phenomena at the 1972, 1973, and 1974 meetings of the American Psychiatric Association, plus some additional invited papers. Some of the major subject areas covered are altered states, psychic healing, psychosomatic medicine, psi and psychotherapy, and psychiatry and mysticism.

46. Ehrenwald, Jan (Ed.). *History of psychotherapy: From healing magic to encounter.* New York: Jason Aronson, 1976. 589p. Bibl. Ind. $20.00.

   This book consists of chronologically arranged excerpts from the basic texts on mental healing, each with an introduction by Ehrenwald, who places it in perspective. Many selections and even whole sections are relevant to parapsychology. One chapter is devoted specifically to parapsychology and covers the work of Freud, Servadio, Ehrenwald, Eisenbud, and Ullman.

47. Krippner, Stanley, and Villoldo, Alberto. *The Realms of healing.* Millbrae, California: Celestial Arts, 1976. 336p. Bibl. Illus. Ind. $6.95 (pap.).

   The authors present a first-hand description of various forms of psychic healing. The evidence for psychic surgery is examined (primarily in reply to the accusations of Nolen [49]). A chapter is devoted to a review of laboratory investigations of healing. There are chapters on several individual healers and a long closing chapter offers a theory of how "healing" happens.

48. LeShan, Lawrence. *The medium, the mystic, and the physicist.* New York: Viking, 1974. 299p. $7.50. New York: Ballantine Books, 1975. $1.95 (pap.).

   The author argues that although PK and ESP do not make sense within the framework of sense-based reality, they do fit in with an equally valid view of reality which he terms "clairvoyant reality." He describes this reality based on similar views of mediums, mystics, and physicists. He tells how he put the theory of clairvoyant reality to the test by using its postulates to become a healer. He describes his success both in healing and in teaching others to do the same.

49. Nolen, William. *Healing: A doctor in search of a miracle.* New York: Random House, 1974. 273p. $8.95.

   Describes his personal investigations of Kathryn Kuhlman, Norbu Chen, and several Filipino psychic surgeons. He found that healers could relieve symptoms and even cure some functional diseases, but he did not find a healer who could cure organic disease.

7.1. Reprints and New Editions

Ehrenwald, Jan. *New dimensions of deep analysis.* New York: Arno Press, 1975 (© 1955). $18.00.

8. Parapsychology and Other Sciences

One of several ways in which parapsychology is unusual is the fact that it interfaces with almost all other scientific disciplines. Two books in this section relate parapsychology to several sciences: the Parapsychology Foundation conference proceedings and Schmeidler. The other titles below stress parapsychology and one other science: biology, Randall; anthropology, Angoff and Barth; physics, Oteri; and sociology, Greeley.

Elsewhere in the bibliography Wheatley and Edge (59) devote a section (7 chapters) to parapsychology and the sciences. Individual sciences and parapsychology treated in other books are anthropology, Mitchell (31), White (36), and Wolman (75); archaeology, Dean (45) and Goodman (61); biology, Beloff (27), Hardy (77), Mitchell (31), Thakur (58), White (36), and Wolman (75); medicine, Dean (45), Ehrenwald (46), Krippner and Villoldo (47), Mitchell (31), White (36), and Wolman (75); neurology, Dean (45) and Wolman (75); physics, Beloff (27), Brier (56), Krippner and Villoldo (47), LeShan (48), Mitchell (31), Taylor (70), White (36), and Wolman (75); psychiatry, Dean (45), Ehrenwald (46), Grof (2), White (36), and Wolman (75); psychology, Beloff (27), Krippner (16), Mitchell (31), Parker (7), Roll (34), White (36), and Wolman (75); and sociology, Greeley (76).

50. Angoff, Allan (Ed.). *Parapsychology and the sciences.* New York: Parapsychology Foundation, 1974. 289p.

   This volume brings together 20 papers delivered at a Parapsychology Foundation conference on parapsychology and the sciences. Two are on whether parapsychology is a science; seven deal with scientific methodology in parapsychology; and 11 relate parapsychology to specific sciences: psychology (3), psychoanalysis (1), meteorology (1), psychiatry (2), physics (1), genetics (1), chemistry (1), and biology (1).

51. Angoff, Allan and Barth, Diana (Eds.). *Parapsychology and an-thropology.* New York: Parapsychology Foundation, 1974. 328p. $9.00.

Nine papers in this conference proceedings were by para-psychologists, three of which are oriented toward empirical re-search. The nine contributions by anthropologists tend to stress primitive beliefs about psi and the supernatural. Several papers suggest psi in primitive societies: precognition and prophecy, divination, weather-changing, healing, and hex death.

52. Greeley, Andrew M. *The sociology of the paranormal: A reconnais-sance.* Beverly Hills, California: Sage Publications, 1975. (A Sage research paper in the social sciences) 88p. Bibl. $3.00 (pap.).

As part of the research program of the National Opinion Research Center, 1460 persons responded to a poll of their views on the paranormal (ESP, survival, and mystical experiences). This monograph reports on the results and analyzes the types of situa-tions which appear to trigger mystical experiences. Greeley dis-cusses significant interactions among psychological, attitudinal, and demographic variables.

53. Oteri, Laura (Ed.). *Quantum physics and parapsychology.* New York: Parapsychology Foundation, 1975. 283p. Illus. $12.00.

The papers in this Parapsychology Foundation Conference deal with parapsychology and physics (especially quantum physics) and also parapsychology and science. Targ and Puthoff describe their "remote viewing" experiments. There are theoretical con-tributions by E. H. Walker, G. Feinberg, C. T. K. Chari, O. Costa de Beauregard, V. A. Firsoff, another by Puthoff and Targ, J. H. M. Whiteman, H. Schmidt, and T. Bastin. Also included is a com-mentary by Chari, and a round table discussion by all participants.

54. Randall, John L. *Parapsychology and the nature of life.* New York: Harper & Row, 1975. 256p. Bibl. Illus. Ind. $8.95.

This book reviews parapsychology in relation to life in general and human personality in particular. Part I presents a picture of man provided by mechanistic science. Part II—the major section—is a review of parapsychology—its problems, failures, and successes. In the third part Randall presents his assessment of the implications of parapsychology for our conception of nature and man.

55. Schmeidler, Gertrude R. (Ed.). *Parapsychology: Its relation to physics, biology, psychology, and psychiatry.* Metuchen, N.J.: Scarecrow Press, 1976. 291p. $11.00.

The papers in this book are the result of a symposium sponsored by the A.S.P.R. in 1974. There are two papers each on parapsychology and physics and on biology and parapsychology. There are four papers each on parapsychology and psychology and parapsychology and psychiatry.

9. *Philosophy and Parapsychology*

The years 1975 and 1976 were unusual with regard to the publication of important books on parapsychology and philosophy. They were unusual in two respects. First, because of the number of books published and, second, because of the technical nature of the books. All four of the books listed in this section are written by professional philosophers for professional philosophers (although this is not to say they would not be of interest to the general reader or specialist in another field). They are also written for professional parapsychologists who cannot be too aware of the assumptions on which their seemingly empirical research rests nor overly cognizant of the implications of parapsychological findings for our understanding of the nature of man and the universe in which he lives. As French puts it: "... understanding this world of the psychical researchers necessitates an understanding of the concepts used to describe such a world. This understanding is at base philosophical" (p. viii). As for the philosophers, as evidenced by many of the chapters in the books below, they are provided by parapsychology with empirical data that not only provide a challenge to thought but also a factual underpinning for certain arguments which could at one time be scoffed at as "mere speculations." Of the four titles, Brier and French are the more technical. Brier's book is devoted to a single topic: backward causation and precognition. French's anthology devotes nearly as much space to philosophy and psychology and philosophy and physics as it does to philosophy and parapsychology, and this, in a sense, is a hopeful sign in a book ostensibly devoted to parapsychology and philosophy alone, since parapsychology hopefully will provide the keystone which will cement the union between psychology and physics. Wheatley and Edge cast the widest net of the four and have gathered together enough fish of the parapsychic and philosophic breeds to keep readers busy for some time to come. Thakur's book is the most eclectic in that, although all the contributors are philosophers, they provide philosophic approaches to a variety of parapsychological subjects such as anpsi and biology as well as philosophy and parapsychology *per se.*

Other books containing significant material on philosophy and parapsychology are Beloff (27), Hardy, Harvie, and Koestler (37), Krippner and Villoldo (47), LeShan (3, 48), Ornstein (5), Oteri (53), Randall (54), and Tart (80), especially the chapters he contributed himself. Roll (40), White (36), and Wolman (75) are particularly useful for models of psi operation.

56. Brier, Bob. *Precognition and the philosophy of science: An essay on backward causation.* New York: Humanities Press, 1974. 105p. Bibl. Ind. $5.00.

   In this monograph, Brier takes the philosophical concept of causation and shows how it could be changed to account for the phenomenon of precognition. He analyzes philosophers who have dealt with backward causation pro or con: Gale, Dummett, Swinburne, Scriven, Flew, Mundle, Broad, Ducasse, Black, Taylor, Chisholm, Dray, Mackie, and Schlesinger.

57. French, Peter A. (Ed.). *Philosophers in wonderland: Philosophy and psychical research.* St. Paul, Minn.: Llewellyn Publications, 1975. 276p. $9.95 (pap.).

   An anthology of 25 "critical examinations into the propositions and beliefs of psychical research insofar as they are related to serious philosophical questions" (p. viii). The topics are dreams, space, time, mind and body, personal identity, psi phenomena and knowledge, survival, and scientific acceptability of psi. However, only 12 selections are directly related to parapsychology.

58. Thakur, Shivesh C. (Ed.). *Philosophy and Psychical research.* London: Allen and Unwin, and New York: Humanities Press, 1976. 215p. Ind. $15.00.

   The chapters written for this book are by philosophers who wrote on the aspects of parapsychology that interested them most. Five chapters are on philosophy and psi, while two deal with parapsychology and religion, two with biology and parapsychology, and one with survival.

59. Wheatley, James M. O., and Edge, Hoyt L. (Eds.). *Philosophical dimensions of parapsychology.* Springfield, Ill., Charles C Thomas, 1976. 483p. Bibl. Ind. $24.50.

   An anthology of 32 previously published articles on philosophy and parapsychology. The section titles and number of papers in each are psi and philosophy (4), psi and cognition (5), psi and precognition (4), psi and survival (7), and psi and science (7). 15-page bibliography.

10. Practical Applications of Psi

One aspect of psi that critics touch upon is the fact that it is capricious and unreliable. It cannot be demonstrated at will. One often hears the taunt: "If ESP is a fact, then why can't you make a killing in the stock market?" It is true that just because a person has one striking spontaneous psi experience—say, a detailed dream that came true—this does not guarantee that he or she will ever have another. And in the laboratory ESP has yet to be demonstrated to order under conditions that always hold true. And yet, there are three new books which suggest that ESP is reliable enough to have practical applications. *Executive ESP* presents evidence that psi may be used in business situations. Goodman's book is about a new field that is opening up—"psychic archaeology"—in which ESP is used as an aid in archaeological research. And Tabori's book cites several cases in which psi was used in criminal investigations. In addition, *The ESP papers* is an anthology of articles by Soviet researchers who tend to stress practical, rather than theoretical, aspects of psi and related phenomena.

Elsewhere in the bibliography all the books in the section entitled "Medicine, Psychiatry, and Parapsychology" (45–49) could be said to deal with practical applications of psi. Also, all of the books on or by individual sensitives and mediums listed in the section entitled "Auto-biographies and Biographies" (11–21) contain some examples of practical psi. In addition, LeShan's method (3) has potential practical applicability; Ebon's book on exorcism (83) obviously has a practical aspect; and suggestions regarding the usefulness of psi may be found in Brian (82), Mitchell (31), Wilhelm (44) and in the Parapsychology Foundation conference proceedings on anthropology (51) and on para-psychology and the sciences (50).

60. Dean, Douglas, and Mihalasky, John, with Sheila Ostrander and Lynn Schroeder. *Executive ESP.* Englewood Cliffs, N.J.: Prentice-Hall, 1976. 290p. Bibl. Illus. Ind. $7.95.

   A popular account of the work of Douglas Dean and John Mihalasky at the Psi Communications Project, Newark College of Engineering. They have examined the role of ESP in daily life, particularly its application in business. They have emphasized physiological instrumentation and computerized ESP tests in their research. Included are interviews with successful executives who also served as subjects in the ESP research reported.

61. Goodman, Jeffrey. *Psychic archaeology: Time machine to the past.*
New York: Putnam's, 1977. In press. ca 224p. Bibl. $8.95.

The author proposes that psychics should be used to indicate
where archaeologists should dig and to suggest what may be found,
as well as to provide background information on how life was lived
in prehistoric times. He describes earlier archaeological attempts by
psychics "John Alleyne," Stefan Ossowiecki, and Edgar Cayce. He
also gives an account of assistance he has received from psychics in
his dig in Flagstaff and closes with a worldwide survey of current
psychic archaeology activities.

62. Ostrander, Sheila, and Schroeder, Lynn. *The ESP papers.* New
York: Bantam Books, 1976. 236p. Bibl. Illus. Ind. $1.95 (pap.).

Soviet parapsychology tends to be much more practical than
research in the West. This is a collection of previously published
materials on parapsychology (i.e., psychoenergetics) in East European countries and the U.S.S.R. Only about half appear here in
English for the first time. However, it does bring together many
otherwise scattered and hard-to-obtain-materials and taken together
they provide a capsulized view of Soviet research in parapsychology
and related fields.

63. Tabori, Paul. *Crime and the occult: How ESP and parapsychology
help detection.* New York: Taplinger, 1974. 260p. Bibl. Ind. $8.95.

This book describes several cases—mostly European—in which
a psi factor may have been involved in criminal investigations. It
covers hypnosis and suggestion, psychometry, clairvoyance, motor
automatisms such as dowsing, and precognition.

11. Psychokinesis

Currently one of the most active areas of parapsychological interest
is psychokinesis (PK), or the ability of organisms to influence other
organisms or objects without using normal sensory means. The theoretical implications of PK have recently attracted a number of physicists, as
is exemplified in the book below edited by Oteri and by Taylor's book.
Research in PK is being conducted on a number of fronts from the use of
modern electronic equipment pioneered by Helmut Schmidt (see his
chapters on PK in Beloff [27] and in Mitchell [31]) to what has been
called "macroscopic PK," or the ability of special sensitives to perform
directly observable PK events, such as moving physical objects without

touching them or if touching, then not applying appreciable pressure. As evidenced by the books below, the recent books on PK deal primarily with the macroscopic variety, both spontaneous and voluntary. Three of the books are on Uri Geller alone (Ebon, Panati, and Randi) and Taylor's book is on Geller and the mini-Gellers. RSPK (recurrent spontaneous psychokinesis) is covered in Roll's book on the poltergeist. Feola has written a survey of all types of PK, both spontaneous, mediumistic, and experimental. Owen's book is about an exciting experiment aimed at finding a repeatable method for producing physical phenomena (paranormal physical effects usually associated with mediumship).

Additional material on macroscopic PK may be found in the autobiographies of Geller (13), Manning (17), and Swann (20). Wilhelm (44) describes some PK research with Geller and Swan at Stanford Research Institute. Hintze and Pratt (30) have a chapter on Kulagina's PK. There are general chapters on PK in Mitchell (31), Oteri (53), Panati (6), L. E. Rhine (33), Rogo (34), Schmeidler (55), White (36), and Wolman (75). Bender has a chapter on modern poltergeist research in Beloff (27). Sibley (91) has chapters on materialization, direct voice, and tape recording of purportedly deceased voices. Christopher (22) has several chapters criticizing the PK claims of Geller, Serios, and others. Every year *Research in parapsychology (RIP)* contains several research briefs and papers on PK. In addition, *RIP 1973* (41) has a symposium entitled "Psychokinesis on stable systems" and in *RIP 1974* (38) there is a symposium called "Energy focusing and lingering effects in poltergeist cases and experimental studies."

64. Ebon, Martin (Ed.). *The amazing Uri Geller.* New York: New American Library, 1975. 168p. Illus. $1.50 (pap.).

    A collection of popular pro and con articles on Uri Geller, including a psychological portrait and chapters on his psychic photography, Geller imitators and the SRI experiments. In a summary chapter entitled "Everybody has his own Geller," Ebon likens the Israeli entertainer to a Rorschach test.

65. Feola, Jose. *PK: Mind over matter.* Minneapolis, Minn.: Dillon Press, 1975. 176p. Bibl. Illus. Ind. $6.95.

    Aimed at high school students and laymen, this book surveys all forms of PK. After an introductory chapter, the next five are on types of spontaneous and mediumistic PK, including poltergeists, haunts, levitation, materializations, and PK effects associated with death. The last five are on experimental PK, including a chapter on PK with animals and plants.

66. Owen, Iris, with Sparrow, Margaret. *Conjuring up Philip: An adventure in psychokinesis.* New York: Harper & Row, 1976. 217p. Bibl. $8.95.

    An account of how eight people created their own "ghost" or postmortem communicator by using the oldtime method of the home circle and the psychological techniques introduced by Batcheldor and Brookes-Smith. Their manufactured ghost, "Philip," communicated by means of raps, and other physical phenomena occurred. Another group produced similar results, and it is suggested that the method described can enable any group to generate psi phenomena.

67. Panati, Charles (Ed.). *The Geller papers: Scientific observations on the paranormal powers of Uri Geller.* Boston: Houghton Mifflin, 1976. 317p. Illus. $10.00.

    A compilation of scholarly reports on Uri Geller, some not previously published. The selections consist of reports, letters, entries from diaries, and papers by physicists, mathematicians, engineers, parapsychologists, magicians, and a professional photographer. Panati's introduction reviews and evaluates the major highlights of the research for the general reader.

68. Randi, James. *The magic of Uri Geller, by the Amazing Randi.* New York: Ballantine Books, 1975. 308p. Bibl. Illus. $1.75 (pap.).

    The author calls this an "annotated anthology." He presents in small boldface type what others have written about Geller and before, after, and interspersed with the quoted material he presents in normal type his own comments on what the others wrote. He says he used this method "to supply the reader with additional pertinent data that often change considerably the conclusion one might come to" (pp. 18–19). In essence, Randi tries to show that Geller is a magician masquerading in the clothing of a psychic.

69. Roll, William G. *The poltergeist.* Metuchen, N.J.: Scarecrow Press, 1976 (© 1972). 208p. Bibl. Ind. $7.50.

    This book, although published in 1972 and 1973 in different editions, was difficult to obtain and so this new reprint is treated here. It is a survey of poltergeist phenomena including cases that Roll, who specializes as a field investigator in parapsychology, has investigated himself. There is a chapter on PK and consciousness and one entitled "The poltergeist: Parapsychology or human potential?" An appendix and reading list offer suggestions for investigating poltergeists.

70. Taylor, John. *Superminds: A scientist looks at the Geller metal-bending phenomena and the paranormal.* New York: Viking, 1975. 183p. Bibl. Illus. Ind. $10.95; New York: Warner Books, 1977. $1.95 (pap.).

   In this book Taylor provides an account of his investigations of both Geller and a number of mini-Gellers. Unfortunately, insufficient information is given on the test conditions and controls. The second half consists of his attempt to explain psi by known physical principles.

11.1. Reprints and New Editions

Adare, Viscount. *Experiences in spiritualism with Mr. D. D. Home.* New introduction by James Webb. New York: Arno Press, 1976 (© 1870). $11.00.

12. Reference Works

Parapsychology has been represented by several of the major forms of reference works since 1974. *The encyclopedia of the unexplained* is the first serious attempt to deal with parapsychology and related subjects by means of a one-volume encyclopedia since Fodor's (still useful) *Encyclopaedia of psychic science* in 1937. And G. K. Hall has come out with two major bibliographic tools, the published library catalog and the annual library-acquisition listing. The Wolman *Handbook* can serve many useful functions: that of a reader, a bibliographic source, a handbook for students and researchers, and a work of general reference on parapsychology. The Popenoe book is not intended as a reference work, but it is included here because it can serve two useful reference purposes: it is a subject guide to available books and it is an acquisition tool.

   Books with useful reference features listed elsewhere in the bibliography are Beloff (27), Mitchell (31), Schmeidler (55), Wheatley and Edge (59), and White (36), all of which contain state-of-the art surveys which, together with their bibliographies, provide succinct guides to the literature of specific aspects of parapsychology. In addition, White (36) has supplementary bibliographies. Mitchell (31) also contains a glossary and a chapter which serves as a directory of the main parapsychological research centers, educational opportunities, library and information facilities, and key publications. Shapin and Coly (35) contains an article on the role of the library which describes general and specific reference tools providing information on parapsychology. *Research in parapsychology* (38, 39, 41) is an annual which describes the major research developments in parapsychology each year. In addition, a number of books have useful and lengthy bibliographies on specific parapsychological subjects: Black (81) on out-of-body experiences; Christopher (22) on criticisms; Krippner and Villoldo (47) on psychic healing; Ornstein (5), Pelletier and Garfield (8), and Smith (9) on altered states; Parker (7) on altered states and psi; Roll (40) on the psi response; Roll (69) on poltergeists and hauntings; Stevenson (93) on xenoglossy; Tart (80) on transpersonal psychology and mysticism; and Wheatley and Edge (59) on philosophy, science, and parapsychology.

71. *Bibliographic guide to psychology: 1975.* Boston, G. K. Hall, 1976. 182p. $80.00.

G. K. Hall plans to publish this volume annually. It covers all books in psychology "catalogued by the Research Libraries of the New York Public Library with additional entries from Library of Congress MARC tapes. Included are works in all languages and all forms—non-book materials as well as books and serials" (p. iii, p. v). Two subject areas included are "Parapsychology" and "Occult sciences." The price prohibits purchase by individuals, but it might be a useful volume to consult in large libraries.

72. Cavendish, Richard (Ed.). *Encyclopedia of the unexplained: Magic, occultism and parapsychology.* New York: McGraw-Hill, 1974. 304p. Bibl. Illus. Ind. $17.95.

The most authoritative of recent attempts to provide an encyclopedic approach to parapsychology (although, as the subtitle indicates, only a third is devoted to parapsychology). The arrangement is alphabetical with most entries less than a page long, but general subjects such as mediums, parapsychology, and spiritualism are much longer. Longer articles are signed and indicate further sources of information. There is a supplementary index of persons and titles and a 521-item bibliography.

73. Popenoe, Cris. *Books for inner development: the Yes! guide.* Washington, D.C.: Yes! Bookshop, 1976. Distributed by Random House. 383p. Illus. Ind. $5.95 (pap.).

This is not a trade book although it is distributed by a trade publisher; nor is it intended as a reference book. However, it is potentially such a useful book that it has been included here even though only a small portion of it is devoted to parapsychology. It is a bibliography of in-print books (including 1976 imprints) arranged under 76 subjects. The subjects most likely to be of interest to readers interested in parapsychology are astral projection, consciousness expansion, death, divination, dreams, humanistic psychology, meditation, mysticism, parapsychology, prophecy, and reincarnation and karma. The compiler has written an introduction to each subject area and there are paragraph-length annotations for each title. It is actually a guide to the books available from the Yes! bookshop, although users are urged to consult local libraries and book dealers before ordering from Yes!

74. Society for Psychical Research. *Catalogue of the library of the Society for Psychical Research.* Boston: G. K. Hall, 1976. 341p. $49.00.

Another volume too expensive for personal collections but which large libraries may purchase is this SPR library catalog. It reproduces the author and title cards in the catalog of the library of the Society for Psychical Research in London, which was founded in 1882. Periodicals are included as well as books and also some books in languages other than English.

75. Wolman, Benjamin (Ed.). *Handbook of parapsychology.* New York: Van Nostrand Reinhold, 1977. 1070p.

This eagerly awaited handbook reportedly will run to over 800 pages, but as this bibliography goes to press only the table of contents is available. However, it is included in this bibliography because due to the authority of the work and its comprehensiveness, it is potentially a major reference work and sourcebook for teachers and students, and because it should be available by the time this bibliography is published. There are 37 chapters, covering all aspects of parapsychology, each written by a recognized authority.

12.1. Reprints and New Editions

Research Library, Council of Psychical Investigation, London University. *Short-title catalogue of works on psychical research, spiritualism, magic, psychology, legerdemain and other methods of deception, charlatanism, witchcraft and technical works for the scientific investigations of alleged abnormal phenomena from circa 1450 A.D. to 1929 A.D.; with a supplement of additional items acquired between 1929 and 1935.* Detroit: Gale, in press (© 1929 and 1935).

13. Religion and Parapsychology

The religious texts of the world are partly sourcebooks on parapsychology, containing examples of spontaneous psi phenomena and instructions concerning conditions favoring success, as well as warnings concerning the dangers involved in dabbling in psychic and occult matters. The aspect of religion most often associated with parapsychology today, as well as in the past, is that which deals with mystical states and religious ecstasy. Tart's book, which interestingly was at one time tentatively entitled *Spiritual psychologies,* views some of the major religions as psychological disciplines. There are frequent references to psi phenomena, particularly in Tart's own contributions. Hardy's book is on the evolutionary significance of mystical and psychic experiences. The most general treatment of religion and parapsychology is provided in the book edited by Higgins. Heron's is on psi experiences in the Bible. Greeley's book could have been listed under Survival or Parapsychology and Other Sciences, but it was decided to put it here because it is primarily about man's *belief* in survival (i.e., immortality).

Other books that also deal with religion and parapsychology are Dean (45), who has several selections on mysticism and parapsychology; Jacobson (89); LeShan (48); Mitchell (31); and Moody (90), who describes mystical experiences associated with the experience of dying. Greeley (76) and Gruss (24) are partly concerned with religion and the paranormal, and religion plays a central part in the lives of Jeane Dixon (82), Sean Harribance (14), Alex Tanous (21), Olga Worrall (12), and, of course, in that of Bishop Pike (19). Several contributions in Thakur (58) are on religion and parapsychology. Finally, persons interested in mysticism should also consult several titles listed under "Altered States and Psi," especially Barber (1), Ornstein (5), and Pelletier and Garfield (8).

76. Greeley, Andrew. *Death & beyond.* Chicago: Thomas More, 1976. 144p. $7.95.

Greeley presents the results of several surveys of the belief in a life after death from several countries taken between 1936 and 1973. In the United States, at least, belief in survival increased slightly in that time period. In a chapter on mystical experiences he reports on a poll which revealed that such experiences foster belief in survival. He devotes a chapter to parapsychology and transpersonal psychology. He concludes that survival is a highly rational possibility.

77. Hardy, Alister. *The biology of God.* New York: Taplinger, 1975. 238p. Ind. $9.95.

    Hardy argues on behalf of consciousness and purposiveness in man and higher animals. He proposes that both man and animals can initiate evolutionary changes through altering habit patterns by means of their purposive, exploratory activity. A chapter is devoted to the relevance of parapsychology to religion and to biology. He describes the work of the Religious Experiences Unit at Oxford which studies psi in relation to mystical experiences and prayer.

78. Heron, Laurence Turnstall. *ESP in the Bible.* Garden City, N.Y.: Doubleday, 1974. 212p. Bibl. $5.95.

    This book is based on the premise that man is able to discern the will of God by means of psi. He proposes that "great religions arise from prophetic experience in extrasensory perception" (p. 17). He provides a survey of spontaneous psi experiences described in the Bible and relates them to similar cases in the literature of parapsychology and also to current findings on altered states and to modern instances of creativity and inspiration.

79. Higgins, Paul Lambourne (Ed.). *Frontiers of the spirit: Studies in the mystical and psychical. . . .* Minneapolis: T. S. Denison, 1976. 133p. $6.95.

    This anthology was compiled to honor the twentieth anniversary of Spiritual Frontiers Fellowship (SFF). It includes a history of SFF, three chapters on parapsychology and religion, one on Christianity and psi, one on Christianity and mediumship, two on mysticism, two on spiritual healing, and four on prayer and meditation. Most of the authors are identified with religion, and this book serves not so much as a review of parapsychological findings as it depicts the meaning of parapsychological findings for the religious community.

80. Tart, Charles T. (Ed.). *Transpersonal psychologies.* New York: Harper & Row, 1975. 502p. Bibl. Ind. $16.50.

    The authors of each chapter in this anthology have attempted to present the spiritual discipline with which he or she is familiar as a psychology. The "spiritual psychologies" presented are Buddhism, yoga, Western magic, Arica training, Christian mysticism, Sufism, Zen, and Gurdjieff. The first 150 pages consist of three seminal chapters by Tart, who is concerned with the development of sciences for various altered states. One is a review of parapsychological findings and their relevance for the spiritual. 11-page bibliography.

14. *Spontaneous PSI Experiences*

Since the late nineteenth century parapsychologists—or psychical researchers, as they then called themselves—have collected and studied spontaneous occurrences of what appeared to be clairvoyance, telepathy, precognition, and psychokinesis. The early journal literature and two of the classic books in the field, *Human personality and its survival of bodily death,* by Myers, and *Phantasms of the living,* by Gurney, Myers, and Podmore—both two-volume works—contain hundreds of accounts of such cases and attempts to verify and corroborate them as well as to classify and analyze them. Although a number of general spontaneous case surveys have been published over the years, both in book form and in the scholarly journals, the trend since 1974 appears to be one of increasing specialization with whole books being devoted to a single kind of spontaneous psi. This is so with all the new books in this group: those by Black and Greenhouse are on out-of-body experiences, Ebon is on possession and exorcism, Green—McCreery and Rogo are on apparitions, and MacKenzie is on precognition. The book by Brian is an attempt to evaluate the evidence concerning Jeane Dixon's experiences. All of the books in this section are popular works except for *Apparitions,* which is a scholarly analysis, and *Riddle of the future,* which falls in the middle.

Additional material on spontaneous psi experiences may be found in Greeley (52), Gruss (24), Hintze and Pratt (30), Jacobson (89), Mitchell (31), Moody (90): spontaneous experiences occurring in near-death conditions; L. E. Rhine (33), Rogo (34), Roll (69): poltergeists; Stevenson (92): cases of reincarnation; White (36): retrocognition; and Wolman (75): research methods with spontaneous cases.

81. Black, David. *Ekstasy: Out-of-the-body experiences.* Indianapolis: Bobbs-Merrill, 1975. 243p. Bibl. Ind. $7.95.

    The author is a free-lance writer who became intrigued by the possibility of OBEs. This book is the result of his excursions in the literature and interviews with persons who have had OBEs and parapsychologists who have engaged in OBE research: Lilly, Morris, Noyes, Osis, Roll, and Tart. Theories about OBEs are considered. 22-page bibliography.

82. Brian, Denis. *Jeane Dixon: The witnesses.* Garden City, N.Y.: Doubleday, 1976. 216p. Bibl. $6.95.

    In previous books on Jeane Dixon no attempt was made to substantiate her experiences. Brian does so in this book by describing many of Dixon's experiences, the testimony of other principals involved or quotes from newspapers or other written accounts as well as questions he asked of Mrs. Dixon and the witnesses, and their replies. Comments by skeptics as well as believers are included.

83. Ebon, Martin. *The devil's bride; Exorcism: Past and present.* New York: Harper & Row, 1974. 245p. $6.95.

This is a history of the phenomenon of possession and exorcism showing how these experiences have been manifested throughout history in various countries and cultures. In addition, Ebon offers his own conclusion on the nature of exorcism and provides a psychology and a sociology of it as well.

84. Green, Celia, and McCreery, Charles. *Apparitions.* London: Hamish Hamilton, 1975. (Distributed in U.S. by Transatlantic Arts.) 218p. Bibl. Ind. $12.50.

This book provides analyses and discussions of firsthand cases of all types of apparitions involving any of the senses. Fresh cases obtained as a result of newspaper and radio appeals are included as well as already published cases. The authors classify and analyze the characteristics of the apparitions and individually describe many cases.

85. Greenhouse, Herbert B. *The astral journey.* Garden City, N.Y.: Doubleday, 1975. 359p. Bibl. Ind. $8.95.

Although somewhat loosely organized, this is the most complete survey of out-of-body experiences in print. It is an historical survey, a review of the evidence, including recent laboratory experiments, and a discussion of the psychology of OBEs. Its strength lies more in its breadth of coverage than its depth. Each example—and they are numerous—was selected to illustrate a particular aspect of OBEs.

86. MacKenzie, Andrew. *Riddle of the future: A modern study of precognition.* New York: Taplinger, 1975 (c 1974). 172p. Bibl. Ind. $8.50.

The author states that this "is an attempt to present the evidence for precognition in everyday life . . . so that readers may make up their own minds on the reality (or non-reality) of precognition" (p. 12). The literature of spontaneous cases is reviewed and fresh cases are described along with previously published ones. A concluding chapter reviews the theories that have been offered to explain precognition.

87. Rogo, D. Scott. *An experience of phantoms.* New York: Taplinger, 1974. 214p. Bibl. Illus. Ind. $8.50.

This is a survey of apparitions of the dead and the living, including those associated with poltergeists, animals, hauntings, and OBEs. It is useful because it draws not only on the most important historical studies but also describes current research and theory on the nature of apparitions and their implications. An annotated bibliography of "suggested readings" is appended.

15.1. Reprints and New Editions

Saltmarsh, H. F. *Foreknowledge.* New York: Arno Press, 1975 (c 1938). $8.00.

Sidgwick, Eleanor M. *Phantasms of the living: Cases of telepathy printed in the Journal of the Society for Psychical Research during thirty-five years,* and Gurney, Edmund, Myers, F. W. H., and Podmore, F. *Phantasms of the living,* abridged and edited by Mrs. Sidgwick. New York: Arno Press, 1975 (© 1962). 2 vols. $56.00.

15. Survival

Although there has been an upsurge of interest in death and phenomena associated with it in many disciplines at the present time, culminating in the new discipline of thanatology, it should be remembered that parapsychologists have been investigating phenomena associated with death and dying since the late nineteenth century. The question of whether man or any aspect of human personality survives death has always been a major area of parapsychological investigation, even though the research emphasis in recent years has been on studies of living rather than the dead. The recent books on survival reflect several approaches to the question. Ian Stevenson, one of the chief researchers in this area, is represented by two books, one on reincarnation and one on xenoglossy. Moody's book is a study of near-death experiences. The books by Jacobson and Sibley are general surveys of the evidence for survival. Bayless presents a survey of direct-voice phenomena, including tape-recorded voices.

Elsewhere in the bibliography W. G. Roll contributes a chapter on survival research to Beloff (27) and one in Mitchell (31). Greeley's book (52) has a section on survival and his more recent book (76) is a discussion of the rational grounds for a belief in immortality. Many of the apparitions described in Green and McCreery (84) are of the dead. LeShan (3) presents a new way of looking at the survival problem and

Hintze and Pratt (30), L. E. Rhine (33), and Rogo (34) discuss aspects of survival evidence. Pamela Huby has a chapter on survival in Thakur (58). There are sections devoted to survival in French (57), Wheatley and Edge (59), and Wolman (75). Rogo's autobiography (18) and the biography of Bishop Pike (19) point up the difficulties involved in obtaining clearcut evidence of survival. The success in creating a "ghost" reported by Owen and Sparrow (66) sheds fresh light on the problem of mediumistic communications. Christopher (22) offers criticisms of individual mediums and investigations of survival. The biography of Lodge (15) devotes considerable space to the experiences and experiments which convinced Lodge of survival.

88. Bayless, Raymond. *Voices from beyond.* Secaucus, N.J.: University Books, 1976. 234p. $8.95.

Interest in direct (or disembodied) voice has been renewed by current claims of tape-recorded voices. This is an historical survey of direct voice emphasizing its relevance to survival. In addition to reviewing the classical cases, there are chapters on fraud, mediumistic controls, and direct voice associated with poltergeists and haunts.

89. Jacobson, Nils O. *Life without death? On parapsychology, mysticism, and the question of survival.* Translated from the Swedish by Sheila LaFarge. New York: Delacorte Press, 1974. 339p. Bibl. Ind. $10.00; $1.75 (pap.).

This survey of parapsychological phenomena and their relevance for survival is in five parts. The first is on death, followed by a survey of the major areas of experimental parapsychology. The third deals with difficult-to-control phenomena which, however, are relevant to the question of what happens at death: OBEs, apparitions and ghosts, spiritualism, possession, tape-recorded voices, reincarnation, and xenoglossy. Part four relates psi to various states of consciousness, and the last part is entitled "How does it look from the other side?"

90. Moody, Raymond A. *Life after life?* Introduction by E. Kubler-Ross. Covington, Ga.: Mockingbird Press, 1975. 126p. Bibl. $2.45 (pap.).

This is a study of near-death experiences which, as described by Moody, share many of the same characteristics as OBEs. Since Moody does not draw on the literature of parapsychology, it is of interest that he has made independent observations on the nature of OBEs and death that are similar to those of parapsychologists

writing on the same subject. Although Moody does not deal directly
with survival, he concludes that the cases described suggest "that we
cannot fully understand this life until we catch a glimpse of what
lies beyond it" (p. 125).

91. Sibley, Mulford Q. *Life after death?* Minneapolis, Minn.: Dillon
Press, 1975. 160p. Bibl. Illus. Ind. Glossary. $6.95.

    This book is aimed at high school students and uninformed
laymen. There are three introductory chapters on the survival
problem followed by nine chapters on specific types of survival
evidence: ghosts and apparitions, dreams, OBEs, materializations,
automatic writing, direct voice, cross correspondences, reincarnation, and tape-recorded voices. A concluding chapter summarizes
conflicting views of the evidence. Five appendices consist of documents relevant to the survival question.

92. Stevenson, Ian. *Cases of the reincarnation type. Vol. 1. Ten cases in
India.* Charlottesville, Va., University Press of Virginia, 1975. 374p.
Ind. Glossary. $20.00.

    The initial volume in a new series aimed at providing detailed
reports of reincarnation-type cases in Asia and the Mideast. Stevenson investigated each case personally, often over a long period of
time. In each instance he provides a summary of the case followed
by complete background material based on first-hand testimony.
Each account ends with a discussion of its weak and strong features.

93. Stevenson, Ian. *Xenoglossy: A review and report of a case.* Charlottesville, Va.: University Press of Virginia, 1974. 268p. Bibl. Ind.
$8.50 (Also published as vol. 31 of the *Proceedings of the American
Society for Psychical Research.*)

    This book provides the most complete account of a case of
xenoglossy in the English language, if not in the literature. It is
about a woman whose consciousness, when hypnotized, was taken
over by a personality giving the name of "Jensen," who carried on
conversations in Swedish with three native Swedes. Stevenson considers counterhypotheses to the survival hypothesis such as fraud,
cryptomnesia, and ESP. Nearly two-thirds of the book is a trans-
cript of the tape of one session. Greatly adding to the value of the
book is a review of the literature and a bibliography of 112 items.

15.1. Reprints and New Editions

Crookall, Robert. *The supreme adventure: Analyses of psychic communications.* 2nd ed. New York: Attic Press, 1975. $7.50.

Myers, Frederic W. H. *Human personality and its survival of bodily death.* Introduction by Gardner Murphy. New York: Arno Press, 1975 (© 1954). 2 vols. $80.00.

Podmore, Frank. *The newer spiritualism.* New York: Arno Press, 1975 (© 1910). $18.00.

Salter, W. H. *ZOAR; or, The evidence of psychical research concerning survival.* New York: Arno Press, 1975 (© 1961). $13.00.

Saltmarsh, H. F. *Evidence of personal survival from cross correspondences.* New York: Arno Press, 1975 (© 1938). $9.00.

Stevenson, Ian. *Twenty cases suggestive of reincarnation.* 2nd. ed. Charlottesville, Va.: University Press of Virginia, 1974. $15.00.

Thomas, John F. *Beyond normal cognition: An evaluative and methodological study of the mental content of certain trance phenomena.* New York: Arno Press, 1975 (© 1937). $19.00.

Name Index

Subject Index